Praise for Rosalie Marsh

"A gifted author who can bring her travels books alive. She has a wonderful sense of the ridiculous and her style as a raconteur means that the reader feels she is talking personally." Judith Sharman. Author on '*Just Us Two*'. judithsharman.com

"The descriptions—so wonderful. I felt I was there, on the motorbike."Jean Mead, Author, on *Just Us Two*. Well worth reading. A wonderful story that takes the reader to the heart of the place that Rosalie Marsh loves so much. Deserving of the five stars. Jean Mead on *ORANGES*. jeanmead.com

"Inspiration for us all to motorcycle touring overseas" Editor Motorbike Search Engine on *Just Us Two*.

"Another great book by Rosalie Marsh that should not be missed. The flow of words employed to narrate it, is in itself most refreshing." Joseph Abela, Author, on *Chasing Rainbows*.

"A great read. Fantastic story." Amazon reader on *ORANGES*

About the Author

Rosalie Marsh is an award-winning author and a native of Lancashire with Irish roots. Today she lives in North Wales where she settled with her husband and growing family. Retiring to concentrate on her writing, her first travel biography, *Just Us Two: Ned and Rosie's Gold Wing Discovery*, Winner in the 2010 International Book Awards (Travel: Recreational category),was also a UK best seller and finalist in the USA Book News 2009 Best Books Awards.

In addition to *Rosalie's Chatter* [blog], Marsh has written a variety of online guest articles and contributed to the Gold Wing Owner's Club of Great Britain (GWOCGB) monthly newsletter.

Marsh has written many academic, vocational, technical, and research materials in her long and varied career in banking, sales management, and further education in work-based learning. The *Lifelong Learning: Personal Effectiveness Guides*, build on her wide experience.

Embracing digital solutions, all books are always available worldwide in print and e-book formats for most devices.

Connect with Rosalie at:
http://www.discover-rosalie.com
http://www.discover-rosalie.blogspot.com
 @RosalieMarsh

 uk.linkedin.com/in/rosaliemarsh/
 facebook.com/rosalie.marsh.JustUsTwoTravel?ref=hl

Also by Rosalie Marsh

Just Us Two Travel Series
Just Us Two: Ned and Rosie's Gold Wing Discovery.
Chasing Rainbows: with Just Us Two.
The Long Leg of Italy: Explore with Just Us Two
Island Interludes: Just Us Two Escape to the Sun.
(Forthcoming. t.b.a.)

Fiction
ORANGES: A Journey

Lifelong Learning: Personal Effectiveness Guides
Lifelong Learning: A View from the Coalface.
Release Your Potential: Making Sense of Personal and
Professional Development.
Skills for Employability Part One: Pre-Employment
Skills for Employability Part Two: Moving into
Employment
Talking the Talk: Getting the Message Across

The

Long Leg

of

ITALY

Rosalie Marsh

C

Christal Publishing

CHRISTAL PUBLISHING
www.christalpublishing.com

ISBN 978-1-908302-39-7 Perfect Bound Soft Cover.
ISBN 978-1-908302-40-3 e-book Amazon Kindle
ISBN 978-1-908302-41-0 e-book PDF (Adobe Digital Editions)
ISBN 978-1-908302-42-7 e book ePub Smashwords Edition

A catalogue record for this book is available from the British
Library.
This book is printed on environmentally friendly paper from
responsible sources.

Some names have been changed to preserve confidentiality.
Facts have been verified by the videos taken at the time and
personal notes, reference to the Internet, maps. Web links are
included.
Some locations and adventures have been described in:
Just Us Two:Ned and Rosie's Gold Wing Discovery.
By kind permission of the author.
Wikipedia references/links courtesy of
https://creativecommons.org/licenses/by/2.0/uk/

WREXHAM. WALES. UK

Photographs.

Acknowledgements

To Allen for his unfailing support in more ways that I could possibly mention and his willingness to follow my optomistic travel plans.
'Do what you can, when you can and then you will not be saying "if only".' *The author.*

Contents

How it all Started

If you have read the first in the *Just Us Two* series, you will know of my husband's aversion to parties. As our Silver Wedding Anniversary approached, he was adamant that he wasn't having a party.

'We will have a little trip,' he decreed.

That is what he thought! He meant a little trip in the UK, not too far from home.

I, on the other hand, had much bigger fish to fry. Our wedding had been a small family affair and, being poor, we did not go away on honeymoon. So, himself wanted a little trip did he? Read on.

I not only like to read about places to explore but also dreamed often of one day visiting these faraway places. A burning need to visit Rome became an insistent call. Off to do a round of the travel agents I went, two winters ahead of the big day. I spent the first winter, (often propped up in bed with brochures, pen and paper my companions, as my husband nodded in dreamland) plotting and planning. I surrounded myself with maps and did many sums as I examined various permutations. We had no calculator then—all sums were mental and worked out the old-fashioned way. On paper.

Not only was Rome a distinct possibility but a three-centre trip would take us to Florence and Venice as well. Three centres? Wow! That *was* adventurous! At this point, we had only been abroad twice in our lives, and recently at that, to Lourdes on a closely organised five-day itinerary.

Every available minute brought me back to my brochures. I knew that if I was to achieve my dream, I must have all my facts and figures ready. Charting out the various trips and combinations, I costed out the various hotels and hotel basis. It was a little daunting to realise that travelling between cities would be on an independent basis: no courier, no one to shepherd us around and guide us, no transfer from hotel to railway station and onward to next hotel. We needed some re-assurance, some kind of security. This really was a leap of faith on our part.

The favourite choice of travel company was Citalia who specialised in Italy. The deciding factor was that—at that time—they were owned by the Italian State, which gave some, not exactly priority, but recognition to the passenger. I bought a Michelin Green Guide and researched each city, matching the maps to the map in the brochure.

Don't forget that it was late 1987 and the World Wide Web had not yet arrived. Google Earth? A foreign language. Multi Map? Didn't exist. AA Route Planner? Unheard of. This was back-to-basics route planning where all aspects and eventualities had to be carefully considered.

In the brochure, I found a hotel in our price bracket that was not too far from the railway station in both Rome and Florence. As for Venice? Well! Dreams of gliding down the Grand Canal came to the fore. I was conscious that there were no roads in Venice. Well not as we know them. It is all water. Cleverly, I plotted out the water stops along the canal. I learned which were the buses and which were taxis. Cost-wise we wanted the cheapest so waterbus, or vaporetto, it was.

I found a reasonably priced hotel at the far end of the Grand Canal near the Arsenale and gardens at stop No 17. It was but a few steps to trundle the luggage to the hotel. I suspected that my husband, like me, would not relish the thought of trundling cases along the canal sides, piazzas and over and down the bridges of Venice.

One day, early in 1988, I waited until my husband had settled down after his evening meal.

'Erm, you said you wouldn't have a party for our Silver Wedding Anniversary,' I began tentatively. 'You said that you wanted a trip.'

'Yes,' the reply was uncompromising. Silence. I waited.

'I want to go to Rome,' I stated firmly before going on in a rush, 'and if we go to Rome, I want to go to Florence and Venice. Something is telling me to go to Rome. I have looked at the brochures . . .,' I trailed off, waiting silently. The air in the room was still.

'I will think about it.'

A few days later when himself came home from work he had barely got through the door when he made an announcement as he was taking off his work boots.

'I have been talking to Charlie in work about cameras. If we are going to Rome, we will need a new camera.'

Whew! I stood in the kitchen, stunned, and with baited breath carried on cooking the evening meal. My joy knew no bounds. In a daze my mind whirled.

We sat down later and pored over the options as we went through all my figures and reasoning and agreed that the Citalia brochure offered the trip most suited to us.

And so began our love affair with Italy.

The Eternal City

On March 25th, 1989 with new clothes, plane and train tickets—for Citalia had booked all the planes and the internal trains for Rome to Florence and Florence to Venice to smooth our journey—suitcases packed and lots of lire (Italian currency at the time) we were ready. Flying from Manchester Airport on a British Airways Super Shuttle Flight to Heathrow, our onward connection was an Alitalia flight to Rome. This in itself was a huge new experience. To land in one terminal, find our way to another in this huge, bewildering airport complex and not miss our connection was a daunting task. Luckily, at Manchester our luggage was booked through to Rome and transferred onto the connecting flight for us. We didn't have the worry of collecting bags in one terminal and carting everything across to another and checking in again.

We didn't have a camcorder at the time but Allen was the proud owner of a spanking new camera. That was splashing out enough for us! Actually, I had won a competition, in the electrical retail superstore where I worked, for selling extended warranties. The vouchers went a long way towards the purchase.

The flight as I remember was smooth with plenty of legroom. The Air Hostesses as they were called then, not Cabin Staff, were chic and well groomed. You can always tell the continental flight teams as they pass through the airport. They have that something special about them with their sharp well-tailored suits and immaculate presentation. We were amazed to find that they served wine in the meal tray as standard. Very continental. On landing in Rome, we cleared customs easily.

There was a coach transfer to our hotel on this leg of the journey; we soon arrived at our Hotel San Remo on Via Massimo. d'Azeglio 36 in the city. How can I remember all this you are asking yourselves? I kept the tickets for the Easter Sunday Mass in Saint Peter's Square and the envelope in which Vatican messengers delivered them to the hotel. That's how! In fact, I made a souvenir folder of the main parts of the whole trip with plane and train tickets, significant photos, and Vatican correspondence.

We were married on Easter Monday in 1964. Our twenty-fifth Wedding Anniversary fell in Easter Week. We wanted to hear Mass in Saint Peter's Square and perhaps attend the Wednesday Audience. I had desperately wanted to surprise Allen with a Papal Blessing but there were a few hurdles to overcome. Reading the procedures for applying to the Prefettura Della Casa Pontifica (Prefecture of the Papal Household) at the Vatican, it seemed a daunting task.

In 1988—the previous year—we had returned to Lourdes on the Diocesan Pilgrimage. At the hotel, when out Parish Priest commented, as we relaxed on a settee with our feet up, that we looked like a newly married couple, one of our party, was amazed to find how long we had been married. We got chatting in the lift and he said he could help in the application for tickets and the Papal Blessing.

Approaching Canon Pelosi nearer to the time, I explained my request whereupon he wrote a lovely letter to the Vatican. Wishing to surprise Allen, I arranged for the reply to go care of my parents' address. (They were thrilled when a letter with a Vatican postage stamp arrived through their letterbox and my father came hotfoot to the store where I worked to let me know it had arrived. For someone who frowned on bringing personal matters into the workplace, this was a big thing on his part. He waited eagerly while I opened it; for my parents, it was a big event to have correspondence from the Vatican.)

As we were going through some traumas at the time, I had also written a personal letter to His Holiness Pope John Paul II. *(Now Saint John Paul II)* Known as Il Papa, I felt that he was approachable. I was astounded to receive a reply from the Secretariat of State together with a personal Apostolic Blessing from the Holy Father and a set of Rosary Beads for each of us.

I also received a reply from the Prefettura Della Casa Pontifica regarding the arrangements and tickets for the Easter Day Mass and Wednesday Audience in Saint Peter's Square. I shared this exciting news with my husband.

What I didn't share with him was the surprise that I had in store. I had wanted a Papal Blessing to be presented to us. The Apostolic Nuncio in London was unable to help with this, other than to make various suggestions to Canon Pelosi, which proved unsuccessful. I did however, collect the Papal Blessing, had it framed and stashed it away to be secreted later into my suitcase. *(N.B. A Papal or Apostolic Blessing is a richly decorated parchment with the words of the blessing and to whom it is for, written in beautiful calligraphy. They are a privilege.)*

Our letter of confirmation from Rome informed us that our tickets for the Easter Day Mass would be left at our hotel. As we checked in, the smiling receptionist reached behind the desk to the cubbyhole for our room and handed us an envelope. Gingerly and with awe, we opened it. Yes, there they were! Two orange-coloured tickets. In flowing script, they each entreated us to enter by Piazza del S.Uffizio at the Braccio Di Carlo Magno. Loosely translated this means that we had to enter by the Carlo Magno gate/branch in the Sant'Uffizio square. A taxi would sort that one out!

Our board basis was bed and breakfast; this seemed to be the norm in most tourist hotels; there are so many places to eat it probably makes sense. Our rooms were fairly large and comfortable with en-suite facilities but I was astounded to find that the bath towels were in fact large sheets of a closely woven fabric. An actual bath sheet.

I soon had pictures running through my mind of centuries ago when the Roman gentlemen gathered in the baths, wrapped in huge sheets. I had never thought of the connection before and that this was a bath towel, Roman style. They didn't dry one as well as a terry towelling one but we soon got used to it. It was an old building and the bathroom was of a more traditional style with high ceilings and windows, and quite basic, if you can imagine that. (On a later visit, it had been modernised.)

We had travelled on a Saturday, the day before Easter Sunday and could not wait to explore. After a meal in a local restaurant Allen looked at the street map, after which we headed towards Saint Peter's Square.

Rome is huge. Not only spread over a large area, it is huge in terms of buildings that are so high you have to crane your neck to see the rooftops. You know how in the films of when the Americans drove into Rome at the end of World War II and the soldiers were leaning over almost backwards to see up to the sky? Well, that is what it reminded me of.

We were slightly bemused that the streets appeared to be so drab. In our planning, we had forgotten that it was a Bank Holiday weekend with everywhere closed up. It was dark by now. The towering buildings cast long shadows across the pavements. In the dark, they looked so dark and forbidding but we were to realise later that everywhere was simply closed up for the Easter weekend.

We had from Saturday until Thursday in which to explore and, being young and fit, we intended to take full advantage of what Rome had to offer; starting bright and early and—after a change of clothes for the evening—planned to stay out late to absorb all aspects of Roman life in this vibrant city. There were many policemen on street corners, usually in two's. One aspect, which I found disturbing, was that they carried guns, although Allen was unconcerned—well, he appeared so in any case. Some of them quite big; not ones you would want to argue with. In the UK, we weren't used to this at that time and I usually elected to walk around the back of the police officers—just in case they went off or something you understand.

Over the next few days, we did explore as much as we could, visiting the Forums, Piazza Venezia where the policeman stood on a box in the centre and attempted to control the traffic, the Vatican Museums, Saint Peter's Basilica, an unexpected trip around the Vatican Gardens, Piazza Navone, Spanish Steps, Piazza del Popolo and much more.

Now, braving the Roman traffic on this dark, still evening where street lamps cast long shadows everywhere we crossed piazzas, streets, the River Tiber, rounded corners, walked down the dark and unnervingly silent Via della Conciliazione until . . . 'There it is! Oh! Isn't it huge?'

We will never forget our first sight of Saint Peter's Square and the Vatican. Truly, a dream come true. A semi-circular colonnade on each side that sweeps round in a huge circle surrounds much of the square, which holds 250,000 people; it was cordoned off ready for the ceremony the following morning. In the middle was an Egyptian obelisk.

'25.5m. tall. 41metres (135 feet) including the pedestal. The obelisk, originally located at Heliopolis in Egypt, was built for Cornelius Gallus, the city's prefect. In 37AD Caligula decided to transport the obelisk to Rome.'

(http://www.aviewoncities.com/rome/piazzasanpietro.htm *sourced 23.12.2011.*)

At the top, near the steps we could see that one area was furnished with chairs. Beyond the ropes where we stood, another area was cordoned off; then behind where we were standing, the ropes left the rest of the square behind us open.

'I think this is where we will be,' ventured Allen with certainty.

'Actually', I ventured, 'I think we will be up there.' I pointed ahead.

'No, we can't be.' Meaning that we weren't important enough.

Easter Day. A dream comes true.

Nevertheless, so it proved on the morrow when the taxi dropped us off in the brilliant sunshine of a Roman Easter Day. The entrance that we had been bidden to use was at the top end, to the left, just where the colonnade started.

The signs and directions from helpful guides were easy to follow; to Allen's astonishment we found ourselves in a roped off area with an excellent view of the altar which was set out on the steps outside Saint Peter's Basilica. I see from my notes in the photograph album that our seats were about ten rows back from the steps of the Basilica. Canon Pelosi must have had friends in high places. (We were very privileged to have seats; they were welcome in the baking hot sunshine that even at this early hour was high in the sky. Those behind the ropes had to stand for hours.)

This was the most amazing experience. Gradually the cordoned areas filled as ticket holders claimed their places. Allen's camera was working overtime and involved many roll changes. The digital age had not yet arrived and the camera held a roll of film, holding about twenty-four pictures, which had to be changed in the shade. With a temperature of seventy degrees Fahrenheit (yes Fahrenheit as in the UK we hadn't then been taken down the metric route) this was not easy. We could not help but be amazed at how close to the front we were. Some people had seats on the steps at each side of the building but really, we had a marvellous vantage point. Someone up there was looking after us.

The organisation at the Vatican is amazing. Twice a week, messengers are running around Rome delivering tickets to hotels for thousands of people from all over the world. During the ceremonies, everything is so smooth and easy. Security is high but undercover. Apart from the Swiss Guards that is who, standing in their colourful uniforms, appear to be purely ceremonial but in fact are highly trained military men.

Shortly before Mass was due to start we heard music. Bands began to play heralding the arrival of the Swiss Guards, the Carabinieri, or National Guard in their colourful ceremonial dress, and different sections of the armed forces: army, air force, and navy. All of them took their designated places behind the cordons. The very cordons behind which we had stood in awe the night before. As the Piazza filled up, flags of many nations appeared; to loud cheers, the flag holder hoisted them up into the air. The atmosphere was electric and yet, there were pockets of silence as pilgrims prayed quietly and absorbed the astounding scene. The flowers, the music, the mix of nationalities, all add to the unforgettable scene.

Some of our photographs show the amazing scene behind us which was just a sea of bodies as people of many nations crammed into every available space in the square and far beyond out into Via della Conciliazione. It was standing room only there and, in the heat, we were thankful for our seats.

After Mass, celebrated on the outdoor altar on the steps, we waited while the balcony high above the main doors was prepared. It was from here that His Holiness would give his Easter Blessing to the world. After a short wait, Vatican officials draped a richly coloured cloth, bordered in a rich red and gold, over the balcony. In the centre was the Papal Arms on a white background.

Soon, soon, we would hear the blessing. Then, there he was; that so humble, approachable man of the people. Speaking in many languages, he gave his blessing to the world.

Easter Sunday Blessing. Saint Peter's Basilica. Rome.

All too soon, it was all over. The armed forces marched off in a colourful display while the crowds dispersed quickly.

It was now time for lunch. Although I could not speak Italian, it had a certain familiarity to me as I had been used to the Latin Mass when I grew up and had learned Spanish at school. Leaving by the colonnades at the left entrance, we spotted a Swiss Guard. I entreated Allen to take a photo. He [Swiss Guard] had his back to me but I did not dare ask him to turn around and pose!

A Swiss Guard at the Vatican. Rome.

Although the Vatican City area is still in the heart of Rome it has an atmosphere all of its own, away from the hustle and bustle of the rest of Rome. For a while, we stopped and just looked in amazement at the seemingly chaotic traffic whizzing around the piazza. Cars and coaches, with lots of noisy horn blowing, vied for space amidst the parked cars as the traffic police attempted to restore order.

With the help of the phrase book and map, we found a typical Italian restaurant for lunch and relaxed over a simple meal and cool drink to reflect on the morning. Looking at the map and remembering what I had read in the guidebook, I suggested that we walk to the Janiculum Hill (Gianicolo in Italian) where there were gardens and reputed to be fabulous views over Rome. It was not far from Saint Peter's Square, just to the south in fact and still west of the Tiber. It is sometimes known as the eighth hill of Rome.

It was a lovely way to send a Sunday afternoon. As we toiled along the path to the top, we passed many Italian families who were also out for a Sunday walk with everyone—mothers, fathers and children— in their Sunday-best clothes strolling in the sunshine along the paths in the park. This was a wonderful sight; it was good to know that we were not the only ones in our 'Sunday-best'. Meandering along the path as it wended its way upwards, we stopped frequently to examine and exclaim over the flowers and trees which grew in abundance and stare at the glimpses of the city and the hills beyond which peeped through the trees.

Consulting the guidebook at every twist and turn, we eventually arrived at the top of the hill. From here, a breathtaking view across the hills of Rome opened up and, dominating the skyline was a huge white building that had been nicknamed 'Wedding Cake'. It was a monument dedicated to Victor Emmanuel II, also called Il Vittoriano, in the Piazza Venice. We have a lovely photograph showing this hilltop view of Rome framed by an old, knarled, and bare-branched tree to one side and evergreen bushes to the other. On our return home, we had this enlarged as one of a set of four that include a favourite view of Florence, Venice, and the Dee Valley where we lived. For many years, they hung in our hall where I could see them from our bedroom as I lay in bed. They always invoked such wonderful memories.

From the Gianicolo we walked down to Trastevere, an old part of Rome. On the way, we passed another of the huge, ornate, ancient buildings that populate Rome. The architecture and statuary are amazing, the craftsmanship so intricate and seemingly everlasting.

As I write this and look into my memory box of mementoes, I find that I have saved a receipt. (In Italy, it was the law then that you take your receipt or you could be fined. The receipt says, 'Bar-Gelateria, Piazza Santa Maria Trastevere 2, ROME. Contantini 10.000 (Lire. No Euro then!)17:42 26.03.89.

I remember that this is where we sat down for a snack and had our very first pizza. I was quite surprised at how thin it was and simply spread with tomato. However, that was a genuine traditional pizza and another new experience.

From Trastevere we wanted to go back through the centre of Rome. We re-crossed the Tiber at the point where the Tiber Island lay sleepy and still in the middle of the river. This brought us to the Roman Forums.

I am not going to bore you with a lot of archaeological history; there is much information on the Internet. I will share with you however how timeless they are; to see these great, white, majestic columns still standing in modern Rome after two thousand years is awe-inspiring. What tales they could tell; what secrets they hold.

Strolling towards Piazza Venezia we came upon the Capidoglio or Capitoline Hill; the smallest of the Seven Hills of Rome. Here, on one side of the beautiful Piazza del Campidoglio is the Palazzo Senatorio that used to be the seat of the Roman Senate. Bordering two other sides are the Palazzo Nuovo and Palazzo dei Conservatori that are now museums. Rounding into the Piazza Venezia our ears were assaulted by the noise of whistles blowing, horns blowing, and cars tooting their horns as they whizzed around the policeman who stood on a box in the centre of the piazza. With white helmet making a focal point, there he stood waving his arms in all directions, blowing his whistle as he started and stopped traffic to make sense out of chaos. Apart from cars, there were many coaches (bus), mothers with babies in pushchairs, horse-drawn carriages, and even people taking some fresh air while they stood at the side of a coach waiting for some movement. We have a photo of yours truly stood in the middle of all this. Well I found a clear space and darted out trusting my safety to fate. When in Rome, do as the Romans do, they say!

In the Piazza Venezia is that wonderful, stark white, ornate building which had just seen from the top of the Janiculum Hill. The 'Wedding Cake', better known as the monument to Victor Emmanuel II is truly awe-inspiring and amazing. What struck me, and probably did you if you have visited Rome, was the age and beauty of the buildings in the Piazza. This one however, was built in the early twentieth century.

From the Piazza Venezia we knew that we needed to head towards the railway station or stazione termini that was fairly close to our Hotel San Remo.

We were confident of finding a restaurant for dinner settling on a restaurant not far from the Via Massimo d'Azeglio and quite close to the Teatro dell' Opera or Opera Theatre. The previous night, our first Italian dining experience, it had been strange to see how not only the menu's differed from British ones, but the eating patterns and meal times. This was all part of our memory box of experiences. In one restaurant, that we went to there was a vertical row of drawers against a column. Ever curious, I opened one to peep inside. All at once, I heard a noise behind me.

'Oh,' I exclaimed to the laughing waiter. 'You made me jump.' No one minded though. Chuckling, my husband shook his head.

It was pleasant to stroll along the streets after dinner, drink in, and savour the sights and sounds of Roman life after dark.

We found it hard to get used to the custom of standing at the counter/bar to drink coffee and have a snack. Evidently, you pay more for a seat at a table.

A word of warning. We took a taxi on more than one occasion and had to cover our eyes in sheer terror. In the end we called these yellow cars 'Banana Cars' as they ploughed their way down the streets of Rome—going one way while the traffic was going the other! Hmm! Scary, what?

Easter Monday.

Bright and early the following morning we set off to explore. As we have many photographs and postcards filed away, in order, in albums, it is easy to follow our route and to be truthful we still have strong impressions etched in our memories.

Our first port of call was the most essential. We wanted to see inside Saint Peter's Basilica and perhaps the Sistine Chapel. However, it seemed that Rome was closed for the Easter holiday. It was Easter Monday after all; the Vatican would have to wait. Taking information from our guidebook and maps, we decided that we would head towards a main road that would lead us to the Piazza del Popolo and the Spanish Steps.

I know that we had our first glimpse of the Coliseum as we struck out in the early morning sunshine so we must have gone down the Via Cavour as our photos show that we came upon the Papal Basilica of Santa Maria Maggiore. Inside the present building, which dates from the early fifth century, is a very long nave that is supported by columns. The high dome seems to go on forever. The altar is a papal altar and very ornate. In retrospect, it reminds me a little of the altar in Saint Peter's but we hadn't at this point been inside there. No description can do it justice. You have to see for yourself.

The Piazza del Popolo is one of the largest in Rome. It contains an Egyptian obelisk that was placed there in the sixteenth century. As with all piazzas in Rome, the Piazza was thronged with tourists, locals, people on bicycles, cars, yellow taxi's etc. who all vied for space. You will find the Piazza del Popolo on the right bank of the River Tiber, near the Villa Borghese at one end of the Via del Corso, with the Piazza Venezia at its other end. The Villa Borghese is now a huge public park with a lake, museums, botanical gardens, and many walkways. Unfortunately, time limitations meant that we were not able to absorb its undoubted beauty and peace.

The Spanish Steps, or Stairway of the Trinity of the Mountains to give them their real name, are famous and popular with tourists. At the foot, in a strategic position in the Piazza di Spagna (Spanish Square), our photos show a row of horse-drawn carriages waiting to carry tourists on a tour around Rome. We declined this opportunity, preferring to explore Rome on foot.

The steps, of which there are many, lead up to a church at the top; it is quite a climb. However, it is from the top that you get the most fantastic views of the streets and buildings surrounding it. Of course, many people sit on the steps and let the world go by. In truth, a short rest is needed as climbing one hundred and thirty steps is quite exhausting in a seventy degree heat. We were in Rome at the end of March, which was a little early for the azaleas that flower in abundance when in season.

Naturally, we were keen to see the Trevi Fountain that was but a short distance away to the south of the Spanish Steps. Disappointingly, we found that it was under wraps due to restoration. In fact, on this visit we found that many monuments and buildings were undergoing restoration. We know that his has to be done sometime but we *had* wanted to throw our pennies in the fountain. I had to be content with some picture postcards! It was strange to compare these with the one in front of us that had had all the water drained from it. We could however, see the statues and get an idea of what it would be like.

Our next stop was the beautiful and jaw-dropping Piazza Navona, which is built on the site of a former stadium. The sheer size is hard to take in. Surrounded by towering buildings including a church, the centre is dominated by the Bernini Fountain where water spouts from four figures that surround the obelisk in the centre. At either end are other fountains—Neptune Fountain and Moor Fountain.

Our feet took us onwards towards the Piazza Venezia, which was as hectic as it had been the day before. Our photos show a mêlée of orange buses and cars going in all directions across the Piazza. Although it does appear that they are all going against each other, there were traffic lights to form some sort of order. One tourist unconcernedly strolled across the centre of the square, camera in hand. One day we saw a man on a scooter with a roll of lino propped between his legs! At that time, crash helmets were not compulsory in Italy and they just hopped on and off with their shopping, children etc. without fuss. Shopping Roman style!

By now, we were footsore and weary, although satisfied and filled with awe at the sheer scale of Rome. Reaching our hotel, we found that the lift was out of order and had to walk up to the third floor. Reaching the first landing, I took off my sandals and leaned on the glass-topped gilt half-table for support. We have a photo for posterity of a very exhausted lady who refused to go another step for a while!

Later when we were refreshed, we strolled out to find somewhere to eat. We also wanted to buy a book of tickets for use on the metro and public bus system as this is one way of covering a large distance.

Rome comes to life.

Tuesday dawned bright and clear as Rome put on her weekday dress. Shutters flew up, doors to courtyards opened, shops welcomed customers, and Rome came alive.

We planned today to visit the Vatican and Saint Peter's Basilica. In order to avoid the searing heat an early start was the order of the day. The metro looked an inviting prospect for getting from A to B. We tried it. Once! Allen is not a good traveller but nothing prepared us for the sheer terror we both experienced as the train descended into the darkest depths beneath the streets of Rome; it bounced and rattled with gay abandon around the sweeping bends of the underground line. Shaken, and with my poor husband turning whiter by the minute, we eventually emerged into the fresh clean air of Rome. Suffice to say that we did not repeat the experience. (Hopefully, things have changed in the ensuing twenty-five years; perhaps we should visit again and check?)

The metro stop Ottaviano San Pietri had brought us near to the Vatican Museums. Deciding that our first priority was to see Saint Peter's Basilica and to go up to the top of the Dome before it got too hot, we headed down the Via Ottaviano towards the Vatican. The high walls along the street reminded us that they protected the Vatican City.

Making our way around to Saint Peter's Square, we climbed the steps before which we had sat only two days earlier. The expanse of the square was a reminder of how many thousands of people had packed themselves into there on Easter Sunday.

Today, all was serenely quiet. Entering the Basilica, our first impression was that it was not as large as we had thought. Due to the perfect proportions of the design, this was a false impression. It is in fact the largest church in the world. The original church was built in the fourth century on the site where Saint Peter is buried. In the fifteenth century, a new basilica was built with Michelangelo as the chief architect.

Saint Peter's Basilica has forty-five altars around its sides, all in little alcoves that make each one private. The dome is massive with a diameter of forty-two metres (almost one hundred and forty feet). It is one hundred and thirty-eight metres high (approx four hundred and fifty-five feet).

'Impressive' does not describe the jaw dropping, awe-inspiring, and sheer wonder of it all. Along the nave in the floor are carved the lengths of the main cathedrals in the world. Saint Peter's Basilica dwarfs them all.

Wandering round in silence, we saw Michelangelo's Pieta (Christ lying in the arms of his mother Mary). On that first visit, it had not been protected by glass as we found it was on a subsequent visit. It was possible then to get close. A Swiss Guard in his red, gold, and blue ceremonial dress stood to attention beside the statue of St Peter. The main altar was inside a canopy, which was supported by four great columns of intricate design. I was enchanted by the holy water basin. Being used to a small font or even a glass bowl in our local village church it was hard to grasp the intricacy and opulence of the Bernini water fountain guarded by two cherubs.

Drinking in all the splendour, the sheer history, and significance of it all to our fill, after a while we ventured to the Dome. Craning our necks, we tried to see right to the top. It was impossible, as we couldn't lean back far enough. The top disappeared from view as the perfectly proportioned curves of the Dome almost meet in the middle giving way to an opening, which rises into the sky. (We didn't know it then, but this was to be our final destination after a seemingly impossible climb.) Taking the elevator we found ourselves half way up the cupola where, from an inside vantage point, we had a perfect view right down into the Basilica itself. Still we could not see to the top of the Dome! The lift stops at the level of the flat roof of the Basilica from where you can go outside and marvel at the view over Vatican City and Rome. Our mission at this point was to climb to the top of the Dome.

But was it possible to go to the top? Well yes, but it really was a surprise. Entering, we found that we were not going round and round the dome itself but going in a zigzag sort of way inside the double skin that makes up the walls of the Dome. On the way up through the Dome, we could see, through slits, glimpses of buildings. It went on forever and, as you can imagine, as you got nearer to the top, you had to bend more and more over sideways as you leaned into the sharp curve. A strong heart is needed! Eventually, we reached a point where we changed from the zigzag stair arrangement—very cleverly thought-out—and changed to a narrow stone circular stairway. As usual, I was wearing a mule style sandal and had to take care that one did not drop off and clatter all the way down!

Eventually, when you thought that you had no breath left, or you would be overcome by claustrophobia or a heart attack, you feel the cool air and realise that you have arrived. Was it worth it? Oh yes, and yes again. Feeling on top of the world, literally, we could see all over Rome and, even more exciting, into the Vatican Gardens. Now that *was* an unexpected treat.

The views from the top were stupendous. Taking care not to lean too far over the protective railings, we could see the contours of the formally laid out gardens; the Governor's Palace, which is the administrative centre for Vatican City; the full beauty and symmetry of the curved sides of Saint Peter's Square and the colonnades. Not only was there an unrivalled view of Rome as it stretched into the distance in the mist, there was the amazing sight of Saint Peter's Square with the Obelisk in the centre leading outwards to join the long straight line of the Via della Conciliazione, flanked on either side by massive imposing buildings. We could also see more of the outside of the Dome with all the intricate detail of the stonework and architectural genius.

Making our way around the narrow walkway at the top, our view changed as we caught more glimpses of Rome and, over the gardens, across to other buildings that proved to be the Vatican Museums. Allen was in total awe at the whole experience and of the workmanship that had been prevalent in days gone by. As a craftsman himself, this all had a special significance.

Our journey down took us in the same zigzag fashion but down the other side of the Dome. Almost bent double as we leaned into the curve of the Dome, this was just as scary as the upward climb. Coming out into fresh air on the flat roof of the Basilica, we caught our breath and rested a while. As we rested, I saw a sign and people coming out of a building with bags. I noticed that part of one of the buildings on the roof had been converted into a shop.

'There is a shop. I have to go in there.'

And off I went to see what was on offer before we took the lift down to the ground floor of the Basilica. I found a well-stocked shop full of mementoes and religious items of all kinds for tourists and pilgrims to buy.

Marvelling again at the sheer size and perfect proportions of the Basilica, we wandered out into the blistering sunshine. Trying to remember that it was still early and only March in spite of the heat, we wandered around to the left of Saint Peter's. I just had to post a card home from the Vatican Post Office. It has its own special stamps. We followed the signs that would lead us to a building on the left of the walkway.

Nearing the Post Office and passing a Swiss Guard in his blue and gold striped uniform, we noticed a mini bus at the entrance to the gardens. They did trips? Around the gardens? Oh, what another unexpected treat. The Post Office could wait!

Hopping onto the mini-bus that was collecting passengers we looked in awe around us as, expectantly, the huge gates to the Vatican Gardens slowly opened. With a Swiss Guard standing immobile to attention but with ever-watchful eyes on us, we sallied forth as the bus slowly moved off into the cool shade of the Vatican Gardens.

Just a point about the Swiss Guards before we go any further. They go back in time to the fifteenth century, serving at various European courts over time. The Papal Swiss Guards are based in Vatican City and are the Pope's personal guard.

Although they wear a traditional renaissance uniform, all the guards are highly trained. There is more on their fascinating history at
http://www.guardiasvizzera.va/content/guardiasvizzera/it.html
The ride around the gardens took us into the coolness of the shady trees, shrubs, and paths. This was something we had never expected to see and had no idea of what was in store for us. Yes, we had had a bird's-eye view from the top of the Dome, but to travel the paths that Popes for centuries had trodden was amazing and the wonder of it still stays with us today, many years later. One startling fact is that there is a Papal railway station with the line running right inside the Vatican City grounds. But it makes sense really, as at one time Popes did not leave the Vatican City State as they do today.

I cannot do this part of our adventure justice but there is an excellent website with many colour photos and explanations at:
http://www.vaticanstate.va/content/vaticanstate/en/monumenti/g iardini-vaticani.html
After the excitement of the tour around the Vatican Gardens, it was time to visit another important place on our list—the famous Sistine Chapel and Vatican Museums.

We were not to know at that point that we would be able to make another visit to Rome a few years hence. For now, we were anxious to see as much as we could, over-awed and happy at the experiences that this trip constantly surprised us with.

Following the signposts for the Vatican Museums, we eventually found ourselves in another world. The long corridors seemed to go on for miles. Craning our necks to get a view of the arched ceilings, we eventually experienced a certain stiffness as we moved along slowly. Along one corridor was a long line of cupboards. Each had the name of a past Pope—a reminder that there was an unbroken line back to St Peter the Apostle (the first Pope) and Jesus when he became man.

Working our way along, we eventually came out into the bright sunshine and welcome shade of a large open space like a courtyard between this and the next museum. How delightful! A welcome resting place for weary feet. There was also a restaurant where we were fortunate enough to find lunch. Never would we have thought that we would ever have lunch in the Vatican City. The organisation of everything was superb with visitors' needs well catered for.

Continuing the tour, we eventually found ourselves near another of our goals. The Sistine Chapel.

It is not allowed to take photographs in the Sistine Chapel. We contented ourselves with some excellent postcards that capture its essence. The frescoes covering the walls and ceiling are out of this world. To think that the artist Michelangelo painted the ceiling by lying on his back on a platform.

Visitors were guided to keep moving as they moved into and around the chapel so that there were no hold-ups for the ones coming in behind. With our minds saturated with all we had seen and absorbed, we found ourselves back in Saint Peter's Square.

It was quite a walk back to our hotel, especially after a long day. It would be quicker to take the metro again. But, looking at each other we laughed.

'No,' was the emphatic answer to my unspoken query.

Even though we had bought a book of tickets for city transport, after our experience on the metro that morning, and given that we were not familiar with where we had to get off the bus, we were also reluctant to use the bus as well. We decided to walk. We were young. We were fit. I assured my long-suffering husband that I would not complain.

'I promise!'

Our hotel in Rome, the San Remo, like many hotels in Rome did not have a restaurant. There were however, many, many eating-places. One evening we found one not far away where, after our meal, we got into conversation with a Dutch couple and their family. The young man, who worked for a large car manufacturer, was happy to translate to the rest of the group and we spent a happy few hours in conversation before returning in the balmy evening air to our hotel.

Wednesday Audience.

Once again, we were up bright and early. As is usual practice for these occasions, our tickets for the Wednesday Papal Audience were delivered to our hotel the day before. Looking at the seat numbers, we thought that we might have good seats again. As the weather was good and due to the heat, the Papal Audience was to be held outside in Saint Peter's Square. To ensure that we were not late or arrived all hot and bothered in the heat, we took a taxi to St. Peter's Square. The taxi driver was used to this and, asking us which entrance we had to use, dropped us off in a very convenient place.

Near the bottom of the steps that lead up to the Basilica, a podium or stage had been erected along with a huge canopy over the raised chair where the Pope would sit. Seating was in sections to both sides and the front. Our seat was to the right and amazingly, we were only a few rows away from the front. While we waited for the Audience to begin, we watched as the seats began to fill.

On time, His Holiness arrived and took his seat. The Audience follows a programme where various people are actually presented in person before the Pope speaks to the crowd. There were various choirs from around the world. They sang their hearts out in the clear air and brilliant sunshine and still it was only the end of March. Unbelievable!

At a given signal towards the end, brides and their bridegrooms who had married that weekend processed, under the watchful eyes of the Swiss Guard, through the crowd to be presented to His Holiness for his blessing.

At the end when people started to move, the Pope spent some time with the Bishops before chatting to the Japanese

Choir on the steps at the side of us as well as to the Canadian Choir. Then, unbelievably, the Pope made his way around the perimeter of the crowd that surged to the barriers. Allen told me to go ahead as he knew what this meant to me; he would catch what he could on the camera while I clambered on to the now vacant seats to get a glimpse of Pope John Paul II. At the last minute, shyness overcame me and I did not lean far enough forward to grasp his hand. An opportunity missed but what an exciting and wonderful experience.

When all this was over and the Pope had retreated into the Vatican, the brides and their new husbands filed out of the Square. The Audience was over.

Wandering away from our post, we saw a well-suited man standing at one side observing the crowd. (Allen said that he was a security man.) Haltingly, we asked him if he would take our photograph and explained that it was out twenty-fifth wedding anniversary that week. He readily agreed and we have as a souvenir of the trip, a photo of us standing in Saint Peter's Square. Truly, a dream come true and one which we had never thought to realise.

As we were again dressed in our Sunday-best clothes and wanted to make the most of our short time in this beautiful city, we went back to our hotel to change into clothes more suitable for sightseeing. This was an occasion for a taxi, even though we had to close our eyes as the taxi went in the taxi lane against the oncoming traffic. Amazingly, there were no accidents!

Consulting our map of Rome, we plotted a route that would take us to the ancient monuments that surprisingly, are not set aside in a special area but are part and parcel of modern day Rome.

As I have said, the Hotel San Remo is situated on Via Massimo d'Azeglio, chosen for its proximity to the railway station from where we would depart for Florence, or Firenze, in Tuscany. It was also quite central and within easy walking distance to many of the sights that we wanted to see and explore.

In the bright spring sunshine, we wandered down the shady Via Massimo d'Azeglio to join the Via Cavour. This was a very long straight one as are most of the streets in Rome. It was also very wide with high buildings lining the street. I was constantly amazed at the sheer size of the buildings that were mainly five or six stories high. When the doors to the courtyards within and the shops were closed, they looked very nondescript. It was a different matter when the inhabitants flung back their shutters and breathed life into the fabric of Rome.

As we made our way down the Via Cavour, we could see the mighty Coliseum in the distance. Coming nearer, we were awed at the scene before us. Standing proud, this once centre of gladiatorial conquests and entertainment formed a huge roundabout where many streets met; where traffic raced round at speed with much honking of horns as the life of Rome went on its way. This today is entertainment of another kind.

Turning right as we took in the sights and sounds of Roman life, we quickly reached the remains of the Roman Forums that was the 'religious, political, and commercial centre of ancient Rome'. Amazingly, after two thousand years, the Arch of Constantine still stands. It was easy to imagine Romans in time gone by, racing their chariots through it for sport; or is that my imagination running riot again? As this reminder of ancient Rome towered above the ruins, the stonework and carvings high above my head fascinated me.

At this point we were able to take photos from the outside of the Coliseum and get a glimpse of what is was like inside. It goes without saying that there was the usual trader selling souvenirs.

Meandering through the ruins and back streets, we eventually came to the Quirinale. The Palazzo de Quirinale is a magnificent edifice. It is the official residence of the President of the Italian Republic. From the piazza in front, we could see ahead, in the distance, to huge white dome of Saint Peter's Basilica dominating the skyline.

Following our usual pattern of striking off down back streets—one of the best ways to see and feel the essence of a city—we came upon huge entrance gates supported by even taller gateposts. Atop of these were huge planted urns. Outside, guarding the entrance was a soldier in blue ceremonial dress with a red stripe running down one side of his trousers. On his head, he wore a brass helmet with a spike on top. With hands resting on the sword, which he held pointed to the ground before him, he looked at us carefully. Sensing that he may think we were a security breach by taking photos, we quickly went on our way. (As I write this many years later, I have found a wealth of information on the Internet of the palace, palace grounds and gardens.)

http://www.quirinale.it/elementi/

This was our last day in Rome. Tomorrow we were to go to Florence or Florence by train. Before that, there was one more surprise in store for my husband. For tomorrow was our actual twenty-fifth wedding anniversary.

Our Silver Wedding Day.

After packing our suitcases the night before, we were all set for taking our leave of Rome. We were both of the same mind that we wanted to hear Mass in Saint Peter's before we did so. Unbeknown to Allen, as I said earlier, I had secretly organised a Papal Blessing when organising to get tickets for the Easter Day Mass and Wednesday Audience and I had this, in its frame, in my capacious bag. I was hoping that I could find an English-speaking priest to present it quietly but that was not to be.

To save time and so that we would manage to fit everything in, we took a taxi from the hotel to St. Peter's and quietly mounted the steps. All was quiet and still. As we made our way around the Basilica, we passed the many side chapels where, at some of them, Mass was being said in many languages. We stood quietly and took this in. The language didn't matter. The Mass was the same the world over.

Afterwards, coming out slowly into the now bright sunshine, I hesitated on the steps; I quietly delved into my bag and brought out my surprise. Allen was overcome. We quietly exchanged a wordless look. Thinking about it now as I write it was good timing as the hour was around the time when we exchanged our vows on the cold and blustery early spring day that was March 30th 1964.

Through the Tuscan Hills to Florence

Checking out of the hotel later, we walked the short distance down the Via Massimo d'Azeglio, turned the corner, and made our way to the entrance of the railway station, the Stazione Termini. Our suitcases were heavy and Allen, who was young and strong, carried the two large ones while I carried our smaller cabin bags. In those days, we did not have suitcases with wheels and a handle to pull along so it was hard work but the distance was too short for a taxi. Or so I was persuaded.

Reaching the station, we parked ourselves in a quiet area. We needed to find the Information Office. Citalia, who had booked all our onward travel as part of our package, had included our tickets with the aeroplane tickets. We just needed to find out from which platform we would leave.

Noticing huge signs along one area of the station, I headed over leaving my husband with the suitcases. The Information Office very helpfully had a different queue for a different language. I joined the English-speaking one. Quickly I completed my quest and headed back to my husband and luggage.

He was in a fluster.

'I only turned round for a moment to see if you were coming,' he said in disbelief. 'Just out of the corner of my eye, I saw a movement. Turning back, I just managed to stop one of the street urchins from making off with a suitcase,' he finished in relief and horror at his lucky escape.

Making sure that we kept everything together, we made our way to the platform where a helpful porter, on seeing our Citalia luggage labels, took charge and stowed our luggage away in our compartment. We had been advised that the Italian State Railway owned our tour operator, Citalia, and that on seeing our luggage labels the porters would look after us. This was true. They did, which was both a relief and a source of comfort to these novice travellers. Citalia had also reserved seats in the first class compartment. We felt like royalty!

As I write, I am checking in the special souvenir photo album that I made on our return home all those years ago. As well as all the tickets and correspondence from the Vatican, I also put aeroplane tickets, train tickets, special photos, and hotel details.

'Yes,! Here it is! The train ticket for Firenze (Florence) which shows that we were to depart from Roma Termini for Firenze at 13:00hrs on 30.03.89, in a Class 1 non fumatore compartment (non-smoking). Lire 8.000!' The ticket also said that it was three hundred and sixteen kilometres from Roma Termini to Firenze. It would go via Chiusi, which is a town in the Sienna province of Tuscany. This route would take us through the Apennine Mountains that form the backbone of Italy. (There is also a photo of my 'guardian of the luggage'— the luggage that he almost lost in his quest to search for me among the throng.) As a reminder, don't take your eyes off your luggage for one second.

Heaving a huge sigh of relief that we had negotiated another hurdle, we settled down for the journey that would take us from the heat and Seven Hills of Rome, north into the Apennine Mountains, through Umbria into Tuscany.

Our journey was a long one but it gave us the chance to relax and, in anticipation, look towards this next part of our Silver Wedding adventure. We had certainly come a long way in these twenty-five years; overcoming many obstacles from our very simple start in married life, we were now at a stage where our family was grown up and we could make plans for ourselves.

Allen, ever the engineer, had to examine in minute detail the nooks and crannies of the railway compartment. He tested this lever and that, finding that the seats reclined somewhat. Even more curious, he fiddled with the catches behind the seat to reveal a hanging space for an overcoat or jacket. Very civilised! He was entranced. The Italians certainly had got it right. Any thoughts that things would not be what we were used to dispersed rapidly. Things were *better* here on the continent.

Gazing out of the window, our impressions were of a lot of undulating hills, lots of tall green trees and lush vegetation.

Looking at my Michelin guidebook now, I can tell you that our journey had taken us through the many vineyards of Orvieto, Montepulciano, and Chianti where, in the hills and valleys of Umbria and Tuscany, such wonderful wines of the same name are produced. It is also interesting to note that here in the Arno Basin, the mighty River Tiber starts its journey as it flows down from the mountain, south to Rome before releasing itself into the sea.

When planning this trip, I had matched up the location of the hotels in the brochure to the Michelin book that I had purchased. As we were under our own steam for our arrival and departures between Rome and Florence, and Florence and Venice, we needed to be central. For some reason, in Florence we were to stay in one hotel for one night, the Albion on Via Il Prato, with the following four nights in the Hotel Ariele on Via Magenta. This was a former residence of the Swiss Ambassador.

Eventually arriving on the outskirts of Florence, we gathered our luggage, preparing to disembark. What a romantic way to spend your Silver Wedding Anniversary! It was hitherto unimaginable! Making our way out of the railway station, we had our first glimpse of Florence. The station entrance was facing, across a huge piazza, the striking Basilica of Santa Maria Novella with its richly decorated facade.

The Albion Hotel where we were to spend our first night, is a tall imposing nineteenth century former private mansion situated only a few blocks away from the Stazione Santa Maria Novella. It is the only 'example of neo gothic English architecture in Florence. It stands on a corner in a central area of Florence. Although there was a restaurant, as it was our special day, we wanted to eat in a special restaurant.

The journey from Rome had only taken a few hours. By now, it was early afternoon with plenty of time to find our bearings before the evening.

Of course, we had to head off to see the famous Ponte Vecchio Bridge over the River Arno. The hotel supplied us with a map. This was our constant companion over the next few days. Arriving on a Thursday afternoon, we had another three full days before leaving for Venice on the final leg of this wonderful adventure.

As is usual on the continent, all the shops and restaurants were closed during the afternoon. This did not stop us window-shopping. Walking from the hotel on Via Il Prato we joined the main street—the Borgo Ognisanti—into the centre of Florence. Stopping to look in the shops windows, our progress was slow. We also wanted to find a good restaurant for our anniversary dinner. Although these [restaurants] were closed until evening, there was usually a menu displayed outside. Taking note of one called El Profeta we agreed to keep it in mind for later.

Wearing comfortable walking shoes, or in my case low-heeled mules, we strolled in the sunshine. Although very warm, it was not as hot as it had been in Rome. Florence of course is in the hills and it was still quite early in the year so we did not have the searing summer heat of July.

Florence is what I call 'get-about-able'. It is not as large as the ancient city of Rome. It is however, no less fascinating being full of its own jewels. And I don't mean jewels in the jewellers' shops on the Ponte Vecchio Bridge!

Florence was thronged with tourists. It was Easter and apart from tourists the city was thronged with students from the nearby University zipping through the traffic without a care. Many of them used bicycles to get around. Really, you took your life in your hands when crossing the road; they knew where they were going and nothing would get in their way. A good recipe for life itself now I come to think about it.

One thing we noticed about the students was that they were not scruffily dressed, as so many students in the UK at the time appeared to be. They took pride in their appearance. Being early in the year, many were still wearing overcoats; all appeared to be wearing well-polished and well-kept good shoes. It was a revelation.

Passing many palazzos (or palaces) and ancient buildings and turning to walk along the banks of the Arno, we came to our destination. Stopping for a moment to take in this ancient yet bustling scene we excitedly stepped onto this famous medieval bridge. We did so reflecting that the inhabitants of Florence had walked this way and carried out their business dealings here for centuries. It appeared timeless, providing as it did then and still does now, a passage from one side of the Arno to the other. In addition there is a corridor above the shops—Corridoio Vasariano—which links the Uffizi with the Pitti Palace on opposite banks of the river. You can just imaging the intrigue which took place amid the dark shadows of the night by people in voluminous cloaks to keep them warm against the chill of the river and messengers running backwards and forward to do their master's bidding.

Awed, we strolled first up one side before retracing our steps down the other. Our progress was impeded by my constant stops to peer into the many jewellers and goldsmiths' shops that appeared one after the other in the huddle of buildings. Such fabulous jewels and pearls. But no prices. They do say that if you have to ask the price, then you can't afford it. True and we weren't about to embarrass ourselves by asking. The bridge was crowded with tourists; here and there were dark-skinned men hawking their wares of watches and other items for sale.

We laughed, as all at once, there was hurried activity as the men folded up their makeshift stalls made of cardboard and disappeared into the crowds. A policeman was on his way.

A must do was to have a photo taken with the bridge as a backdrop. This was such a romantic city; a dream come true.

Ponte Vecchio, Florence.
Showing the Corridoio Vasariano.

Heading from the Ponte Vecchio back into the centre of Florence, we soon came upon the Piazza Della Signoria—the historical centre of Florence. (The Signoria of Florence was the government or ruling body of medieval Florence.)

What an education! I didn't quite know where to put my eyes, as all around me were white statues and sculptures of almost-bare famous figures and the impressive Neptune's Fountain. One sculpture was a copy of Michelangelo's David in all his glory! My husband, busy with his new camera, was busy snapping away and cheekily got a shot of me with my back to one of the statues of a giant of a man, surrounded by other fierce figures. I wasn't looking. Honest! I was studying the map!

We had hoped to see the original Statue of David in the Accademia during our visit but when we did eventually make our way there, the queue, mainly with students, was so long that we decided against it.

At one side of the piazza are the arched columns of the fourteenth century Loggia della Signoria, a former assembly hall, which affords some shade; open-air restaurants abound in the piazza where locals and tourists alike could rest their weary feet and refresh themselves.

Dominating the Piazza della Signoria is the Palazzo Vecchio. This medieval palazzo built in gothic style, is impressive with its square, stark shape in warm-coloured stone topped by battlements and crenellations. Its tall, square, bell-tower rises high into the sky at ninety-four metres; the clock shows its face just above the battlements of the Palazzo.

Strolling back to our hotel, we caught a glimpse of the famous Duomo and the Baptistry. This part of our adventure is not meant to be a guidebook. Many excellent websites and guidebooks give an authoritative account of the history and importance of these famous buildings. I am simply relating our impressions and sharing a little information.

Anxious to find out where our next hotel in Florence was, we passed the Albion Hotel, which was our abode for the night, and carried on down Via Il Prato. We had made a note of possible restaurants for our special meal that night and decided that El Profeta would be our choice as it was not far to walk.

Heading away from the city centre, we realised that we were coming into the more residential part of the city. The shops were of a more general nature. For example, there was a hardware shop, selling all kinds of implements and appliances for the kitchen and home in general. The colourful and exciting designs of cookware and implements were unlike anything we had seen before.

We found the Hotel Ariele in a quiet street between Via Il Prato and the river. Satisfied that everything was in order we retraced our steps to the Hotel Albion to get ready for the evening. We were also satisfied that we were coping well in this ancient but enchanting city. It was only the third time that we had been abroad and the first time that we were travelling independently, on our own. Just us two.

A celebration meal. Italian style.

Dressed in our best finery—Allen in a nice suit, shirt and tie; I in a white two-piece floaty skirt and a top with a draped scarf effect which set off my silver necklace—we strolled out of the hotel and headed for the restaurant. Not having been able to book a table we hoped that we would be in luck. Entering the restaurant, we could see that it was busy. Standing just inside the door, we waited. A smiling waiter hurried across; perhaps it was because we were so well dressed, we don't know, but he was effusive in his greeting as he showed us to a table. He told us that his name was Pasquale as he showed us the menu. He helped us to choose and when we began to order the second course, he stopped us.

'The first course,' he said, 'and then we choose.' Notice the 'we'. It was a partnership to go on a journey to discover and enjoy tastes and textures of food. He to advise and bask in the praise of our enjoyment and discovery.

How civilised was that. After all, you don't always know what you have room for until you have consumed the first course. Dinner at El Profet was not only excellent but the whole dining experience was a revelation; it was so unhurried with the focus on enjoying the food.

Pasquale was very helpful and translated the menu for us, telling us what was in the various dishes. The experience all those years ago is so etched on our minds that I have no trouble recalling it as I write this.

We were to eat there on another night before we left Florence. Moreover, I have the receipt from April 1st.1989. There was the usual cover charge, one wine and one mineral water, one antipasto and one minster or soup for the first course, two pietanza or main course, two dolce or sweets, two caffè, and two service charges. All this came to a huge amount made even more startling as it was in lire, so there were lots of noughts at the end! The bill doesn't show a 'Digestivi or digestive but we were offered one—'to settle the meal you understand'. We have often found this. That when you return you get a little more for your money.

However, on this Silver Wedding anniversary night we really did not care what the bill came to. We were celebrating.

Exploring Florence.

The following morning we packed and checked out of the hotel. Although it was only a short distance to the Hotel Ariele, with a large suitcase each and a flight bag, it was too far to walk. The hotel supplied us with a welcome taxi.

The Hotel Ariele, a plaque on the entrance wall informed us, is a former palazzo and former residence of the Swiss Consul. The entrance straight off the street took us to a reception area. We found that there were many pieces of antique furniture, which appeared to have been there for many, many years. The rooms were simply but comfortably furnished. The two single beds with wrought iron bed heads had an intricate wall light over each and a bedside cabinet. The wardrobe and dressing table were of beautifully carved wood. The bathroom was very modern and met all our needs. Each floor of the hotel had a large landing area furnished with mirrors, tables, and chairs. It was lovely and truly like being an honoured guest in someone's home.

After settling in, we must have strolled around the area but I seem to remember that we had to meet the Citalia Representative at a hotel in the city. She had to explain that, on the Sunday we would not be able to eat in a restaurant in the city as they were all closed on Sundays. The company however, had arranged for us to eat in the restaurant of one of their other hotels.

On Saturday, after a buffet breakfast, we set off with a purpose, heading right into the centre of Florence. My green Michelin Guide Book was proving invaluable—as it is now as I write and refresh my memory, needing to get my facts right!

Heading down the Borgo Ognissanti to the city centre, we came to the Piazza Sante Croce near the river. This huge square with many streets running off it features many palaces.

The church of Sante Croce is immense. The map shows it as a convento (convent) but Franciscan monks look after the church and cloisters. *In the UK, we would call this a Friary, convents being for nuns.*

Inside the church, all was quiet and still as it should be. Wandering round, we came to an entrance to the cloisters. Following the sign for the Leather School, we realised that there was a treat was in store, and an unexpected chance to do some shopping for souvenirs. Now, I don't really like to buy souvenirs with the place name written all over them. I prefer to buy something that reminds us of the place we had visited. On occasion though, I deviate from this habit. On this occasion, I did.

The leather school was fascinating. At a long table sat monks who were working on pieces of leather. This was not the leather that we are used to in a cold northern Great Britain. This leather was of wonderful rich and vibrant colours. For a time we watched as the monks/friars put a pattern onto various articles. I chose a beautiful red leather bookmark with the intricately tooled pattern in gold leaf and a blue colour. The leather is so soft and flexible and I have used it constantly in the ensuing years. It does have the word 'Florence' in the middle with a coat of arms but is still tasteful and so beautiful that I leave it out on a small table as a wonderful reminder for us of our time on Florence.

After we had wandered around the parts of the cloisters and museum allowed, we re-entered the church. Wandering around, admiring the frescoes, Allen was fascinated to see a glass display cabinet holding a very old book. It was of music with words underneath each bar and all hand written and drawn. Of course, he had to take a photograph.

Out in the piazza, it was now quite busy with cars, bicycles, and people strolling around. In the Piazza Sante Croce—don't forget that these piazzas are huge—we found a jeweller's shop called The Gold Corner. Allen had used his engagement signet ring, with small diamond in the corner, as a wedding ring when we were married. I wanted to buy him a ring, not to wear on his wedding finger, but just to wear. In The Gold Corner, we found a lovely signet ring with a pattern across one corner consisting of three colours of gold. He would wear it on his other hand.

Making our way out of the piazza, we found ourselves in a narrow street and there it was—the famous Duomo with its huge, distinctive, red dome dominating the city and the surrounding area.

We were surprised at its location, as we had expected a spacious piazza to be in front. But no! Here in the very centre of this wonderful city was Florence Cathedral with an imposing facade and the Duomo behind standing proud and timeless. The crowds were quite thick; we decided not to go inside. In truth, our minds were so soaked up with culture, frescoes, the sheer size of Rome, and a whole host of impressions that we could not take in much more. We elected to wander at will and absorb the sights and feel of Florentine life.

As I mentioned earlier, we ate that night in Il Profeta where we were well looked after again by Pasquale.

One Sunday in Florence.

Sunday dawned without a glimpse of sunshine. It had become cooler in the hills of Florence, necessitating the use of a light jacket. We didn't mind as it made sightseeing a little more comfortable. This Sunday however the sky was overcast so I wore a light waterproof coat and Allen the warm jacket he had worn on leaving the UK. It was still only April 2nd. As long as it kept off rain, that was the main thing.

We had decided to cross the Arno and go to the Boboli Gardens and the Pitti Palace. As we strolled into the city centre, we saw a man dressed in a wonderful uniform, carrying a big trombone. Although his actual uniform of jacket and trousers was unremarkable, his headgear was another matter.

It was a kind of flat helmet with a brim all around. From one side, there was a massive cascade of shiny black feathers. Stopping in our tracks, we were entranced and he very obligingly stood still for a moment while Allen took a photo. He was outside what must have been an official building as we also caught an officer in the photo as well. From *his* uniform of smart black trousers with a red stripe down one leg, I think he was a Carabinieri or Military Police—one of the four types of policemen in Italy.

The Boboli Gardens are vast; they also rise up to a fair height with many terraces. That means lots of walking and climbing. From my photographs, I have recorded that we went right up to the old Kaffe House or Coffee House. We didn't go in to sample coffee, contenting ourselves with absorbing from the terrace the most wonderful panoramic view over the city and across the hills of Florence. Dominating the skyline was the brilliant red dome of the Duomo as well as other bell towers.

View of Florence from the Kaffe House.

The sky was now grey with black clouds scudding along; we prayed that it wouldn't rain.

We spent some time wandering around, trying to follow the simple map. From our vantage point from the Kaffe House, we could see the tops of people's heads as they climbed the steep steps up. Behind them lay a huge lake and, beyond that the famous Pitti Palace. We used a photograph of this scene as part of the set of four that I mentioned earlier.

Wandering along many paths with their statuary, hedges, and trees, we came to a long avenue—sloping downwards—which seemed to go on forever. I don't think that we ventured down there though. There were welcome stone seats here and there. We do have a photo however, of another avenue of trees, which seemed to meet overhead. This made a lovely setting for a photo with me in the middle to give some perspective.

At the time that we took these photographs, cameras used a roll of film that you had developed into negatives in the camera shop and the photos printed out onto special paper. Not the digital cameras of today! I am so glad that I wrote little notes on the back of them and recorded details in the index of the photograph albums (of which there were many).

Gosh! It sounds as if we are out of the Ark. It just demonstrates how quickly and how far technology has advanced in recent years.

We did not go into the Pitti Palace. Our brains couldn't absorb any more frescoes and sculptures; they felt fit to burst with all the cultural experiences that we had avidly pursued. Instead, we went from the Pitti Palace at the end of the Boboli Gardens, across the Ponte Vecchio Bridge to the market.

A tourist with whom we had got into conversation had told us about the figure of Il Porcellino—the wild boar in the market place. The story goes that if you stroke the nose of the wild boar you will come back to Florence at some point. We stroked and we did come back.

The market place or Loggia del Mercato Nuevo was very busy. The wild boar was having lots of attention from young tourists who made his very shiny nose even more polished and shiny. We have a wonderful photograph of the roof of the Loggia with its fantastic decorated arches and paintings.

I have said earlier that I like to take home a souvenir of the place we have visited. Now I love lace. Lace mats, tablecloths etc. On our strolls through the streets, I had looked at tablecloths in shop windows. In the UK at that time, it was difficult to get a tablecloth that covered the table when it was extended for family events. I had noticed how large some of the cloths on display here were. It would be wonderful not to have to match up two tablecloths and have odd napkins.

Looking around the stalls in the market in Florence, I saw a good selection of tableware. I was quite taken by the huge tablecloths that were large enough to cover my extended table with enough material to give a good drape over the edge. The one that took my eye was a natural linen colour with extensive cutwork and embroidery. It also came with twelve napkins. Haggling a little, we made our purchase.

Around this time, at one of our stops for a rest, Allen made an unexpected announcement.

'We will do this for our thirtieth wedding anniversary.'

After a short pause while I absorbed what he had said and did a few quick calculations, I responded robustly.

'In that case, when we get home we will open a special savings account and save ten pounds (GBP) a week. In five years we will have enough money.' This is what we did.

On Sunday evening, we made our way to the hotel where the Citalia Representative had made dinner reservations for us. (Due to restaurants being closed.) We were greeted and shown to our table. Choosing meat, we asked for 'well-done'. It came running red and we could not eat it. Other diners had the same problem. We however, sent it back to be cooked properly according to our request. Other diners soon followed.

Later, in the evening, back at our hotel, we relaxed in the lounge with a quiet drink. I had noticed from our bedroom window a tree with a profusion of pink blossom mingling with pale green conifers in a delightful small garden at the back of the hotel. This picture made a lasting memory of our time in Florence.

One last look.

The following day, Monday, was our last day in this wonderful medieval yet modern city and we decided to wander at will. As what became our usual pattern when in a new place, we meandered down back streets. Here you get a glimpse of daily life as you peer into antique shops, carpenter's and restoration shops, and car repair shops etc. It was quite a contrast.

At some point, we went into a museum or old palazzo in the city. I know this because the tickets are in the indexed photo album but I haven't noted what the building was— unfortunately. But then, I didn't know that I was going to write about it one day. Strolling back to our hotel, we went on a little further, past the Teatro Comunale Florence, to see where the road led. Just past Via Magenta, it joined a major road that circled the city, passing over the railway station.

After dinner that night, it was time to pack and say good-bye to wonderful, unforgettable Florence. Until next time. We knew now that out plans included a next time.

The Romance of Venice

Our train tickets were again first class. They stated that it was two hundred and fifty-seven kilometres from Florence to Venice, Stazione di Santa Lucia or S.L. We would travel via Vernio in the Province of Prato to the north before going northeast via Padua, west of Venice in the Veneto region of northern Italy.

Having negotiated Italian railways once, we weren't as daunted this time. Nothing is usually as daunting the second time around. Reaching the railway station—Stazione Santa Maria Novella —we quickly found out from which platform our train would leave. At least, I did. My other half, as usual, took a seat and guarded the luggage while I went off on an expedition of exploration. (I seem to remember that I also bought something for our lunch.) He watched our luggage carefully; he had learned his lesson. I eventually wandered back and informed him that there was a train on the platform that I thought was ours and we should make a move. It did appear that trains arrived quite early to wait in the station while passengers arrived. I was nervous that if we did not make a move we would miss the train altogether. Helpful staff soon put us right.

The journey was uneventful but we spent time reflecting on our adventures so far and admiring the changing scenery. The landscape became flatter as we left the mountains and hills and entered the plain of Po. The Po River runs across the top of Italy from west to east (below Lake Garda) before spilling out into the Adriatic Sea south of Venice. Passing Padua, I again began to link places that I had heard about as I grew up, mainly from where saints had lived, with their actual location. Nearing Venice, we left the mainland at Mestre and hurtled over the stretch of water that separated it from our destination.

Arriving in Venice was an experience that neither of us will ever forget—for all the right reasons. To this day, the wonderful and unexpected experience is still as fresh as ever in our minds.

I had longed to ride down the Grand Canal in Venice and was hoping that we could do this by Gondola—at least for part of the way, as we knew that they were very expensive. However, we were in for the treat to end all treats.

Passing through the station barriers, we made our way to the exit expecting to find an area from where signs would direct us to the waterbuses or vaporetto. As you know, I had planned our hotel for ease of transport from the station and near to a vaporetto stop so that we wouldn't have too far to carry the suitcases and hand-baggage. As we were travelling independently—just us two—we did not have transfers provided for the travel between railway station and hotel. We had to negotiate this for ourselves. In reality, this was a big challenge for inexperienced travellers.

Hotel transfer via the Grand Canal.

Moving through the huge entrance of the station, onto what we thought would be the usual type of concourse, the most wonderful sight met our eyes. As we drew breath on a gasp, we looked at each other. It was beyond our wildest dreams. The whole of the Grand Canal lay before us with all the hustle and bustle that a waterway being the only means of transport brings.

I was thankful that I spent so much time on research beforehand. Having a somewhat photographic memory, I had a clear picture in my mind, drawn from the maps and guidebook information, of the different types of transport that plied up and down the Grand Canal as well as the stops for the various types of boats.

Standing for a few moments to absorb the colourful and noisy scene before us, we took note of the various modes of transport: vaporetti, water taxis, private launches with a pilot and a proud well-dressed man standing at the rear, and of course the gondolas gliding smoothly along as the Gondoliers expertly manoeuvred them along.

When the next vaporetto came along, we clambered aboard. With little room for luggage, we had to store our cases in the front of the boat while we found a seat inside. It was a little nerve-wracking, we kept a careful eye on them, but they were safe.

Our stop—number seventeen, Arsenale—was right at the other end of the Grand Canal. We started at stop number two, Ferrovia or Station. With our heads twisting this way and that in wonder and excitement as the boat plied its way in a zigzag to reach both sides, we were in a state of suspense and wonder as if it was all a dream.

There are many different 'lines' just as we have with motor buses. Our line was Linea One that started at the Piazzale Rome near the car park by the railway station. (Apart from a rail link from the mainland there is also a road link.) Our Arsenale stop was right at the other end on the Canale di San Marco but not as far as the Giardini or Gardens. Many of the lines or routes took passengers to other islands in the lagoon or took shortcuts through the network of canals to reach other parts.

In a dreamlike state, we watched as the vaporetto glided past the ancient palazzos (or palaces) for which Venice is renowned. I often think of Venice as being shaped like two spanners that fit together. This imagery might give you some idea of the journey. Sweeping under the Ponte di Rialto (Rialto Bridge) between stops six and seven, we carried on past endless palaces that in a brilliant array of colours slept timelessly in the water. The owners of many had their own boats and launches that either were moored up outside or were disgorging well-dressed passengers. Some palazzos were now hotels. Here and there, tucked away between the palazzos we were treated to glimpses of unexpected gardens planted with tress, flowering bushes, and lush vegetation under which smooth green lawns carpeted the ground. Landing stages lined many parts of the canal, which is approx three kilometres (just over two miles) in length.

Gently sweeping around another curve between stops ten and eleven we were approaching the Ponte di Accademia (Accademia Bridge) and a wonderful sight ahead of the huge white dome of the Basilica di Santa Maria della Salute on the right, at the point where the Canale San Marco blends into the start of the Grand Canal (coming the other way).

I sensed that we were not far from Piazza San Marco or St Mark's Square; my excitement knew no bounds. All along this route were many churches and around two hundred palaces. The island on our right—the left bank— was, we were to find later, the workday part of Venice and different to the area around St Mark's Square. From stop number fourteen at Santa Maria della Salute, we crossed the canal again to stop at San Marco.

Then, we had our first glimpse of the huge piazza on the edge of the water with its tall Campanile or Bell Tower pointing high into the sky, the Basilica di San Marco, and the Palazzo Ducale (Doge's Palace). Here, there is a landing stage for gondolas, but more of that later. These are our first amazing impressions.

Stop number sixteen, San Zaccaria just past the Doge's Palace, appeared to be a main terminus for many of the different routes around the islands in the lagoon. It allowed passengers to step onto the wide Riva degli Schiavoni from where you can stroll right to the gardens at the far end of the canal or towards the more famous attractions before branching off to explore the many smaller canals that make up the fabric of this most wonderful city.

Catching each other's eye, with a silent nod and gesture we connected that the next stop was ours. Retrieving our luggage, we eagerly and carefully stepped onto firm land. Looking at our map and the directions we had written down, we bounced our cases up the steps of the little bridge, which goes over the Rio dell'Arsenale and down the other side. This small canal led up the side of the Naval Museum and on to the Arsenal at the other end After negotiating this small bridge, it was then simply a few minutes to our hotel, the Pensione Bucintoro on the water's edge. We were, at that point very travel weary and so glad that we had chosen a hotel near to a 'water stop' and not one in the middle of the maze of canals where we would have had to trundle our cases along many small canals and up and down many bridges.

Mindful of our budget we had chosen the Bucintoro not only for location—that apart from its convenience to the water stop, proved to be beyond our wildest dreams—but for cost. At that time, the Pensione Bucintoro was classed as a two star hotel, family run and simple. That was fine by us.

Reality was so much more than we could have dreamt. It was in what we thought must be the best location in Venice. Allen congratulated me saying that I could not have chosen better. It was, quite simply, wonderful.

In front of the hotel, spread out like an apron, was a big square or campo. One part of the hotel had a narrow frontage facing towards the Grand Canal and St Mark's with a long side running along the waterside of San Biagio. This is the historic Castello area of Venice. Adjoining it was the Church of San Biagio[1]. We were told that part of the building had been joined with the Bucintoro to make a most unique experience. Looking on the Internet now, I can see that the hotel has been

---

[1] *San Bagio - The Rough Guide to Venice and the Veneto. Jonothan Buckley.*

extensively renovated and re-furbished and is now a four star hotel with a nautical theme plus enhanced rates to match!

The receptionist greeted us smilingly before we were taken, on what only can be described as a journey, to our room. I say a journey because we went up stairs, down a step—the floors of the two parts of the hotel did not quite marry up, one building having floors of different heights to the other—up more stairs, along a corridor and so on until we came to our room. It was very compact or in other words, tiny!

The rather cramped conditions were more than compensated for by the stunning view that greeted us. We had an unparalleled vista right down to St Mark's Square. Turning the other way we had the most wonderful, panoramic view across to the lagoon, Santa Maria della Salute, and Isola di San Giorgio Maggiore with its campanile not unlike the one in St Mark's Square.

One other important aspect of this tiny room with its unexpected treasures was the bathroom. Bathroom? Is that the right name? Allen still doesn't know and shakes his head in wonder at how they managed to fit in a washbasin, toilet and shower in such a small cupboard. Because 'cupboard' is the only name for it. Well, we could wash couldn't we? We could not complain; only add it to our memories and experiences.

After settling in, I imagine that we would have strolled out to stretch our legs for a while, eager to see our surroundings.

At dinner that night, the owner, who was obviously highly trained, served us a typical Venetian meal. On asking about wine, he suggested a Pinot Grigio. This dry white wine comes from the Veneto region. We have found in later years that restaurants usually served wine from their own region, which is a good opportunity to sample something different. In fact, this was the first time I tasted Pinot Grigio and find that it makes a very pleasant summer wine. I have also recently tasted Pinot Grigio Blush—a Rosé wine. What better place though to have your first taste of such a fine wine than in Venice itself?

Moreover, I still have the receipt for the wines and coffee we had during our stay that shows that we paid 18.000 Lire.

(Back home, every time I have Pino Grigio, which is now readily available, my mind flies back to our first restaurant meal in Venice where we were offered Pino Grigio by a very correct restaurant Manager.)

It is now time to take you on a journey. A journey through Venice through the eyes of these inexperienced tourists who had, all at once, been let loose, on their own; it really was just us two.

From the Naval Museum to St Mark's Square.

Next door to the hotel was the Naval Museum. Allen loves this kind of thing; he will spend ages looking at every nut, bolt, weld, screw, and the intricacies of the design. Although I have a fleeting interest, I am not as immersed as he is. I soon work through the rooms, coming back to find that he had hardly moved from where I left him It was however an education.

Huge canons from ancient ships were on display. Allen patiently explained to this ignoramus how they worked and how they would be on the ships. Piles of cannon balls were on display along with a ship's anchor. There was a beautiful display of elegant ship's lamps and, in one central showcase, a replica of the Doge's ship—the Bucintoro. Heavily gilded with gold, the whole design was intricate and sumptuous with the oars lined up neatly as if ready for action by those poor souls down below whose job it was to row.

It was now early April; in the north of Italy on this overcast and grey day, a jacket or something warm was needed. I remember that I had had a heavy, uneasy, feeling for a couple of days which I could not shake off. As if, I was coming down with something. As we strolled along the Riva degli Schiavoni after leaving the Naval Museum, I confessed that I didn't know what the matter was but I felt fidgety and troubled. Here I was in one of the most beautiful, romantic cities on earth; on a wonderful trip, which we never thought to even think of, let along make–and I was feeling miserable. I wanted to ring home to check that everything was in order. Our son was holding the fort. Allen vetoed that idea stating firmly that if something was wrong I could do nothing about it; if there were an emergency, we would be contacted.

Reluctantly I agreed. Perhaps the overcast weather after the heat of Rome and all the excitement was catching up with me. I shrugged the feeling off, determined not to spoil our last few days. My premonition was, in fact, to be proved to have foundations.

Strolling down to St Mark's Square, we turned amidst the pavement cafés, to take a photo. I knew that we would find it hard to explain just how wonderful was the location of our hotel; from where we were standing, it was clearly facing us in the distance. Moving on, we took every opportunity to peer down the side canals. From the outside, many of the buildings did not look much. However, the odd motor launch moored outside with an arched entrance by a landing stage told another story. In the distance were the bell towers of many churches.

Nearing St Mark's Square and the Doge's Palace, we peered down another canal surprised to see the famous Bridge of Sighs. This canal was narrow with tall buildings standing quietly as they had for centuries as the water flowed along to the other side of Venice. We could see an opening in the wall of the building on the left, which was actually the back of the Palazzo Ducale. Looking up, we could see the famous limestone Bridge of Sighs, or Ponte dei Sospiri, with its small windows covered with stone bars. The top was quite intricately formed which made the bridge pretty to look at. It led over the Rio di Palazzo canal to the prison on the other side. The story has it that prisoners would sigh as they saw their last view of beautiful Venice before entering prison.

Reaching St Mark's Square we could see a lot of water. Yes, I know, Venice is surrounded by water! As you know, it consists of a series of small islands in the sea. At times, the high water would flood over into St Mark's Square. Then, boarding would be laid down for people to walk on so that they would not get wet feet. Looking back at this point, we had a wonderful view of many colourful gondolas bobbing about in the water where they were tied up at the landing stage. Behind, forming a wonderful backdrop was the island of San Giorgio Maggiore on the Guidecca Canal with the snake-like shape of the Guidecca Island disappearing to the west. On the island of San Giorgio Maggiore there is a huge church with a Campanile and massive white dome. In addition, there is an open-air theatre called the Teatro Verde. The Canale della Grazia separates the two islands; the island of San Giorgio Maggiore sits in splendid isolation, accessible only by boat.

Isola San Giorgio Maggiore from St Mark's Square.

Tearing our gaze away from this timeless view, we turned around to our first view of the unimaginable splendours of the Doge's Palace and the Basilica of St. Mark greeting us. Facing us at the far end of the Piazzetta near to the Basilica, we could see the famous Clock Tower and the dramatic blue clock face incorporated with the signs of the Zodiac. High above stands a huge lion. On top of the tower is a massive bell. On either side is a tall lifelike figure that strikes the bell on the hour. These are known as 'the Moors' because the bronze of which they are made turned black.

On our left was the square Campanile soaring high into the sky. Reaching this, we were astounded as we turned the corner to see the huge unexpected expanse of the Piazza San Marco. It seemed to go on forever as it played host to all manner of shops and cafe's with offices above bordering the three remaining sides.

The Piazza was busy with tourists and locals going about their business. We did not manage to go inside the Basilica or the Doge's Palace; there was so much to see in such a short time. We did however, get some wonderful photos of these magnificent buildings and, unbeknown to us, a greater treat was in store.

It is impossible to describe everything about this part of our adventure. I can however, direct you to our old friend the Internet where you will find a wealth of information for you to peruse at will if you wish.

http://en.wikipedia.org/wiki/Piazza_San_Marco

There were still a lot of puddles from the recent high water; it was an education to see how the Venetians coped with this by placing many raised platforms over the ground to provide dry progress across the Piazza.

One feature of this famous Piazza is the hundreds of pigeons that strut around looking for food.

In the middle of a group of them, we saw a little girl who was oblivious to everything around her, so engrossed was she in talking to her feathered friends. It was a captivating scene.

The pigeons in St Mark's Square, Venice.

We decided that we could not pass up the chance to go up to the top of the Campanile. Allen wanted to see the engineering in the bells and the views would be tremendous.

We were not disappointed.

Eventually reaching the top after a strenuous climb, we entered the cramped room that held the bells. Working our way around the four sides of the room, we had a bird's eye view of Venice. So high, were we that we had a view of the rooftops of not only the Basilica but of all Venice stretching right out into the lagoon.

The Moors on the top of the Clock Tower were plainly visible. A fantastic picture of the Clock Tower (Torre dell'Orologio) with the ornate buildings of the Procuratie Vecchie at the side completed the picture. It was an amazing sight.

These ornate buildings were the administrative buildings of the old Republic. St Mark's Square is regarded as the heart of Venice, being the political, religious, and commercial centre. It is also, still today, the place to meet.

I was fascinated by the rooftops. It was like another world. Down below you have the ornate and colourful buildings of the Piazza. Behind, the red tiled roofs of all shapes and sizes huddle together complete with chimney pots and television aerials. Here and there, we could see the bell towers of the numerous churches that abound in Venice.

Moving round the room, we were now facing the other way. Ahead was the beautiful white church of Santa Maria della Salute. Having seen it from our journey down the Grand Canal on our arrival, we found it amazing to have another perspective. It was like a 3D map. The sky was still overcast but the clouds were moving away. With more rooftops and chimneys to look over, in front of us we could see a vaporetto on the Grand Canal gliding past. Behind the Basilica of Santa Maria della Salute, we had glimpses of the Guidecca Canal, Guidecca Island, and another smaller island in the lagoon beyond.

Looking down through the windows of the Campanile, we had an unparalleled view of the edge of St Mark's Square where it meets the Riva degli Schiavoni. We could see the tops of the tall white columns in the Piazza, and details of the intricate architecture and colours of the Doge's Palace; a long row of gondolas, moored up, and covered against the threat of rain. Far below, the many people moving around appeared tiny and the many pigeons were like moving dots.

The canals were busy with water traffic. As well as the vaporetto, other boats served other transport lines as well as private launches. We could see how the lagoon was marked with buoys and posts for safe passage of boats.

All at once, amid the quiet chatter of tourists, we heard a whirring and clanking sound; the bell mechanism began to move. Then, all hell let loose as the great bells began to swing and chime. Everyone clapped their hands over their ears and all these years later, I can still hear them in my head (when I think about it) so deep was the unforgettable impression they made. Laboriously swinging this way and that, we got a view of their insides as they sonorously chimed out the hour. As it was twelve o'clock, we had to suffer twelve big 'dongs'! Allen of course, was in his element as he examined all the workings; that is why we have lots of photos of bells and their mechanisms in our box of memories.

There was still a lot of water lying around in the Piazza but turning back to the other side we could see a lone gondola gliding along the canal. Two vaporetti were coming in the other direction looking as if they were going to collide but just in time disaster was averted. A launch came from the other direction making a lot of wash behind it as it sped along. It would have made for a choppy ride for the gondolier and his clients whom he was possibly serenading. Ahead, a massive long low boat was making for Guidecca Island. It seemed to be a working type of boat as it had tall structures like lifts.

It was now time to make our way down to the ground and out into the emerging sunshine to find lunch.

In the afternoon, greatly refreshed, we carried on with our Venetian discovery. Wandering along the streets and smaller squares or Campos as they are knows in Venice, we came to the Accademia Bridge that spanned the Grand Canal joining the two 'spanner-shaped' islands.

Looking across and down the Grand Canal, we had a clear view of the beautiful ancient palaces with their wonderful architecture, gardens, and landing stages marked out by red and white poles. Through the side gate of one of the palaces was an unexpected sight of a garden where many trees; some of them flowering with blossom, formed a frame for the huge lawn. Such a pretty picture. Some of the smaller canals leading off the Grand Canal simply appeared to give access to buildings before leading to a large square or campo, a church, and other streets.

Now at the other side of the Grand Canal, we could look across and see where we had been that morning. It was also quite an experience when strolling around to see the palaces from their back.

We took dinner in the hotel again and finished off the day with a stroll out into night-time Venice. Near our hotel, just along the Riva degli Schiavoni was a church (how did you guess?) that held concerts. It was lovely to hear the music floating out. We did not stay out late, as Venice appeared to go to bed early. On the other hand, perhaps we did not venture far enough along the dark canals to find life.

One night we stood by the little bridge (by our hotel) which crosses the Arsenal Canal and watched a man fishing. He was quite unconcerned that a boat might want to use the waterway. With his little lamp, fishing rod, and bait, he was happy in his own little world.

The Murano experience.

Venice is renowned for its glass. The glass-making factories are on the island of Murano and our quest today was find our way across. Thanks to our trusty green Michelin guidebook and maps, we had the information we needed. Apart from traversing around the canals of Venice and going across to Guidecca Island, Line five had a route that started at the S.Zaccaria stop a short stroll away near St Mark's Square. From there it went through the Arsenale to the other side of the island before turning north to pass the cemetery on its way to Murano.

Going through the Arsenale was another new experience and one that Allen found very interesting. It didn't really move me but then you wouldn't expect it to! Would you?

As we passed through you had a feeling of what it would have been like when ships set sail all those years ago to fight for Italy. Turning left, the boat went along the Fondamente Nuove where it pulled up to disgorge and take on passengers. On this side of the island, you would also see many signposts for the hospital that is situated here. This area appears to be the more workday part of Venice. In our quest to see all the tourist sights, we can forget that Venice is also a working, living, breathing city and needs all the facilities those inhabitants would expect.

After leaving the Fondamente Nuove, the boat turned right to head for the Isola de San Michele or Island of St. Michael. This is now the cemetery and something that hadn't entered my consciousness until now. But of course! Where else would Venetians bury their dead but on an island. This is where you begin to realise that all traffic and transport is by water. We even saw a milk float one morning; but it was a boat. Even the milk is delivered this way.

How else?

Setting off again from the cemetery, the boat was soon pulling in at the island of Murano. It is not very big, less than a mile (one and a half kilometres) across. Bridges connect lots of little islands here.

We soon found the glass-making factory. Tentatively entering, the intense heat from the furnaces struck us forcibly. We watched at a safe distance as men, at various stages of the glass-making process, heated molten glass on the ends of a rod; they expertly twirled the rod and, pointing it to the floor, blew down the rod to expand the glass. At various stages, they hammered, cut, and blew again to get the shape they wanted.

From the outside, as we wandered along, we could see an old warehouse sprawled along the edge of water. Then we came upon a newer building; the Linea Mazzuccato Centre had been set up a few years previously to bring together highly skilled people to work on new ideas. We weren't able to visit this unfortunately.

I just had to take some Murano glass home with me so before leaving I bought what I refer to as my Cinderella slipper. It is a backless shoe with a small curved heel and a frill across the top edge where the arch of the foot would be. The base is pink with the top having stripes of teal, black, and pink.

Arriving back in Venice, we strolled down to the far end of the Piazza to explore the shops. Finding a shop that sold a wide selection of glass and wanting a souvenir of our time here as well as commemorating our special anniversary, we chose a sherry decanter and six small glasses. The shop owner assured us that they would not break; they had been fired twice during the making and they would bounce if we accidentally dropped them. Not that we wanted to risk it! The decoration in gold on the deep purple glass was very effective. Tall and elegant, the stopper of the decanter was covered in gold leaf. We placed an order, as the set would be made specially and, on hearing that it could be inscribed, left details for an inscription to be engraved underneath the base of the decanter.

During our visit to Venice, we did manage to pay a visit to the Basilica of St Mark and to take a few photos. The workmanship was breathtaking and sumptuous. The artistry employed in making the many mosaics on their golden backgrounds on the walls and cupolas is unbelievable. We were so glad to have made the time.

There was another bridge that we hadn't seen and that was the Rialto Bridge near vaporetto stop number seven. From this end of the Piazza, it was a meandering walk; following the signs, we caught a glimpse of Venetian life as our route took us through many streets, shops and over canals.

Across to the Lido de Venice.

Today was Friday; this was to be our last day. The weather had improved with lots of sunshine. We had decided to go across to the Lido de Venice.

The Lido de Venice is one of the sandbars that separate the lagoon from the Adriatic Sea. As well as many hotels and beaches, there is the Casino and a palace where the International Film Festival is held each year. Overlooking the Adriatic Sea on the other side from the lagoon is a sandy beach.

As we headed across the lagoon, we had a view of our hotel and the beautiful boat moored up in front of it. I was happy to sit outside, wind blowing through my hair as I excitedly absorbed another new experience.

After the narrow streets and numerous canals of Venice itself, we were surprised at the difference and contrast of the Lido. Wide tree-lined boulevards shaded the building set back off the road. The Casino sits beside the Cinema. After the ancient buildings and palaces of Venice, it was a shock to see a modern building such as the Casino.

Strolling around, we saw a cafe. I promptly sat down while Allen went to order cool drinks. As he made to take them back to the table, the young waiter stopped him in his tracks.

'No! No! You pay, I bring!

He was adamant and of course, in Italy, if you sit down you pay a different price. Many stand at the counter drinking their coffee and pay the 'stand-up' price. After more walking around in the sun, I lay down on a wall overlooking the sea for a little nap. Railings to stop me falling into the sea protected me.

The journey back from the Lido was uneventful but we looked eagerly for firm land. Allen, not least, because he can't look at waves and is not a happy bunny on a boat. As we approached we saw the masses of greenery of the Isola di Sant'Elena before we reached the Giardini Pubblici or Public Gardens near vaporetto stop number eighteen—a short way before our stop at number seventeen.

Later that evening, after dinner we strolled along to these gardens before walking around to the canal at the side of the Naval Museum. Here we heard music as locals and tourists gathered at bars and cafes. We didn't linger. Not being seasoned tourists, I was a little nervous of the dark shadows cast by the intermittent lights, and brooding buildings standing silently in the dark of night along the waterways.

It was time to pack and say goodbye to enchanting Venice and head for home. We said our good-byes though knowing now that we planned to return.

The following morning, a wonderful sight greeted us as we peered out of our bedroom window for one last look. Being so high up, we really did have a wonderful view and never tired of drinking it in. And there we saw it; steaming slowly and grandly towards the Guidecca Canal was a cruise liner. The Orient Express. That, quite simply, rounded off our trip and, taking one last look of our panoramic view from this well-placed hotel, we said a final good-bye to Isola San Giorgio, Santa Maria della Salute, Piazza San Marco, the Campanile and Venice.

Citalia had arranged a taxi transfer to the airport. I truly can't remember anything about this but is must have been smooth; otherwise, it would not have been such a shock on our return journey to find how the land lay!

Arriving at Heathrow Airport, I was adamant that I would brook no argument. I insisted on ringing home. I was sure there was something wrong. Our eldest daughter answered and at once, I knew.

'How is—?' giving our son's name.

'Oh, Mum, I was dreading telling you.'

He had had an accident and was in hospital on traction. Returning to my husband, I shared the bad news.

'I just knew that something was wrong.' We were eager now to catch the shuttle flight back to our regional airport and home.

More Flavours of La Bella Italia

In the ensuing five years, we did what we had planned to do and saved hard for a return visit for our thirtieth wedding anniversary. Life was busy with a wedding, a car accident, more trips abroad (we both worked hard and travel was of the essence) visiting Lourdes, Portugal, Madeira, moving house and jobs, winning a free flight to Spain in a sales competition; you know, the usual kind of things that happen. Then it was time to book our thirtieth wedding anniversary trip.

This time we decided to do it the other way around and see Venice and Florence with clear brains before they got addled with all the stupendous culture of Rome. Then, I declared that we would need a rest after all that culture and that we should have a week in Sorrento. Also, we would go a little later when it would be a bit warmer in Venice. So that is what we did.

By now, we had a camcorder. I had won it in another sales competition that had involved making a film to promote an electrical item of a major electrical manufacturer. I chose to set a scenario of selling a dishwasher to a single man (a colleague) who didn't know one end of a washing up bowl from another. He preferred to play golf. The store manager filmed the whole thing on his new camcorder. Well that was once he had read the instructions, but then again, he had to as he had told me that I was going to win the competition. They liked the reflected glory you see! The results of the competition came on Allen's fiftieth birthday and I presented him with an extra present. He was so good with his camera I thought that he would make an easy transition to a camcorder. Not so. It lay unused until I picked it up and fell in love with it. So himself carried on with the point and shoot business while I captured all I could on the camcorder.

Once again, we chose Citalia who made all the arrangements as before, booking all the tickets for transfers between cities. Deciding on the same hotels in Venice, Florence, and Rome was an easy task as we had been so pleased with them; for Sorrento, we had chosen the Hotel Tramontano for its central location and romantic history.

As you have just explored with us, this return journey will be all the more special as you will be familiar with some of the places mentioned, especially if you have been following our steps on a map. There will also be a lot of new places to explore in these wonderful cities.

An Unexpected Arrival in Venice

The flaps came down on the aeroplane wings. With rising excitement, I knew that we were not far away from our destination.

'Passengers are reminded that it is not allowed to take photos whilst flying over Italy.'

The firm voice of the Air Hostess, as they were still called then, came over the tannoy. Giving a start, I looked up and found her staring down the length of the cabin, straight at me from the front of the aeroplane. We were flying over the massive Dolomites and with their snow-capped peaks and mountain lakes showing clearly through the clouds, I just had to capture the scene. Would we ever be able to visit those?

Marco Polo airport lies on the edge of land in the Gulf of Venice, which is at the top end of the Adriatic Sea. The lagoon is only part of the Gulf of Venice. This stretches across from the Po in the south west to Croatia in the southeast.

Eagerly anticipating the next leg of our journey as we left the airport, we made our way as directed to where a private launch would be waiting to would take us across the lagoon to our hotel. But what a shock we had.

We found ourselves on the very edge of the land. There was not at a proper landing stage or jetty with the launch waiting ready for us to simply step onto it as we expected. (Or rather *I* had romantically expected.) Where was the boat? The boat was bobbing about on water far below where we were standing on the landing stage. The tide must have been out!

Horror stricken we watched as, quickly and efficiently the porter, at a shout from the boatman below, threw, yes, *threw* our cases down onto the boat, which was rocking wildly in the choppy water. They left us to fend for ourselves, clamber down some slippy steps, and hop onto the boat. It was all in a day's work for them.

I was not really wearing shoes suitable for that caper; I was also carrying a beautiful wide-brimmed straw hat lent to me by our daughter to wear against the anticipated fierce Italian sun. With a stiff sea breeze coming in over the water, it was too breezy to wear it. In addition, I wasn't dressed for clambering down a landing stage; if I had known I would have worn trousers. Actually, I may have had second thoughts if I *had* known!

Gingerly, with Allen in front ready to catch me if I fell—I am not noted for my agility, rather a distinct lack of it—I negotiated the rickety descent and nervously clambered onto the boat that was swaying and bobbing up and down.

Safely ensconced on a comfortable seat inside the launch, the journey across the lagoon was, however, unforgettable. With its flag at the back of the boat proudly fluttering in the breeze and the water churning as the pilot swept the boat into an arc, we soon left the imposing modern building of the airport and dry land far behind. I love to see the froth of water in the wake of the boat and I filmed all I could through the windows and gaps in the curtains. Yes, feeling like very privileged people we were travelling in style, the boat even had curtains at the windows in the cabin.

To avoid the shallow water the pilot followed the huge markers, which denote a safe passage across the lagoon, thus avoiding the sandbanks. These markers consist of huge beams of wood driven into the sandbank, with two spaced a little apart and topped by another for support. Altogether, they form a roadway in the water.

It was very overcast and drizzling with rain at this point, which was disappointing, as we had expected better weather in May. The route from Marco Polo airport was swift and, passing the little island of Murano, soon reached the northern side of Venice. With land and smaller canals on our right, we passed the Ospedale bus stop but didn't stop, as this was a private journey. The bus stop however, was similar to the ones, which we have on dry land with. It had seats inside for protection against the weather, and for waiting passengers to rest while they waited.

Making a right turn, we entered a long narrow canal—I don't remember going through the Arsenale so possibly it was the Rio di S.Giustina which then crosses the canal called San Giovanni Laterno to meet the Rio dei Greci—passing high buildings with lots of what looked like secret doors. But of course, we were passing the backs of the buildings. They open out onto the streets formed between the numerous canals.

Soon our pilot was turning into the Grand Canal where we he quickly deposited us at the Pensione Bucintoro as it was named then.

Following our booking with Citalia, I wrote to the manager of the Hotel Bucintoro to explain that we had stayed five years previously for a special anniversary. They been given us a room at the top of the hotel. I asked if we could have a similar room with a view over towards St. Mark's Square and the islands. A room on the side of the hotel would not have had the same panoramic view.

How thrilled we were to find that they had allocated us a corner room on the first floor with wide windows that gave a stupendous view of Venice. What a lovely present!

Unpacking, we quickly stored away our fine new feathers. Himself was busy with the camcorder, recording my activity in the wardrobe! Then, panning the camcorder over to the window, he caught the memorable and fantastic view, right down to St Mark's Square, of the busy Venetian life on the Riva degli Schiavoni The top of the Campanile appeared to be covered in scaffolding. How glad we were that we had climbed to the top and taken such good shots on our last visit.

Below our window, was the water bus stop just by the bridge where many boats of all kinds had moored up. This part of the Riva degli Schiavoni is quite wide; the space was full of market stalls, awnings, and a band playing a rousing tune, which mingled with many voices. The bridges here were very wide and ornate with wide shallow steps, unlike some of the narrow ones over other canals. Blended in with their surroundings they added to the romance and atmosphere of the city.

Turning to the window on the other side, we took in the wonderful view across the lagoon to Isolo di San Giorgio Maggiore, and then panning across, to the wide expanse of the Canale di San Marco meeting the Guidecca Canal with all the markers in the water to ensure safety. A vaporetto was just coming in to stop. In the distance was a large boat like a ferry. Some of the boats were very large, depending on the distance that they travelled around the islands, and some were smaller and faster.

The zoom facility on the camcorder allowed us close-up views of buildings quite far away, which gave us a different perspective to that of five years previously.

We were up bright and early at 5:30am the following morning, unwilling to waste a minute. Actually, we were probably woken by the noise and bustle as Venice woke up; one morning we saw the milk float going under the bridge; yes a refrigerated boat.

Now, at this early hour, a huge cruise liner was making its way into the Guidecca Canal. After cruising overnight, an early arrival would give passengers a good day to sample Venice.

'It is a beautiful day to day. The sky is so clear.' I announced as I filmed the tranquil scene outside our window. The birds were singing their hearts out as they welcomed the morning.

A Sunday pageant and St Mark's Basilica.

After breakfast, it was time to find the church as we usually do. Wandering down the Riva degli Schiavoni, we stopped about halfway between our hotel and St. Mark's to listen to the band that had gathered to play. They all wore those big flat hats, held on by a strap under the chin, with those lovely feathers draped down one side. *You remember? I told you about those on our last visit to Italy when we were in Florence.* They also wore tight red jackets and fitted black trousers.

Their noisy greetings to each other competed with the clamour of church bells ringing out joyfully; tourists mingled among them, stopping to take in the scene; market stalls appeared as if from nowhere.

At a signal, the band began to play a lively tune. The strident notes of trumpets and trombones mingled together, drowning out the peals of church bells as the men played on in the early morning sunshine. The instruments had a heavily embroidered trumpet flag hanging down proclaiming that they were from Venezia. The heavy gold embroidery was very effective against the rich red velvet material. What a festive air they gave to this wonderful sunny Sunday morning.

Turning to look back from where we had started out a little earlier, we could clearly see our hotel, our spacious corner room on the first floor and, high up, the tiny window in the middle of the building—part of the original church—the room on the front that we had been given on our first visit. The view just reinforced what a good spot the hotel enjoyed.

Coming up to the Doge's Palace we were able to zoom in and film all the intricacies of the wonderful white and pink marble in the geometrical architecture; the birds flying in and out of the windows; the wonderful white larger-than-life statue at the very top. Last but not least, were the well-fed pigeons that were still busily pecking at as many crumbs as they could. We had planned to go to church in a small church we had found nearby. However, we were waylaid.

The Grand Canal was busy for the time of the morning with many gondolas and ferries moored up and many bells ringing out their message across the lagoon and the canals of Venice. As we watched, first one gondola and then another came across the water to moor up near to where we were standing. The teams of rowers were all dressed differently. The bells of the Campanile rang out in greeting while many smartly dressed policemen kept an eye on proceedings.

More and more gondolas with teams of men rowing in unison came closer across the water. These gondolas were not the small ones that gave tourists a ride along the canals. These were seriously long! In fact, they were huge, with about fifteen men rowing.

On the landing stage in front of the Piazza, a man in medieval dress stood watching the busy, vibrant scene. A Police launch came up at speed followed by a private launch that appeared to be flying its own personal flag at the back. Boats of all kinds joined the throng. Bells tolled—there are many churches in Venice!

Vaporetti moved serenely across the water; in the space between two landing stages, a man was polishing his motor boat; yachts with their tall masts reaching to the sky, bobbed about where they were safely moored. Not all public transport uses the vaporetto for their journeys across Venice. (Waterbus.) Other lines require a larger boat such as a motoscafi (motor boat) or traghetti (ferry).

A fantastic ornately-gilded boat carrying Neptune in the front was next; ten rowers in brightly coloured costumes of an ancient or medieval style stood proudly. As they moored up, they unfurled their flags and draperies for the boat. Another ornately decorated boat was dressed with a seahorse at the front. Later, we found that this was the annual Festa Della Sensa, now held on the Sunday after Ascension Day.

Originally, the ceremony of the marriage of Venice and the Sea was held on Ascension Day itself—a Thursday. The Doge sumptuously dressed in cloth of gold would sail in his state galley, the Bucentaur, into the sea to perform the ceremony. Boats filled the whole expanse of water between San Marco and the Guidecca Canal. Big boats and little boats proudly flew their many different flags. Some were very ornate with one sporting a replica of a tall Venetian lamp on the back. Everyday transport carried on its business. After all, there was enough water for them all. In one boat, everyone carried a red and gold flag with the blue European Union (EU) flag flying from the front. In the middle of all this activity sat a man in a little rowing boat.

A group of men—dressed in richly coloured doublet and hose, swinging a cape from their shoulders, and a hat of the era covering their heads—paraded onto the landing stage. Each carried a large flag on a flagpole. One carried a huge banner in red and gold, which they proceeded to secure onto the sea-horse boat. The men with flags followed to stand in the well of this boat.

'You know,' I interrupted our perusal of this scene, 'I think we should walk back down to that square there.'

Turning to look at the gathering throng in the Piazza, we had a wonderful sight of important looking men and ladies in sumptuous medieval costumes. Some of the men looked as if they were 'Merchants of Venice'; one appeared to be a cardinal. The richly robed ladies wore low cut dresses of all colours, each with a well-fitted bodice and a wide skirt sweeping to the floor. They wore jewels in their hair in the manner of days gone by.

All at once, a trumpet sound rent the air. Together with the sea-horse boat, the regatta moved off into the open lagoon to the sound of rousing music. After watching this spectacle the cardinals, merchants and richly dressed Venetian ladies turned away to walk across the Piazza towards the centre of the city.

We decided to see if we could hear Mass in St. Mark's as it was nearly eleven o'clock by now. The crowds of tourists in the entrance were held back behind red ropes that formed a passage, as sightseers were not allowed inside during a service. We simply passed through feeling very special.

It was such a treat to be able to experience the wonderful acoustics for which the Basilica is rightly famous. The priest sang out the chants that resonated through the building as his voice reached high into the dome before the congregation sang the responses. High up to our left, almost into the roof, we could see the choirmaster as he conducted the choir. At the end, of the service everyone clapped. The expanse of mosaic and marble in the domed blinded us with their gilded backgrounds. The camcorder actually captured much more than we could see with our naked eyes, as it was quite dark in there.

As Mass ended and the Basilica emptied, we stayed a while to absorb this wonderful, building. Making our way outside, we found that the Piazza was even more thronged with tourists than before. Looking up to the Clock Tower, we found that the Moors appeared ready to strike the hour.

Burano.

The following day dawned with the sun rising slowly, its fingers casting fronds of light into the Venetian sky portraying a warm day.

Five years previously, we had visited the little island of Murano and a glass-blowing factory. This time, I wanted to visit another island in the lagoon—Burano— which is famous for its lace. Burano is further north than Murano, making a longer journey from Venice.

We realised too late, that we had not changed travellers' cheques into local currency. We only had a little money on us. We had enough for the boat fare but if we turned back, we would miss the boat. If we couldn't find an exchange bureau, we had enough for one of us to come back, get the passports and return. What to do? What a to-do as well! We decided to risk it and find a Bureau de Change or at least a bank when we got to Burano. That was wishful thinking on my part.

The fishing village of Burano is quite a long way from Venice, being more to the east near Torcello amongst a group of islands sheltering behind the Lido di Jesolo. The boat was a different one from those that spend their time weaving in and out of the canals of Venice such as the vaporetto. This one had two levels, and inside cabin and an open-air deck on top. I was able to sit in my favourite spot on top in the open air; I could watch Venetian water life go by as launches and delivery boats vied for space in the marked-off traffic routes. To this day, I find the fact of deliveries being made by open boat fascinating. For me, it was truly an unexpected fact of Venetian life. Yes, I know! I ought to have realised as my husband incredulously and laughingly pointed out.

Passing the cemetery on the island of San Michele, with its ornate church at the water's edge, once again a speedboat claimed superiority over this slower boat as it bounced along the water, soon disappearing into the distance along the designated lane. Then we were passing Murano with the huge Marco Polo warehouse and lighthouse on the water's edge. Here a few passengers alighted to sample the delights of the glass-blowing factory and shops. Another ferryboat decked with bunting passed us as passengers waved and whistled a greeting.

Arriving on this pretty island with its many canals and coloured houses, we made it our priority to find somewhere to get money. Not finding a bank or bureau de change, we did find, a travel agent I think it was who was prepared to exchange our travellers cheques for lire.(Euros had not been brought in at this time.) Although we did not have passports, we were able to prove that we were genuine. Thankfully, one of us didn't have to return and I know that that would have been yours truly as himself wouldn't have survived another boat ride so soon.

Burano was enchanting. With the sun shining it had a quietly festive air. Awnings were pulled out over the shop fronts to shade shop windows, and flower boxes overflowed with geraniums and other plants. Every house appeared to be painted a different colour. The scene is the kind you would find on a jigsaw puzzle or chocolate box. Small squares had shady trees to form an umbrella over you while you rested. The sounds of children vied with the twittering of birds and women having a loud-voiced conversation as they exchanged the gossip of the day. One, resting on her broomstick as she broke from sweeping her shop frontage to greet and chat with her friend who was out shopping.

It is so pretty with its narrow canals and wide walkways either side bordering the many shops decked out with lace goods of all kinds. Not only lace mats but also baby clothes of dresses, rompers, and christening gowns. Coming across these embroidery shops, I was in my element.

As is quite common in these sunny climates where local women make the lace, one lady was sitting outside in the shade of the awning. On her lap was a large firm pad on which she had tracing paper.

'This is the authentic lace of Burano,' I recorded at the time. 'It is all done on tracing paper and when the lace-work is finished, they pull the paper away and what you have is a piece of work crafted completely out of the thread.'

There were many examples of lace framed to make a picture that you would display on the wall. Ladies blouses were another example of lace items. Some of the shops displayed a profusion of glass and silverware items and, of course, Venetian masks.

We crossed from side to side on the little bridges that spanned the canals. These were not the ornate stone or wrought iron bridges of Venice but plain wooden ones so ancient you wonder if they are safe. I do assure you that they were. Some of course were stone. All spanned the long narrow canals that wended their way through the island to the sea.

Finding a cool spot in a pavement cafe, I viewed the scene. 'Smile!' I called to the waiter as he turned to go back inside. Obligingly he turned. 'Smile? Aha!' he responded with open arms giving a huge happy smile for the camera.

Coming across another lace shop, we went inside so that I could explore, see the lace at close quarters, and perhaps buy. Perhaps? That did not come into the equation! It was a certainty.

I was surprised at the lace. I had always imagined it *all* to be very fine. In contrast, some of it was quite heavy. (Oh! I have found the card that they gave me. We were in a treasure trove of a shop called "La Perla".) An old lady sat in a comfy chair and, while she worked, customers could look on. She had a thick, firm roll on her lap over which she draped her work. She was working on some drawn thread work.

The owner explained to me that there were seven stitches in Venetian lace and the price you paid went up accordingly the more stitches you had in the piece. I wanted a small lace mat for each of our handcrafted brass toffee trays at home. The two mats that we chose had three different stitches in each. The pattern was intricate and the mats very firm and thick. I also wanted a table runner for our dining table that was new, being purchased when we had moved house a few years earlier. The long table runner, which took my eye, had five stitches and of course, was more expensive. The work on this was more open which made the runner more flexible. I didn't dare ask how much the items with seven stitches were. I didn't want to risk my luck!

The owner also explained that if the mats became damaged in years to come, I could return them for mending and they would be returned back to me. That is why I have kept the little card. Of course, it is also part of our memory box of adventures and experiences.

Before we took our leave, I could not resist. With our first grandchild due in the summer, I bought the most delectable pair of lace baby bootees, which in the event our little cherub never wore, as they would not fit.

As we strolled along, we looked in one shop window to see a glass blower had set up a little studio. Sitting in the window, he set about making articles of various kinds, using a blowtorch to heat the molten glass. On a large glass dish, there was a huge selection of sweets with wrappers of all kinds and colours. However, these were not sweets for eating. They were made of glass, complete with a twist at each end just how sweets have their wrappers twisted.

With a captive audience watching, the glass-blower deftly used a pair of tweezers or pliers to grip the ends of the still warm molten glass to expertly twist the ends into the shape he wanted before the glass cooled and hardened. We thought that they would look good in our handcrafted brass toffee trays which himself had designed and made when he was an apprentice many years previously and studying for his exams. Together with the lace mats that we had just purchased they would be a reminder of Burano.

While we were in there, a man came in asking the glass blower if the glass pens he was making could be made into perfume stoppers for young ladies in his country. Communication was difficult as neither spoke each other's language. Somehow, they managed but we eventually left them to it.

Wandering through Venice at will.

Today was to be a 'wander about Venice' day. Heading towards St Mark's Square, once again as we turned into the main part of the Piazza, we were over-awed by its sheer size; the perfect proportions of these old buildings with their intricate architecture are overwhelming. We did not venture into one of the cafés, as they are so expensive, although it would have been nice to visit the historic Venetian coffee bar—Caffè Florian—just for the experience and hang the cost!

Wandering over to the streets that lead off the Piazza, we were soon among the shops and everyday life of Venice. It was Market Day; the streets were thronged with people who browsed, chatted, crossed the many bridges over the smaller canals, and generally enjoyed life. The famous Rialto Bridge is another 'must do' in Venice and we happily strolled along, mingling in the sunshine with the crowds.

Our mission today was to head across to the Piazalle Roma. I recorded on the video that, 'Allen wants to see how the cars come in off the road bridge next to the railway station. Allen wants to see how they get the cars sorted out.'

Our maps showed that the car park was next to the railway station but on an artificial island called the Isola del Tronchetto with access from the road bridge. Between this and the Piazzale Roma was the Stazione Marittima which is the cruise terminal and ferry port.

Standing on a bridge we took in the scene of shops, their blinds pulled out over the street against the sun protecting the goods on display outside, and market stalls with all manner of goods such as you find in any market. Walking along a street that ran forever parallel to the Grand Canal, we had glimpses of the many side canals for which Venice is famous.

With bells ringing out from different churches to add to the vibrant and noisy scene, we eventually came out to where we could see in the distance that the railway station was down there. Here was a campo or square with seats under shady trees. A man stopped by a newsstand to purchase his newspaper of the day, reading a little before folding it and heading back to whence he had come. There were massive old houses with ornate flower-decked balconies. Some were in a good state of repair with a lovely pink colour-wash on the walls; others were crumbling. It was a shame to see this. The video shows that we both also had brown hair—and a lot of it.

Eventually we reached the Piazalle Roma where at last himself could satisfy his curiosity, but only by way of meandering along, past intriguing gateways set into the walls of a palazzo behind which lay a private, shady garden.

From the Piazalle Roma, seeing a water bus stop—just like our bus shelters at home—we took a vaporetto back down the Grand Canal. You will recall that on our first visit, we arrived in Venice by train and our first views of Venice were when we sailed down the Grand Canal to reach our hotel. We had been so glad that we had chosen one on the waterfront, as we didn't have to trundle suitcases down narrow streets and up, over and down bridges to a hotel amidst the warren of canals.

We were now treated to another Grand Canal experience only this time, we were able to capture it all on film for posterity. In awe and wonder at the tales they could tell, we glided past ancient palaces that dipped their feet into the water.

Some of these ancient palaces had their own landing stage in front that was marked off with a series of red and white striped poles in the water. Here and there, a motor launch was tied up, bobbing gently in the water as it waited for its master or mistress to instruct it on its next journey.

We had glimpses of private gardens lying between the palaces and here and there a narrow passageway leading straight to the water's edge. The rooms on the first floor of many of the palaces were blessed with long, narrow windows that seemingly could open out onto an ornate balcony. It must be wonderful at night to observe the stillness of the Venetian air from these vantage points.

Regardless of tourists, Venice went about its daily business while boats pulled over to tie up and deliver goods to customers. We have one photo, which shows a boat laden with furniture. Just as we all do, or should do, they used a trolley that they lashed to the front of the boat when not in use.

Passing stop number nine—S.Angelo—we soon rounded the bend from where, in the distance ,we had a glimpse of one of the landmarks of Venice, the beautiful church of Santa Maria della Salute framed by the famous Ponte dell'Accademia or Accademia Bridge. This is one of the four bridges spanning the Grand Canal. Unlike the many ornate stone bridges in Venice, this one is made of wood and appears to be quite plain.

With the waterway widening out as the Grand Canal met the Canal of San Marco and the Guidecca Canal, we passed many gondolas guided along by the skill of the gondoliers who, dressed in red and white striped tops and black trousers, plied their oars into the water as they vied for space with all the other water traffic.

The terrace of the famous Gritti Palace Hotel basked in the sunshine. Can't you just see in your mind's eye the days when richly dressed Venetian men escorted their equally richly dressed, jewel be-decked ladies, to balls, and danced the night away as music travelled over the night air?

As the church of Santa Maria della Salute reared high above us, the Vaporetto crossed the canal to stop number fourteen. From here, the massed old buildings formed a wonderful backdrop to this famous waterway.

Back in the centre of the canal, the Isola di San Giorgio with its famous Basilica and Campanile came into view. Heading towards St Mark's Square and using the zoom feature on the camcorder, we could see in the distance the banks of trees beyond the Naval Museum, which mark the Giardini or gardens.

As St. Mark's came closer, we could see the Doge's Palace behind the tourists thronging the water's edge. From our viewpoint, with a row of gondolas in front of it, it seemed to sink into the water.

Looking back from where we had come there was that wonderful view of the white Basilica di Santa Maria della Salute, standing still and quiet where it jutted out into the water as it watched over the activities of the three canals of Canal Grande, Canale di San Marco, and Canale della Guidecca.

Later that evening, we enjoyed after-dinner coffee and drinks on the terrace in front of the hotel while surveying the life of nighttime Venice as families strolled by in the light cast by many lamps bordering the water's edge, and a singer somewhere in the distance sang out her story.

The following day was another day of wandering and exploring. Once again, we explored the Arsenale at the side of our hotel but did not go into the Naval Museum. We were content to simply wander and recall places we had visited on our last visit. Actually, on our last visit we did not visit the Arsenale on foot. We had passed through on the boat to Murano so Allen was keen to examine it more at close quarters.

Our aim was to head across the Accademia Bridge to the area of Dorsoduro on the other side of the Grand Canal. We wanted to see Venice without its tourist hat.

Looking upwards from our vantage point at a small canal side cafe, we could see a profusion of greenery poking out from the rooftops. Yes, rooftop gardens, and terraces on the top floor of the buildings. How wonderful.

Across the canal the buildings were colour-washed in pastel shades; wrought iron balconies—those beautiful bulbous curved balconies—hung over the water. Here and there, small ledges—too small to be a balcony—supported troughs of colourful, flowering plants. And what are those shops displaying? Decorating the window were artisan creations of masks, glassware and all kinds of object d'art.

Strolling along the maze of streets, we came upon a stone object with a covered top standing, in the middle of a small square.

'Do you think that is an old well?' I enquired of 'him who knows everything'.

'Filled up with rubbish,' was the reply.

'There are quite a few of these old water pumps,' I observed as we came upon one standing in a pool of water as water gushed from it.

Thankful for the map, 'We have now found where we are and are not lost anymore,' I satisfyingly told the camcorder.

Unexpectedly, huge modern buildings vied for space with older, more medieval buildings along these narrow side canals.

'Are those traffic lights at the T-junction on a bend?'

I was surprised to see a bank of traffic lights on a curved pole high above the water on a bend.

'Allen, you are going to be in the way.' My chiding comment came as a figure loomed in front of the viewfinder.

'If you have a bend in the canal like that you need traffic lights, or they will all crash,' came the patient response.

Rounding the bend, we could see that we were in a more workday part of Venice. The canals and waterways, spanned by narrow bridges, were narrow with dark alleyways leading off the canal side walkways. Through decorative wrought iron gates that confronted us at some of the alleyways, we could see gardens and sunshine casting light onto the open spaces. The heavy clanging of metal being dropped, suggested that there was a workshop nearby. What a warren and conglomeration of life.

Rounding the corner, a boarded-up hole in the wall sent me dreaming of how boats would perhaps pull up in the dead of night as locals loaded and unloaded their cargo, or the family would clamber into a boat to sail down the canals for a family outing. In addition, over the wall peeped the tops of trees, hiding the garden beyond.

All at once, we found ourselves in a large campo or square, vibrant with life as Venetians went about their daily business. With fantastic displays of fruit and vegetables on open-air stalls, newsstands, shops with fully extended colourful blinds shading their window displays of goods, tall leafy trees, pigeons strutting about, we truly had a wonderful flavour of the heart of Venice.

Continuing our wanderings, we came to some truly wonderful artisan shops. One in particular—and I have to mention this it was so amazing—had the most wonderful display. At one side were sunflowers; hanging up on the wall, a jacket; here a furled umbrella; in pride of place at the front, a large open book on a lectern; on the window floor a group of love knots and of all things, a display of fruits such as bananas, apples etc., a pair of slippers, and a satchel. All made from beautifully carved wood.

Tearing ourselves away from this craft that we had never before seen, we found ourselves watching delivery boats working their way up and down the canals, carefully avoiding the boats at the side, moored up and covered against the elements.

Stopping on a brick bridge, we worked out where we were.

'We came over that bridge,' Allen informed me pointing to a bridge in the distance.

'Are you sure?' I asked doubtfully.

'Where do you want to get to?'

'I want to get the boat to go across to Guidecca Island.' I explained.

There was a pause, accompanied by the sound of Allen whistling tunelessly through his teeth.

Laughingly, I observed that, 'We could probably do with that map now.'

We must have found our bearings as we soon found ourselves in a large square where adults were escorting, past a large church and through an alleyway, a crocodile of children. A local hailed one of the ladies and passed the time of day.

Coming upon a huge wooded shed-like building, Allen was in his element. It was a workshop where men were making gondolas. Now this truly was the *real* Venice. Of course, we had to stop and look and I have to say that, watching, we were fascinated as the men smoothed the wood using a tool called a plane to shape the traditional curves of a gondola. It is good to see how these things are made. It makes it all the more real and meaningful.

Outside the work shed, lay a variety of gondolas in various stages of completion by the waterside. One, a gleaming shiny black, sat on a frame; others lay still with bottoms upended to the sun.

A gondola workshop. Venice.

Crossing the Guidecca Canal and coming to shore at the Redentore stop outside the church, we were startled to see a boat rocking in the water as a man got off it. It was like home from home.

At that time, I was working in electrical sales; I was used to having what we called 'white goods' delivered to households. Dishwashers, washing machines, cookers etc., were commonplace items to go on the delivery vans. I had never given a thought as to how these would be delivered on this city built on water where no motor vehicles are allowed.

Now, I saw a large box with the name 'Candy' written on the side and other kitchen equipment in the boat. Two men took charge of a huge wide cooker with a hob, which surely must hold quite a few cooking pots. It looked to be the width of two cookers. Carefully the men lifted it up before swiftly stepping onto dry land and placing the items on a trolley. One man went back for another, lighter, box as the other man picked up a tool bag and slung it over his shoulder. With the boat rocking furiously in the water, it was fortunate that the other items were securely tied down.

'A television,' I commented noting the details on one. 'A chest freezer.'

'They are going to install it [cooker],' Allen explained as the men moved off, pushing the trolley with their cargo to their destination.

Outside the church on the waterfront—the Chiesa del Redentore—a purple-robed priest came down the wide steps. With a bell tolling, he turned to watch as three men guided a coffin carrying the deceased to the top of the steps. Wondering what was to come next, the coffin you understand was resting on a wrought iron stand, we watched in awe and amazement as they simply picked up the coffin together with stand and carefully carried it down the fifteen steps to the water's edge. Mourners filed out as the coffin was placed on a funeral hearse—a boat—for its journey around the Venetian islands to the cemetery on the Isola di San Michele.

After they had all moved off, we mounted the steps to peep carefully into the church. Workers were removing the vases of those glorious tall, waxy, white Easter lilies that had flanked the coffin during the service.

Standing at the water's edge of Isola della Guidecca, we had a panoramic view of the Doge's Palace and Campanile across the water. The sky was overcast at this point; the funeral cortege boat bobbed and dipped across the water. From where we stood, it looked as if the coffin had to be held in place to stop it slipping off into the water.

One last dream to fulfil before leaving Venice.

Venice is famous for its masks that are worn at carnival time. Wandering around Dosoduro yesterday, we had seen a tiny artisan's workshop and wanted to return to purchase a mask. We felt that this would mean more to us—to buy from the artisan—than from a tourist shop no matter how authentic. Crossing the Accademia Bridge once more, we found ourselves in a small campo and yes, there it was. The small shop we had seen the day before. Behind the window display of masks covered in shining gold leaf, the mask maker was working delicately on a full-face mask. Onto this, she carefully applied sheets of brilliantly shining gold leaf, layer by impossibly thin layer until she achieved the desired result. Hanging in the window and around the walls were other masks of all kinds. Some were half face, just enough to cover the eyes; some were quite ornate. Against one white-painted wall was a set of stepladders, a shelf to hold her bottles of mixtures etc., and a workbench with shelves to hold her tools and implements.

In fact, the workshop was quite simple and basic but it appeared sufficient for her needs. This was not an affluent area. The front wall of the shop under the window appeared to be in a state of renovation as if she was rescuing it from dereliction, because the ancient brickwork needed plastering or rendering. Other buildings in this small area appeared to be in the same condition. It was wonderful to see that it was being rescued.

The mask-maker's name was, as I remember, Martina. I have searched and searched for her business card that I have kept safe for years but to no avail. But just a minute! I have had a thought! Going to the wall in my study where the mask is still hanging, I can see her name where she signed the mask. Is she now famous I wonder? Yes! Her name is clearly signed 'Soccorola M.' Result! If by any chance you read this one-day Martina, we hope that you have had the success that you deserve.

The mask we were to choose had to be original enough to be special. On the other hand, it had to be of a design that would withstand a long journey: a journey down the Grand Canal to the S.Lucia railway station in Venice, a journey on a train to Florence, a taxi ride to our hotel, another train journey to Rome plus taxi to hotel a journey from Rome to Sorrento which was to be by train and coach, another journey from Sorrento to Naples airport and onwards to Heathrow in the UK. Finally, a shuttle flight to Manchester, before arriving home in one piece—hopefully.

However, more of that and the brush with Customs later. For now, we were concentrating on choosing a mask.

Allen was happy, within reason and the above, to indulge me in choosing the mask I wanted. This is a full-face mask, moulded to fit the shape of the nose and mouth. The shaped eyes are cut-out holes. (If I was to wear it, I fear that I might suffocate, as there are no holes in the nose area to breathe through.) The base of the mask is of a pale cream mottled colour. Starting at the forehead and travelling all the way down one side of the face, is a painting of a harlequin figure.

My harlequin wears a wide-brimmed hat with a feather at the front. It is tipped back on his head to make way for his own mask. This again is full-faced with a sad look, a drooping moustache, and huge curved eyebrows. Around his neck he wears a pleated, double ruff. His costume of red trousers and long jacket are decorated with diamonds of green, outlined in yellow. The same pattern is along the front of the sleeves that are yellow. On his feet, he has the most wonderful yellow slippers, topped off with a huge red bow. In one hand —at least I think it is one hand, as this falls where the eye is cut out so I can only guess—he holds a big stick behind him. The edge of the mask is finished with gold braid. The mask maker had attached a black ribbon at either side so that the mask could be worn. The masks are made of plaster but inside a thick, blue, paper-like substance that is moulded to the shape covers the whole surface.

Carefully, with the sound of bells ringing out in the early morning sunshine, we watched as Martina (and I will call her Martina) packed the inside of the mask with layers and layers of folded white tissue paper. After this, she carefully wrapped the whole package in patterned white wrapping paper before carefully sealing it.

Carrying our precious parcel, we made our way back to our hotel. As I had come armed with my daughter's best straw hat with a shady brim against the hot Italian sun, I carefully placed the mask in its crown. I felt that I could carry it safely this way.

This was our last morning in Venice; we had to catch a vaporetto to the railway station for the next leg of our second Italian cities tour. Old hands at this now, safely and more confidently that before, we caught our train after another memorable journey down the Grand Canal to the railway station, my mask safely nestling on my lap.

From the Veneto to Tuscany and Florence

Being able to capture our journey through Veneto and Emilia-Romegna to Tuscany would give us lasting memories and joy. Indeed, as I have re-visited this wonderful trip through the eyes of the camera, I have become very emotional and even more so as I draft and re-draft our story. It really was a moving and adventurous experience.

As the miles, flashed by to the sound of the train wheels on the track, the countryside changed from the relative flatness of Veneto to the verdant green hills of Emilia-Romegna and Tuscany as we entered the Apennines that form the backbone of Italy, running as they do through its whole length down to the foot. Swooping down into valleys, here and there we could see green fields, shrubs, and farmhouses sitting square and solid with their cream coloured walls contrasting with the brown roofs.

Re-discovering Florence.

We decided that the day after our arrival was to be a day of re-discovery as we delighted in feeling at home in this beautiful city. We had chosen to stay in the same hotel as before. The Hotel Ariele on Via Magenta was virtually unchanged and was as comfortable as ever. We had decided that we just had to re-visit La Profeta Restaurant on Borgo Ognissanti for an evening meal and hugged this to ourselves. (Now, many years after our last visit we notice on the Internet that it received a Certificate of Excellence in 2014. I wonder if Pasquale is still there?)

Re-tracing our earlier steps to the Piazza Santa Maria Novella, we took time to absorb the sights and sounds of rushing traffic mingling with the chatter of birdsong and local dialect. The Piazza Santa Maria Novella is a huge square dominated by the thirteenth century church and monastery of the same name. Its facade of geometrical design in white and green marble is an arresting sight.

Looking down a street, we caught a glimpse of the famous Duomo, which crowns the Cathedral of Santa Maria dei Fiore, one of the largest cathedrals in the world. The zoom facility on the camcorder comes into its own here as the magnification enables you to see much more than you can with the naked eye. Multicoloured marble decorates the geometrical facade of the Duomo. Due to time constraints, we didn't go inside. It was enough to savour with awe the sheer beauty and intricacies of the outside architecture.

From our viewpoint, the Baptistry appeared to be quite small as it sits at the side of this magnificent building. It is however quite large which demonstrates the sheer scale of the cathedral with the Duomo at the end. Overall, it is 'one hundred and fifty-three metres long, thirty-eight metres wide and one hundred and fourteen and a half metres high (max.)'. The Duomo is topped with a huge orb and cross.

The Duomo is the largest brick dome ever constructed. The outside of the building is covered with marble mosaic decorations.

The Baptistry and the Duomo. Florence.

In contrast to this magnificent sight, you will see a row of modern scooters parked up on the pavement along the length of the cathedral as lorries, cars, and other traffic vie for space with tourists as they zoom around the city. Yes, both traffic and tourists.

Everywhere in Florence, narrow streets were home to a long line of parked scooters and bikes as that is how most Florentines get about—especially students. We had planned to go to the Academy Gallery to see the famous statue of David but in the end decided not to bother. There was so much else to see, we had seen copies and no doubt there would be lengthy queues.

Instead, we found ourselves in the cool cloisters surrounding a huge Piazza where young students and school parties were on their cultural sightseeing trip, their excited voices clamouring to be heard in the babble of noise within and the traffic sounds of beeping horns and squealing brakes outside. The walls beneath the shady arched roof were covered with frescos. The silence inside the church of Santissima Annunziata di Florence was broken only by the footfalls of tourists slowly circling to take in the magnificent building.

Outside the Duomo, standing proud is a huge statue of a man on a magnificent horse. As you step back and crane your head to admire it, you feel so small in comparison.

The best way to appreciate the sheer size and grandeur of the Duomo and indeed all of Florence is to go across the river and climb to the Piazza Michelangelo. From your vantage point as you rest among the gardens, you will sweep your eyes over all Florence. Catching sight of the Church of Sante Croce, you will no doubt draw breath as the Duomo towers majestically, head and shoulders above the rest. The timeless scene of the Ponte Vecchio with its bustling shops and other bridges spanning the Arno complete the scene.

Incongruously, amid all the Renaissance buildings a huge crane rose into the sky. Life goes on.

Turning back, you come back to earth as you cast your eyes over the balustrades down to the car park full of modern day coaches and cars.

Naturally, after such a long climb, you will be ready for a refreshing drink or ice cream. The Piazza Michelangelo is well equipped with tables and seats in which to enjoy and reflect. Cypress trees form a lovely backdrop to the formal gardens.

Leaving the Piazzale Michelangelo, we came to Forte di Belvedere or Fort Belvedere. Fort Belvedere is a sixteenth century fortification built for the Grand Duke Ferdinando which, lying between the Piazzale Michelangelo and Pitti Palace, has some fantastic views. It also has a huge wooden door with the largest bolt you ever could see I am sure. Allen of course had to examine the workmanship of the ironmongery on the door while I had a go at trying to move it. Without success, I might add.

Through the door, a very long flight of steps leads you inside. There are two rows of grooves in the stone where the carts would have travelled up and down. Arriving at the top of the flight of very steep steps, Allen examined a huge ring set into the wall.

'There is a rope at the top to pull the carts up the steps. They would have used a rope and block.'

All I could be heard to say was 'yes, yes,' as I listened to the explanation. After a small silence while I was trying to work this out I voiced my thoughts.

'They must have been very fit.'

It was all too technical for me.

With the delay-start function on the camera, Allen was able to set it and catch a rare shot of us together. Usually it is me on the camcorder taking him while he takes me on the point and shoot camera.

We have a lovely shot of us, together, in the grounds of the Belvedere and in the background peeping over the low wall, the top of the red Duomo with the Bell Tower of the Palazzo Vecchio at its side; the rooftops and hills of Florence spread out behind in one glorious backdrop. (It is just a shame that we chopped part of our heads off.)

'You feel that you can reach out and touch the walls of the Bell Tower [Palazzo Vecchio] from here,' I commented in awe.

'We could walk across the Vecchio to the shops. The shops might be open by then,' I remarked into the camcorder. 'We can look for my pearls.'

(Being our thirtieth Wedding Anniversary it was called Pearl Anniversary and fitting that my husband bought his beloved a string of pearls.)

'And go to the Gold Corner for something for Allen,' I continued to narrate. 'The film is coming to an end, Allen has just finished his film as well. I will fade out.'

We did stroll to the shops and down the Via Condotta where we saw a lovely selection of pearls in a shop called Moranduzzo. (I still have the box.) This was an unusual sight for us. In the UK at that time, pearl necklaces were more than likely the standard graded rows with small clasp already fitted. The pearls on display here were simply rows and rows of pearls of different types without a clasp. We were enthralled by the notion that you chose which pearls you wanted, how many rows and then the assistant brought out a huge tray of ornamental clasps of all shapes, sizes and design for you to make a selection and complete a unique piece of jewellery.

After making our selection and giving instructions that I wanted the rows of the small river pearls that I had chosen to be twisted before the clasp was fitted, we left the shop to return later when the job was done. The clasp is golden with a pattern of petals in the middle on both sides. Each petal has a different colour glass. It is all quite chunky and we had seen nothing like this in the UK. I still wear the pearls which look great with the clasp either at the side or the front—usually the front.

Festival of Flowers.

A wonderful surprise greeted us as we strolled into the centre of Florence the following day. The main street was closed to traffic, as there was a festival, or competition of some sort, taking place. As it was a Saturday, there would not be as much disruption as there would be during the week.

All down one main street, laid out on the ground, were the most beautiful floral displays. Not small ones but enormous ones; some of a great height.

A impressive one, made of red and white flowers, depicted the Duomo with the orb and cross on the top. At its side, to set it off was an informal display of flowers and foliage. Each display was laid out on a green baize cloth. One display at the other end of the street consisted of four pillars at four corners, each holding a tall floral display. There was a garland between each pillar and in the centre a huge container with yet more flowers. The artistry was wonderful and breathtaking.

Festival of Flowers. Florence.

I do remember that on this visit we simply strolled around exploring, poking our noses into shop windows, looking into antique shops, and the wonderful art galleries and workshops to be found down narrow streets. Allen was, as usual, in his element when he found a workshop be it a joiner's workshop, metalworker's shop, picture restorer, you name it he loved it. It is down these side streets off the beaten track that you find the shops that sell the kind of furnishings you would have in your home and the more select businesses. Where you have a taste of real life in the town or city.

On this return visit, we found that one of our expandable suitcases had been badly handled during transit at the airport. We were concerned that the expandable locks would not hold if we packed too tightly so we had to find a baggage shop to purchase a smaller case to take our overflow. Just another shopping experience.

Crossing over the Ponte Vecchio we found some lovely leather shops where I was able to buy a leather belt and a small bag of soft leather. I insisted that I would not over-fill it but, in truth, once we got home and it became in daily use I did to tend stuff it with all kinds of what I found to be necessities.

The street traders on the bridge were as active as ever and kept a watchful eye open for a hovering policeman so that they could pack up swiftly and move on. They appeared to keep everything in one fold-up container.

All too soon, it was time to leave this wonderful timeless city, pack up, and head to Rome. We also had our precious cargo to carry. My Venetian mask!

Before leaving the Hotel Ariele, I just had to film some of the furnishings of what was formerly the residence of the Swiss Ambassador. It truly was like being in someone's home as it appeared to have been left just how it had been with all the antique furnishings.

Stepping out into the tree-lined Via Magenta, I captured the sounds of birdsong competing with the roaring of the never-ending scooters as they roared past.

A glimpse of the River Arno revealed the timeless Ponte Vecchio that was backed by a bank of cypress trees and the Tuscan hills that rose into the distance.

Tuscany to Rome

We reached the railway station S.M. Novello without incident. It is always nice when you have been somewhere before and actually realise that you know what to do and where to go.

I remember that, as usual, I had to go exploring while Allen sat quietly with the luggage. He is not a happy traveller and likes to keep calm. I was able to check the times and platform etc. and buy a sandwich for lunch. I love shopping abroad don't you? You know, the excitement of working out the money, reading the labels on bottles and packages and imagining what it was like where the food was grown or produced?

The Hi-speed train sped through the Tuscan hills with the miles flashing past. The landscape changed again as fields growing vines came into view. Here and there, poppies grew beside the track and waved their heads to the passing train as the breeze blew them about.

Once again, we passed by Montepulciano (lovely red wines of that name produced here), and Orvieto in Umbria before the train entered Latium and turned towards the coast and Rome.

Leaving the station without incident, we were soon settled in our nearby hotel. On arriving at the hotel, the receptionist had a message for us. We had asked for tickets for the Wednesday Papal Audience and had expected tickets to be waiting for us. Actually, we did wonder if it might go ahead and as we had feared, the Audience that week had been cancelled as His Holiness was still in hospital. It was disappointing but at least we had been fortunate enough to attend one five years previously.

Once again, we had chosen the hotel in which we had stayed on our last visit. We were not disappointed. On the contrary. The Hotel San Remo had been re-furbished and updated. It was sumptuous with fitted furniture made in a light-coloured wood, plenty of mirrors and the most beautiful bathroom. All bang up-to-date. It is amazing what you film when you are excited isn't it and I just had to have proof that standards were as good as ours if not better.

The Forums, Coliseum, and beyond.

The following day, strolling into the centre of Rome, we were once again astonished at how the old, the ancient, and the new were all thrown together with traffic weaving in and out of it all.

Reaching the Forums, we had a glimpse of the 'Wedding Cake', the aptly named monument to Victor Emmanuel who was the first king of a unified Italy. I am always lost in wonder to see the huge warriors on chariots atop each end. The building really does stand out above all of Rome and you can see it from a great distance.

In the Forums we strolled around, re-visiting parts we saw previously as well as new ones. We saw the Basilica Emilia, or what is left of it, as we walked where Romans had walked two thousand years before. At one point, we were walking on a marble floor.

'I wonder if our marble hearth will last this long,' I commented as I filmed.

In the Roman Senate, we could examine the mosaic floor. A guide was busy informing her party of all the important facts. No Allen, you can't tag along! There is a well-preserved statue that was recovered from the area behind the Curia. Parts of it, which the description says were probably made from different materials, are missing.

I was, and am still, over-awed by the entrance arch that towers into the sky. The zoom function on the camcorder brought up the bas-relief inside the roof. And to think how long ago all this was built. And the craftsmanship, well!

Reaching the Capitol, the powerful microphone, as I filmed, caught birdsong that, in reality, we did not hear. When watching the film later, it was wonderful to listen to their songs as they tweeted and twittered.

Entering the water garden in the Casa degli Vestali, or House of the Vestal Virgins, caused us to pause by the pool to reflect. Mostly, there are remains of statues but one was still complete—after all this time.

House of the Vestal Virgins. Rome.

The ruins of the Forums, backed by trees, rose higher up the hill causing you to reflect and wonder about life in Rome in those triumphant days.

We reached the Tempo di Romerus and the Arco di Tito which has beautiful carvings inside the roof.

'It is truly amazing isn't it?'

For once, that was all I could say.

The stones or boulders—once part of a building—which lay around on the ground gave testimony to the craftsmanship of people of that time as they all had beautiful carvings of flowers and leaves.

And all the while, the sounds of not so distant traffic encroached on the silence of this ancient place.

Observing the wide roadway that runs from the Arch of Titus I, ever the dreamer, had to comment.

'He must have ridden up here in his chariot mustn't he?'

'Who?'

'Titus of course.'

Shaking his head at me with a smile, we left the Forums and came to the Coliseum. Last time if you remember, we didn't venture inside but this time we did.

Allen was keen to explain it all. (He really is far cleverer that I am.) Through the gaps, we were looking under the floor where the animals and slaves were kept. There is tiered seating and it is much preserved inside. The construction is amazing. Through the railings I filmed how close were the nearby Forums. It put it all into perspective.

It was so hot that I was thankful of the wide-brimmed straw hat that I had borrowed from my daughter. It had been useful for carrying my Venetian mask but today, that had another resting place. A passer-by took a photo of us both at the Coliseum. That was lovely. Outside, it was time to look at the map to see what was next.

'Where are we?' I asked.

'Well, we are here (pointing to the map). We have to go up there. We are all right, we are not in a rush.' Allen kept folding and re-folding our excellent map of Rome as we plotted our next route with a pointed finger. All the while, there was lots of whistle blowing as traffic thundered around the Coliseum.

With one last look at the ruin of this magnificent building, we turned and followed the route on the map. Reaching a huge square—isn't everything in Rome huge—cars set off with a squeal of brakes as they raced along going this way and that even though a moped was stationary in the middle of it all.

In the Piazza Venezia, seeing a bus disgorging a lot of men in their ceremonial uniforms I had to ask.

'What are they all doing dressed like that?' I really had confidence that Allen would know.

'It is not their standard uniform,' he thought.

'Well I wonder what they are doing in their best uniform.' I would not leave it at that.

Some of the police were in quite plain uniforms while some were very ornately dressed. One had a white hat—he would be for directing traffic. Horse and carriages, cars, wagons, orange buses, scooters, and tourists, came from all directions. Two men were on horses. The National Guard wore hats like Napoleon, medals and suchlike. One contingent carried a flag each. Another wore a quite sober uniform with a flat cap. Some cars were being stopped and re-directed as the policeman pointed down the street. There was much blowing of whistles and directing of traffic. We could have watched the show all day. You really have to experience Rome, and Piazza Venezia in particular, to appreciate it.

Crossing the River Tiber (Tevere), we now saw the dome of St Peter's Basilica rising above other buildings in the street. Using the zoom facility, I captured the one hundred and forty larger-than-life sized statues depicting saints, martyrs, popes et al that look out over the square from their position atop the colonnades.

Coming nearer, I was able to film the Great Door and inside the entrance. Quietly, we approached and entered, savouring the stillness. The Pieta was now behind glass. We were so fortunate to have seen it before this happened. Approaching the cupola, we could see the tomb of St Peter. We were able to see again the marble plaque on the wall which lists all the Pope's going right back to St Peter in 33AD.

Later, we walked down the streets with all the expensive shops such as Bellini as we headed to the Spanish Steps. This steep stairway of one hundred and thirty-five steps climbs steeply from the Piazza di Spagna at the bottom; it goes right up to the church at the top in the Piazza Trinità dei Monti. From the top of the steps, as you rest and catch your breath, there is a wonderful view over the rooftops that are dominated by the dome of St Peter's, which rises high above them in the distance. The Spanish Steps are a wonderful and popular meeting place, which as usual, was crowded with tourists, many resting their weary feet. One young man quenched his thirst by supping water from the fountain at the bottom of the steps. This fountain is the Fontana della Barcaccia or 'Fountain of the ugly Boat'. On a high plinth further down the street was a huge statue of Our Lady watching over everything.

Looking back up the steps, the twin towers at either side of the wonderful facade of the church with the obelisk in front are an unforgettable scene.

It was a footsore and weary couple who made their way back to their hotel that day!

Trastevere.
Today we were to cross the river to the Trastevere area of Rome. As the Wednesday Papal Audience had been cancelled, we had, in effect, and extra day for sightseeing.

Our route from the San Remo took us west to the southern end of the Tiber. At a bend in the river is the small Tiber Island, connected to both sides of the river by bridges. Crossing onto the island, we came across the church of St. Bartholomew.

'It is all marble inside isn't it?' I can be heard saying to my husband.

'It is a beautiful church but they were waiting for a funeral cortege to come in so we couldn't really film anything,' I recorded.

'We are back on the other side of the river,' I went on, 'in the area of Trastevere.'

In a little open-air cafe, its garden bordered by green shrubs and filled with umbrella-shaded tables, we rested a while for a cool drink. This also gave me the opportunity to capture the buildings and the sights and sounds of this very old and traditional Italian part of Rome. It is said that some of the people who live here have never crossed the river into the city. Their life is there. In Trastevere.

Charming colour-washed buildings with sloping red-tiled roofs were home to arched, flower-decked balconies high up in the walls built to give some shade to the inhabitants.

'Look at those little chimney pots up there,' I cried out. 'They have got little roofs on top.'

Modern day television aerials joined the chimney pots on these ancient rooftops. The chimneys looked like little houses.

'I think they are more for ventilation than chimneys,' observed my husband.

It was so peaceful here in the Comparone Ristorante Gelateria with the sound of birds singing out to each other in their joy of the day only broken by the constant roar of traffic.

(At the time I captured on film the writing [name of ristorante] on a serviette or napkin. I knew it would come in handy one day, even if it was twenty years later.)

Making our way through Trastevere, we came upon a workshop. Allen was even happier now that he had a workshop to catch his interest. This one was a woodcarver's workshop and we stood awhile to watch as he created his wonderful objects from wood. In the window and just inside the shop that was all glass-fronted, there was a very long piece of life-like rope, a trinket box, and a swan bending its head with each feather carved perfectly. It looked as if the woodcarver was also restoring picture frames. There were marvellous carvings of fruit dishes adorned by huge bunches of grapes. Wood shavings littered the floor of his little workshop as he worked in the warm sunshine. This reminded us of Venice where had seen a shop full of carved articles only a few days ago before we bought my Venetian mask.

We came to the Piazza di S.Cecilia with its ninth century church dedicated to Saint Cecilia. Passing open gates, we had a glimpse of a courtyard with a huge important looking building in the distance. Amid this wealth of ancient Rome a little boy, pedalling furiously on his little trike, rode around the courtyard.

Wandering around the church with its expanse of marble floors, arched columns around the sides and an intricately painted ceiling, we spied an open door. A nun was on the telephone. A nod to the present day. It was interesting to see that this church did not have rows of pews, as do most churches. Instead, there were simply rows of chairs. I can't help thinking that the marble floor would be hard on the knees.

Outside in the cloisters, a clamour of bells rang out noisily telling us that it was twelve o'clock.

It was also market day. In the streets, as you see the world over, a jumble of market stalls spilled out onto the pavements; mopeds were parked up in any space left vacant amid the trees, pavements, and shoppers.

Crossing the river again, we had an uninterrupted view along the riverbank to the white dome of Saint Peter's Basilica rising above the trees.

'We are now in the Piazza Navona,' I recorded. 'The fountain you can see there is one of the two designed by Bernini. The other one is right at the other end.'

In the middle of this huge open space, built on the site of Domitian's Stadium in the first century, is an obelisk surrounded by the Fountain of the Four Rivers. Surrounding the square are many churches and palaces and of course, open-air cafe's where you can rest under the welcome shade of an umbrella as you sit and take in the awesome grandeur of it all. I commented that it was much quieter than on our first visit but that, of course, it was school holidays then [Easter], and everyone now is getting about on scooters. A street-trader was busily polishing his wares.

On one side is the Baroque church of Sant' Agnese in Agone. The equally sumptuous Palazzo Pamphili is adjacent to it. Other buildings are not quite so ornate although equally grand and it all adds to the flavour of this wonderful piazza.

The fountains here are not the kind that we are used to in the UK with water shooting up into the air. These Bernini fountains consist of huge figures of animal and man with water gushing from apertures into the bowl below. The low walls of the fountain provide a handy resting place for weary, sun-drenched sightseers.

Later, in the evening, much refreshed we made our way to the Trevi Fountain. Last time we were here, as I said earlier, it was under wraps. Now, fully restored to all its glory, we could absorb this wonderful experience.

With Allen behind the lens he was filming; I was posing.

'It is all right, I have gone past you now.' He panned the camera past me to capture the sight of the water cascading over the statues and basins into the huge bowl below. The coolness of the early evening vied with the chatter of tourists who thronged the whole area.

After finding a ristorante for dinner, we returned as dusk was falling. What a sight! The Trevi was now floodlit and I, in my white pleated palazzo pants, yellow overshirt, little bag from Florence, and no doubt stiletto heels, climbed down the steps to the edge while Allen filmed the whole scene. Well, there are some things you just have to do aren't there. Just to tuck away in your box of memories.

Over in the distance we could see two young lads chatting up a very elegant policewoman. We wondered if one was our son who hadn't told us he was here; this was just the kind of thing he would have done at the time. Actually, there were two policewomen and they weren't being chatted up; they were laying down the law.

The Vatican Museums and climbing the Dome.

Not again! I can hear you groaning. Well, actually, yes but this time it would be different. We decided to visit again and capture it all on film. We also wanted to go up to the top of the Dome while we were still fit enough to do so.

The Swiss Guards in their distinctive uniforms were stopping everyone at the entrance gates. While one stood in the sentry box, another checked over everyone before they would let anyone pass. On through the Basilica we went, once again awestruck by its sheer size. We headed to the lift that would take us to the roof.

'So we are now on the roof and then we start climbing,' I recorded.

'We go up those steps there,' Allen pointed to a flight of steps outside the base of the Dome.

'Right up to there,' I pointed up the walls of the Dome. 'Up to those windows.'

'Oh, past those, up to those little whirls,' was the reply.

'And those are the tops of the little chapels, aren't they? Little domes,' I continued. 'It gives you some indication of just how big they are when you see what is outside.'

On the roof, we were now looking down over the little domes or cupolas of the smaller chapels to the view over the gardens and Rome.

'That is the top of the monument of Victor Emmanuel with the horses on top.' I was busy filming. We could also see the backs of the statues atop the colonnades that surround Saint Peter's Square.

'We are now looking over the balcony which surrounds the base of the Dome,' I again recorded as we went back inside.

The camcorder caught the design and workmanship of the fascinating mosaics in all their glorious detail.

'They are gorgeous aren't they?' I breathed.

With the camcorder, I was able to capture much more detail of the inside of the cupola than could be seen with the naked eye from this distance. It was wonderful. All the sculptures, paintings, and gold leaf right up to the very top in wonderful precision and beauty were now clearer to us through the viewfinder.

'And that is the top of the canopy down there, isn't it?' I went on as I filmed through the protective grille to the scene far below. 'Over the altar which is over the tomb of Saint Peter.'

We now started the climb of three hundred and thirty steps as we zigzagged inside one side of the double skin of the Dome.

'Can you hear me puffing,' I called.

A lot of heavy breathing shows up on the recording; thankfully, a helping hand was not far away, as a stranger stopped to see that I was all right. Allen was ahead of me and turned to see what was going on. He does look after me.

The steps were very narrow indeed and steep. As the dome was curved, so were the walls. As you went higher and higher, the curve became more pronounced and you had to lean over. It also got darker with the only light from those little windows that you can see are dotted around the outside of the dome.

The steps were now extremely steep. There was a lot of laughter—if you had the breath—as all those climbing huffed and puffed.

'That's me falling up the stairs. Now, we are going into a bit of a passageway. Up a staircase, a steel one not the stone one, I can't see much. Probably see more with the camera. The heavy breathing is me,' Allen went on [for the camera].

The curve of the dome was now very pronounced; there wasn't a lot of space to move. Looking at the camcorder film as I write and refresh my memory, it is fascinating to see how the dome was built, the complex shapes, and the tiled walls inside the double skin.

'It has just tapered off,' I can hear being said. The camcorder was picking up mostly a blur in the dark confined space.

'We have a bit of a normal staircase here,' I heard as we turned a corner and saw a straight stretch.

Then, just when we thought that we could climb no more, we came to the spiral staircase.

'The smallest, narrowest, winding staircase you have ever seen in your life. I can't tell what I am photographing. I can't get my head around to it.'

At this point Allen must have taken the camcorder so that I wouldn't drop it. His very un-agile wife needed two hands and all her concentration at this point.

Help was at hand, as there was something with which to grab whilst you hauled yourself up the last few steps. With shaking legs that threatened to give way and laughter, we emerged into the sunshine.

'We made it! It was as bad as last time,' I laughingly observed as I turned to the view over the railings.

Allen was capturing the numerous cupolas on the roof of the Basilica. People below made their way to the doorway of a small building.

'Go on, tell me again,' Allen urged me.

'Those people, going through that doorway, are on the top of the roof. They are not on the pavement down below.'

'Yes, that's right.'

Far down below was the car park and nearby the new Audience Hall. In the piazza, we could see what looked like a lot of ants scurrying around. They were in fact people but we were so high up, they looked like ants. Moving around, being so close to the tops of all the smaller cupolas or domes and the tops of buildings below, there is a wonderful opportunity to study the architecture. From our vantage point we could see, and were awed by, the sheer magnificence of the design and build of this great Basilica.

There was also a picture postcard view of the geometrically balanced design of Saint Peter's Square as it flowed out from the Basilica into the streets of Rome near the Tiber. The Egyptian obelisk in the centre was casting shadows in the sunshine. Also visible was the Vatican railway line behind the gate in the wall; there we saw a rooftop patio just below one of the smaller domes, complete with tables and chairs and the gardens in-between the palaces that form the Vatican Museums. A peep into another world once again.

We negotiated our way down the other side of the dome, in the same zigzag fashion, coming back into the Basilica with shaking legs.

In the Vatican Museums, the staircase fascinated us.

'It is a double spiral staircase. One going up and one coming down.' Allen explained. This was not the narrow one we had just negotiated. This one was wide with shallow steps that rose and fell in a huge circle. The sides of the staircase were ornately carved.

'It is clever isn't it?' I commented in wonder as, looking up, it seemed to go on forever in seemingly never-ending arcs.

'We are now on our way, up the spiral staircase, to buy tickets for the museums.'

I filmed up the staircase and caught Allen at the top catching me on his camera.

Again, we wandered through those remarkable corridors. This time, passing through hall after hall I walked with my head tipped backwards as I caught the awesome beauty of the artwork on the curved ceilings. As I described much of the same earlier, I won't dwell too much now but I do have to share this next snippet.

On the wall was a relief map of Venice and, as we had recently visited there, were excited to see, not only the layout, but also our hotel the Bucintoro by the Naval Museum. The map also showed all the little islands that you don't always see on maps.

You will have to see the artwork, tapestries, statues, and plasterwork in this wonderful place yourself; I cannot describe it adequately to do it all justice.

From one of the windows we had a good view of the Dome with all the intricate stonework and reflected with awe on our adventure in going up there—not once—but twice. We were so lucky.

All too soon, it was time to leave Rome behind and head off to a new adventure in the Neapolitan Riviera and Sorrento by the sea.

South to Sorrento from the Hills of Rome

Sorrento has a local railway that runs to Naples, however there was not a direct line from Rome to Sorrento at that time. Our travel company Citalia therefore, had booked us onto a coach of theirs that was part of another tour. The journey from Rome to Sorrento was about four hours.

We left Rome and the region of Latium in bright sunshine. Our Rome hotel was near the railway station so meeting the coach was not a problem for us. After all, we were old hands at this by now. Learning from our earlier experience in Rome, we knew to guard our suitcases with our life. And, guard my Venetian mask that I now carefully carried in a canvas bag that I had bought in the Vatican Museum. I would need my hat to shade me from the hot Neapolitan sunshine.

Travelling smoothly on the motorway, we soon passed the historical town of Cassino in the distance (the tour guide pointed it out). Monte Cassino was the scene of a great battle in World War Two. In the heat of the mid-day sun, we left Latium, crossing into Campania, as we headed to Naples. After a short stop at the Terminus in Naples, the driver continued on the motorway heading towards Salerno on the Gulf of Salerno but turned off the motorway as we approached the Sorrento Peninsula that forms part of the Bay of Naples. It was only here that the journey became more interesting as we drove along a scenic route along the coast to Sorrento on the northern side of the peninsula.

When planning this addition to our previous Italian adventure, we looked carefully through the Citalia brochure and the Green Michelin Guide Book, deciding that we would like to stay as central as possible.

I was enchanted by the romantic history of the Imperial Hotel Tramontano and its location in the very centre of Sorrento overlooking the sea. Formerly a private mansion as well as hotel, it has played host to many famous guests including royalty. The celebrated sixteenth century poet Torquato Tasso was born in Sorrento; a plaque in his honour has been placed on a wall in one of the public rooms. The public rooms, and indeed the rest of the hotel, are filled with priceless antiques, frescoes and more, leaving you to feel that you have stepped back in time and are visiting someone's home. The restaurant overlooks the sea and we usually enjoyed after-dinner drinks on the adjoining terrace, watching the entrancing sunsets as an enormous red sun sunk gradually over the Bay of Naples.

However, for now, back to the present. Approaching the hotel after negotiating the busy streets, a porter came out to take our luggage. We found that our room was in the older part of the hotel, in an excellent position overlooking the sea. This was perfection itself. There was no balcony as such but the long windows opened up to allow us to stand at the wrought iron railings which prevented us from falling down to the sea and gaze into the distant shore.

Everything was delightful. Wandering out of the hotel onto a narrow street after settling into our room, we rounded a corner to find ourselves in a small square with a public garden, the Villa Communale, on the left. To our right, the thirteenth century cloisters and the church of St. Francis stand cool and serene. At the end of the square, a panoramic scene of the Bay of Naples with Vesuvius beyond came into view. This square overlooks Marina Piccolo, which is actually quite big; it is where the jet foil and ferries leave for the island of Capri and others destinations. Marina Grande to the west of Sorrento town is actually quite small and more of the type where locals go to fish and women sell their lace.

The hotel itself had a wonderful swimming pool set in lush, cool gardens. We found that it was best to do our sightseeing in the morning, unless we were too lazy and opted just to relax after our exertions of the previous two weeks. Arriving back in time for lunch on the pool terrace always seemed a good option and one that we usually took.

Exploring Sorrento.

I seem to have a lot of film from all angles of the hotel, so I must have taken a tour to film out of the windows set in the hallways of the newer part of the hotel that was built onto the original building. I captured views of the hills above Sorrento and the hotels dotted around them. After arriving the day before we had wandered and talked and, on entering the hotel afterwards, thought that we would never want to leave.

This morning though we were eager to explore and were up bright and early. We enjoyed an excellent breakfast in the restaurant overlooking the sea, after which we wandered around the reception rooms of this magnificent nineteenth century former mansion.

The doors of the elegant lounge were open, leading onto the terrace overlooking the sea that stretched out into the Gulf of Naples. I broke off from my filming to comment on what I could see.

'That is Vesuvius over there, coming through the mist.'

From the far end of the terrace, we could see down onto the jetty and bathing platforms of the Marina Piccolo. You have to lean over with care or you will fall down the sheer drop into the sea!

'There is Peter's Beach.' A sign on a diving platform sitting in the middle of the water, proclaimed this. Beyond that we could see that at the jetty, a sleek boat was waiting for its passengers. It was the jetfoil fast boat to the island of Capri. A trip there was on my list of things to do!

Wandering out of the hotel, we dodged the succession of noisy scooters that came flying past and headed towards the square. Following the road round from the Villa Communale, we came to the Piazza Tasso.

The Piazza Tasso is the vibrant, busy, and entrancing centre of Sorrento from which the main streets through Sorrento meet. The Corso Italia, long and straight, was a hive of activity. At one end was a splendid view of the three-story bell tower of the cathedral. From where we stood, it appeared to be in the middle of the street.

The sights and sounds, the hustle and bustle all around us, especially the colourful old-fashioned ice-cream cart on wheels, enchanted us. The Piazza Tasso is an ideal place to people-watch and find out what goes on, especially how mothers and fathers transport their children.

'That scooter has a little kid standing up in the middle,' we commented to each other in wonder. It was so different from home.

We found that this was a feature [at this time]; Mums and Dads zipped around on scooters with one child in the middle in the safety of their parent's legs while another often perched on the back holding on to the adult's shoulders in front. It gave a whole new meaning to the term 'school run'. Yes! I do think that there was school on a Saturday.

We had time to take in the elegance of the Piazzo Tasso with its tall, elegant, square buildings; the abundance of shady trees; the whistling of the traffic police; the nearby hotel that flew flags of many countries at its garden entrance.

The purpose of this break in Sorrento, as I have said before, was to relax after our three-centre journey through Italy. Sunday therefore was a quiet day by the hotel pool. We were not troubled by people putting out towels very early. If the pool attendant found them when he came out early in the morning to tidy up the pool area, he quite simply removed them and heaped them onto the railings.

Back in time to Pompeii.

One of our promised visits was to the excavated city of Pompeii. We had found that from the railway station in Sorrento we could catch a train to Pompeii as it ran past there on its way to Naples. The railway station was but a short walk from our centrally based hotel.

As usual, I was exhorted to get up (almost) at the crack of dawn and make an early start. This made sense really, given the heat of the day as the sun rose.

After an early breakfast, we strolled along the deserted streets in the cool of the early morning while Sorrento appeared to be still sleeping. It was not really so early but it seemed so as the shops were not yet open. It was an easy matter at the booking office to purchase tickets as the prices were listed both for single and return. The ticket officer was used to tourists as well. The train journey was uneventful but it was good to see the countryside and coast outside the town from the train as it followed the coast.

Arriving at Pompeii, we were soon at the entrance. Allen was eager to go exploring. I, on the other hand stood; I looked around at the vast expanse of what seemed, to me, like nothingness but in reality was a large expanse of stones and boulders.

'Can we go now?' I asked hopefully. 'I have seen it now.' Ruins are not really my cup of tea.

With a withering look of disgust came a response.

'You haven't seen anything yet. Come on!'

So I did and was pleasantly surprised as, with a huge sigh of resignation, I meekly followed. With straw hats shading us from the sun, we plotted our way using the map and guidebook.

Railed walkways had been constructed to allow tourists to walk around in safety along the tunnels connecting various areas and up different heights.

Allen was in his element. At one point, he tagged onto a party of tourists with an official guide. He learned about how the stone formations in the roadway were to guide horses and carts and to allow people to cross the street thus avoiding the sewage. The road apparently was also part of the sewage and disposal system. It is marvellous when you think of all the design and construction that went on two thousand years and more ago.

The guide eventually realised that she had an interloper.

'My party only please,' she commanded. Whereupon, one sheepish young man came back to my side.

I caught on camera, the formation of walls where thin, red, narrow slabs alternated with larger blocks of grey stone.

'Are they breeze blocks?'

'They are not breeze blocks. They are lava aren't they?' My fount of knowledge answered me.

'How did they build with lava before it erupted?' I was showing my ignorance.

'Well, it has been erupting for many years,' was the patient response.

Pompeii was a whole town, destroyed by lava when Mt. Vesuvius erupted in 79AD. There had been one some years earlier, in 62AD, and building work was still in progress to repair the major damage from that one. This one caused destruction with people and buildings covered in hot lava and rock up to twenty-five metres deep.

Surprisingly [to me] many buildings were fairly intact. It was thought provoking to think of those poor people who were obliterated during the eruption of nearly two centuries earlier.

'They haven't just plastered the walls, they have plastered and decorated. They [walls] are not just bare stone.'

I was starting to absorb this peep into the past of another life and culture.

'Yes, yes,' agreed Allen.

All the while, during this tour of devastation, birds were twittering loudly as they embraced the day. Amazingly, beautiful mosaics laid into the floor of houses were still intact among the ruins. The inside wall of one building was painted with a picture of bulls, or cattle of some sort, in flight, the rich colours still visible, and other panels of decoration.

'It is beautifully decorated, isn't it?'

This fell on deaf ears as Allen, meanwhile, was engrossed in the workmanship while I chattered on. Outside, among the trees, we came across the amphitheatre. Much of the outside was intact. At the top of the steps, you could see how the rows of seats would have cascaded down to the stage below.

I, as usual, did not climb without a small huff and puff.

'I thought I had done my climbing when we went up the Dome,' I got out between breaths. 'In Rome,' I added.

The view was incredible. Allen drunk it all in and, I must say, so did I.

It was tempting to linger but, deciding that it was getting too hot, agreed that we would return to our hotel for lunch by the pool.

As we neared the exit, a coach was disgorging its passengers. We were thankful (and still are to this day) that we had arrived early. We felt sorry for them having to tour around this ancient place in the searing heat of the afternoon sun. It was only a short stroll to Pompeii Scavi, Villa del Misteri station. We patiently waited here for a train back to Sorrento.

There is a wealth of up-to-date travel and other information at *http://wikitravel.org/en/Pompeii*

Later that night, we again enjoyed the blood red sunset from the terrace of our hotel and the uninterrupted view across the Gulf of Naples. Allen was behind the viewfinder and using all sorts of functions to try and capture the scene.

'I hope that this turns out.'

'Do you know what you have used? Which buttons you have pressed,' I queried.

'Yes,' he assured me.

'If it doesn't turn out you know which buttons not to press don't you? I could not resist adding.

'Exactly, and we will have to come back and do it all again. But it is never the same,' he concluded.

To the Island of Cápri.

We awoke to another day of sunshine and anticipation of the day ahead. Today was Cápri day! That famous, little island off the Sorrento Peninsula.

It could not be avoided! We had to go across the water by boat and elected to use the hydrofoil. This hi-speed ferry went from Marina Piccolo at the front of the hotel. Well, to be exact, from the jetty in front of the hotel which we could reach either by clambering down numerous steps or by using the lift which went straight down the sheer wall of rock on which Sorrento is built. There is also a long winding road.

Looking back from the jetty far below, the view of this sheer wall of rock with the hotels perched on top and the many inlets in the coast, is unforgettable. Interestingly, trees covered some of the wall of rock.

People of many languages filled the early morning air with great excitement and anticipation as they chattered away, watching the comings and goings of slower ferries and other boats coming into harbour from the sea.

Leaving Marina Piccolo and Sorrento far behind across the increasing expanse of water, we had a wonderful view of the tree-covered land rising up from Marina Grande. In this little fishing port to the west of Sorrento town we could see the multitude of boats of all sorts tied up in the harbour; houses, shops, and market stalls of local fishermen and lace makers vied for space as fishermen mended their nets and spread them to dry in the sun.

Reaching Cápri (pronounced Caapri not Capree) on its northern shore, we disembarked at Marina Grande, faced with another sheer wall of rock.

'Where is the town?' you may ask? We soon found out.

In order to ascend the sheer cliff face to Cápri on the plateau, we had to take a ride on the funicular railway. This was an unexpected treat; the ride afforded the most unforgettable views of both the island and the boats out to sea.

The towns of Ana Capri to the west, with Capri to the east of this island, sit serenely on the top of this plateau while the perpendicular wall of rock dips into the clear blue waters of the Tyrrhenian Sea.

The funicular from Marina Grande on the northern shore, took us up to the centre of Cápri town on the island's southern side. We could see the harbour below and a big ship. I was busy narrating as I recorded.

'That island straight ahead would be Ischia wouldn't it?' (I could see the hazy hump of a small island ahead.) 'And Procida, and that would be the mainland,' I finished as I swung round to the northern coast of the Gulf of Naples.

Soon, we were wandering around the flower-decked streets and squares, peering into shops as we went. The jeweller's shops were like nothing that we had seen before. Everything was just, well, more such as larger pieces of jewellery and longer necklaces of the most beautiful pearls and coral. We were outside the Casa del Corallo. Corallo being Italian for coral. No prices but if you have to ask the price then, they say, you can't afford it.

With palm trees waving their fronds against a brilliant blue sky, flower-decked railings protecting you from the sheer drop, and white houses sparkling in the sun, we thought that we were in paradise. (Our travel adventures at this time were only just beginning.) Oh, the romance of it all. It took my breath away as I was lost in a dream.

Wandering on and climbing higher, we came to where we could see out to sea on the south side. The sheer rocks as they rose up were huge. Far below, a luxury private yacht that was more a huge boat, not a sailing yacht with sails, lay at anchor. How some people are able to live! There is another world out there.

Looking down, the water as it washed over the boulders was crystal clear.

'You know, you could drink that water.' I commented. 'It is so clear.'

We had been able to clamber down some steps to the water's edge where we could see that another boat tied up behind rocks, its furled masts telling the tale of rest and relaxation. We were at a little cove with a shingle beach where a line of sun beds waited for occupancy.

On the way back, we passed an old, classic, open-topped red car with an awning over the seats against the sun, parked up so that its occupants could savour the view. The view of the little cove below, protected by walls of sheer rock, was so beautiful. Actually, the car was a taxi which ferried tourists around the island and up (and down) the steep gradients. The driver turned the ignition and started up the engine of the protesting car with a grating sound. He zoomed off down the hairpin bends at speed, followed by an orange bus. There wasn't room on the bend for both vehicles.

Back in town, in Piazza Umberto I the clock on the bell tower told us that it was nearly midday. It was time for some refreshment. We have never forgotten the shock when, stopping at a pavement cafe and on asking for two cans of cola and two ice creams, we were charged ten pounds (our money). It was still lire in Italy then so it would have been lots of noughts! That was nearly twenty years ago as I recall this little snippet. I dread to think what that simple order would cost in 2014.

In any event, we decided that we would head back and have lunch on the terrace by the pool in our hotel in Sorrento. At the time, I think that an omelette and salad for two was about ten pounds. Much more reasonable.

Making our way down narrow streets where flowering shrubs trailed over garden walls, and the beautiful passion flowers tumbling over walls to face the sun were in full bloom, we marvelled at the sheer abundance of it all.

I got a shot of Allen's watch. It said ten to two. It was time to go back and savour the day quietly while soaking up the sun.

Farewell to Sorrento.

There was time for one last look before leaving for the airport. This last leg of our trip included transfer to the airport. Although my borrowed very posh straw hat (my daughter's best wedding guest hat) had been in good use while in Sorrento, it now reverted to being a careful depository for my Venetian mask. Still wrapped in the layers and layers of white tissue paper and outer wrapping paper, it was safely packed in the crown of the hat so that nothing would damage it.

Now, tucking our memories inside my mind, I wandered around the Villa Comunale (public garden) at the side of the hotel, capturing the sheer abandon depicted in the statue of a lady as, on tiptoe, she flung her arms wide. The majestic sounds emitting from the organ in the ancient church of San Francisco to my right where the organist was practising, rent the air. I strolled in the Chiostro di S. Francesco (Cloisters) where the coolness and peace were a contrast to the bustle outside; I drank in the timeless picture of the flowering shrubs which cascaded over the old stone of the high inside walls down to the lower arches which surrounded the peace and seclusion of the central courtyard.

Replaying the film I took all those years ago, transports me back to that time; I feel that I could reach out, touch, and smell all this beauty. I can just imagine how the monks would have strolled around as they engaged in contemplation or quiet conversation, their sandals making little noise against the cool stone floor.

Reluctantly tearing myself away, I quietly made one last foray into the gardens for a final look at the stunning, panoramic view over the Bay of Naples before I went back into the hotel for our departure.

Here, I recorded the inscription on the plaque to the sixteenth century Italian poet Torquato Tasso who was born in Sorrento. You will have to go and see it for yourself. When we were there, it was on a wall in the elegant sitting room, which overlooks the sea.

We had spent much of this part of our anniversary adventure just strolling around and relaxing by the pool. After the sights and sounds of Venice, Florence and Rome, we were thankful for this oasis in our lives.

'There goes the boat to Cápri,' I recorded, 'just past the headland. We will come back to Sorrento and explore a little further.' The camera then faded out.

Then it almost all went wrong.

Well, as you will see shortly, we did come back and what an adventure it was. First, though, there were other happenings in our life.

On arriving at Heathrow, we blithely sailed through the 'Nothing to Declare' channel. Unfortunately, the customs people had other ideas. Ordering me to one side, they took my straw hat and proceeded to take out the parcel within the crown.

'You had better let her do that!' warned my husband.

'I have carried this all the way down the Grand Canal in Venice,' I protested. 'I carried it carefully to Florence, 'carefully

~ 123 ~

to Rome, and then to Sorrento and stowed it safely on the aeroplane. It is a Venetian mask!' I was outraged but in retrospect could see the problem.

Reluctantly they let me undo the parcel, all the while watching me with eagle eyes. I was proved innocent of carrying anything dangerous or obnoxious. I realised that all the white tissue paper probably looked like a mass of white 'something'. Thankfully, my Venetian mask was unharmed and my harlequin still watches over the comings and goings in my study.

Later that year our first grandchild was born. We revelled in being Granny and Granddad and were still young enough to enjoy the experience. Work and family commitments increased. Sorrento pulled at our heartstrings and in 1996 we did return. This time for a longer stay where we intended seeing and experiencing all that we could.

We did not know what perils awaited.

Return to Sorrento

There was no contest. It had to be the Hotel Imperial Tramontano again. The location was so perfect. Choosing to travel later in the season when the sun would not be so hot, we had again booked with Citalia as we had previously had such a good experience with them. Again, they had given us a room with a small balcony, overlooking the bay. We planned to go to Amalfi and this time to see Ercolano (Herculeum), another city covered during the volcanic eruption of 79AD.

In the evening, we introduced ourselves to Alfonso the Bar Manager. In Italy, as in many Mediterranean countries, bar work is a sought-after career. Alfonso's son also worked in the bar and his ambition was to take over from his father after he had gained experience in another hotel.

We spent a couple of days just wandering round and exploring in more depth. This time we were on a regular scheduled holiday, not tailor-made one as we were previously, so the Citalia Rep took other guests in the hotel and us on a walking tour of the town. This is always useful as the Reps are usually a fount of knowledge.

One shop that sold only lemon-based (limone), products enchanted us. And not only liquers, but soaps, creams and more. One wine and spirits shop, called the Pink Elephant, had a huge pink elephant outside—not a real one, I hasten to add. The owner was adept at reeling off his sales patter. But ask him a question which wasn't in his repertoire and he couldn't answer. He didn't otherwise speak a word of English.

Sorrento is noted for its inlaid woodwork. We were taken to one of the showrooms in town called A Gargiulo Jannuzzi. Here one of the staff gave us a fine demonstration on the process of inlaying different shapes of wood into tables, chairs, other pieces of furniture and other articles. The salesman also told us how to spot a fake. The inlaid wood pictures took our eye. One was of Venice with the gondolas bobbing by the water's edge of San Marco, a Campanile in the background.

We were entranced and excited to see a picture depicting Marina Grande with Mt. Vesuvius in the background. In the foreground lay a small fishing boat, steps up to a huddle of houses and . . . 'the pole'.

'Look! That is exactly the picture we caught on camera last time. The trees on the high wall and, look, the cat balancing on the pole!'

We were astonished. These two were something to think about. Needless to say, some heavy negotiating followed in the days ahead. With each other I might add, not just the salesman.

From Marina Piccolo to Marina Grande.

We were happy to stroll leisurely and soak up the scene and atmosphere. The Marina Piccolo lies below the Hotel Tramontano, far below the sheer rock face that is a feature of this coastline.

As explained on our last visit, you had a choice of taking the lift down from or negotiating steps. There is also a long winding road. Carefully we arrived at the edge of the water and wandered along looking at the boats and bathing platforms. It was all so quiet and serene as the sun rose higher to warm the water and early bathers.

We found that the Marina Piccolo was unchanged. The cool, clear, green water was also unchanged. Although named 'Marina Piccolo', it is in fact quite a large marina but more given over to jetties for pleasure craft, fast ferries to the islands, and bathing platforms for sun-seekers and those swimming lazily or otherwise in the cool clear water. For the energetic, there are many steps down to the water, and back up again!

In contrast, the Marina Grande to the west of the town is more like a little fishing village unchanged by time. To reach Marina Grande you have to walk downhill, out of town, before turning towards the sea. A huge promontory of rock, topped by trees, separates the two marinas.

After exploring a little, we made our way back up to street level, heading west along the main road with the sea on our right. Walking along in the shade cast by the high walls of buildings and trees, we reflected on the heights, and distance from the town, of some of the hotels. The views from their terraces would be stupendous but what a trek every time you wanted to go into town. No wonder some ran a bus service for guests or advised on the public service. You would need to be fit to tackle the steep climb up to some of them.

Turning off the main road, we now had to negotiate the steep path down towards the harbour. The wall of rock was now to our right and reared high above us. The roar of traffic now a distant rumble in the stillness of our surroundings.

It was a tranquil scene at the delightful Marina Grande as locals carried out their daily business of fishing and mending nets; trading from stalls on the waterside; catching up with local affairs and gossip as they [ladies] worked steadily at their lace-making in the shade of houses which were built against the rock face. These lace items, hanging invitingly from the few stalls huddled in the shade of the houses and shops, are soon on sale to tourists as they pass by. Of course, I had to wander over and buy a couple of lace mats to take home. Just a couple, you understand. I was sure that I could find use for them.

With the water lapping at the shore, many fishing boats bob at anchor or lay pulled up out of the water. Bathers can spend hours soaking up the sunshine, taking refreshment at the waterside seafood cafés or, possibly at a beach hut that they have hired. Even in a restaurant that, built into the rock face, may have a terrace extending out over the beach.

Although there were not so many holidaymakers now that the season was ending, the seafood cafes were still open for business. I eagerly caught much on camera.

'The rocks rise high up to the road above,' I recorded. 'The lamps attached to buildings are ornate (they added to the timeless scene). On the pier there is a row of bathing huts.'

Across the clear water as the sun rose higher into the sky, we could see Vesuvius in the distance above the rugged coastline that sent fingers of land out into the sea.

A bell is ringing out. Listening, I counted to ten. Time to climb the steep path carved into the wall of rock to the road high above.

Near the huge wall of rock jutting out to the water's edge, we were entranced again to see, on a series of poles tied together by rope, a cat playing before it fell asleep in the sunshine, balancing easily on the rope that was running from the poles to 'somewhere'. Was it the same cat?

Flavours of Sorrento life.

We also found that there were a lot of weddings taking place at this time of year. Perhaps it was because the end of the tourist season was near and hotel families and staff could be released.

From our vantage point in the garden of our hotel, we or I, let us be honest about this, were able to see the comings and goings of the wedding parties arriving at the church next door; also the excitement as the bride and groom came out of church to the joyous sound of bells ringing out their happy message.

As well as Saturday weddings, we found that there were weddings on a Sunday. Not all weddings were during the day; some were in late afternoon or early evening when the heat had gone out of the sun. [We found the same some years later in southern Italy but then it was in June at the start of the season.]

Today though was a Monday. Later that day, as we strolled through the centre of town, we wondered why people were gathering and lining the streets. Then we heard the sound of clapping and cheering and the clip-clop of horses' hooves. Into sight, driven by a burly man to handle the reins, came a horse-drawn carriage. Its precious cargo was a newlywed bride and groom dressed once again in all their wedding finery. Holding on to her wedding veil with one hand and clutching her wedding bouquet in the other, her new husband placed a protective arm around her as he waved at the crown to acknowledge their cheers. Their happy smiles as they paraded through the town, shed a little of their joy among the crowd. We found that this kind of parade was a tradition here.

What a delightful surprise!

Through the Olive and Lemon Groves.

There was a wealth of information available from the hotel staff and tour operator on how to get to various places. And of course, I had the ever-important map.

Having visited Sorrento previously, we were ready to explore further afield. Setting out early before the sun was too high in the sky, I was dressed appropriately in my usual footwear of wedge-heeled mules, flowing cool skirt, and sleeveless top. Planning to walk down to Sorrento through the orange and lemon groves, we caught the bus up into the hills above Sorrento to the mountain resort of Sant'Agata sui Due Golfi.

Now, as well as not being happy on boats, my husband is not happy on buses that twist and turn and shake you all about and the road up to Sant'Agata was full of sharp bends two thousand feet up the mountain.

As the road climbed and twisted, the views across the bay were breath taking. Thankfully reaching the end of our journey, we alighted from the bus ready to spend a short time leisurely exploring this delightful mountain retreat. We could only marvel at the views that, at every twist and turn, are out of this world.

As it was early we, or rather my husband (I am 'encouraged') likes to start out before the sun gets too hot. And of course, he is right. We have found that by doing this we could be back at the hotel in time for a lazy lunch by the pool followed by an afternoon of sunbathing and sleep. What we called having the best of both worlds.

Once again, we had set off before the sun became too hot; the village was only just slowly coming to life after the late night before. After exploring the village a little, the adventure now began, as we didn't have a clue as to how to get back to Sorrento. There was no need to worry though as the road, well a track really, was well signposted even if the signs were rough and ready. Venturing on to the path, we started to make our way down following a signpost that assured us was the way to Sorrento. My map shows a more direct route than the bus had taken on its main route. That route had a number. The secondary roads were yellow but this path was just a thin red line. Hmm.

But what an adventure! Working on the premise that if we kept going down we would eventually arrive at Sorrento we set off. Down and down we went. We knew that as long as we went descended, we would reach to coast at some point. We found that we were picking our way down paths that ran through orange and lemon groves, down narrow farmyard paths to seemingly, a road to nowhere.

Actually, I have said orange and lemon groves and there were certainly some of these, but Allen was sure that there were olive groves. He also remembers nuts. Checking our photographs, I have to say that he is right. There were olive trees, probably oranges as well and there were most certainly lemons, but you could clearly see the nets placed under the trees to catch the olives as they are harvested. I can't verify his claim to nuts.

Negotiating this very rough, uneven downhill path took concentration especially if, like me, you are wearing your favourite holiday footwear of wedge-heeled mules about two inches (five centimetres) high. Laughing all the time, we mused that we would reach civilisation sometime; when not stopping for a drink of water or to take in the fantastic view as we twisted and turned that is.

'Oh! A sign,' we called out to each other.

'Well, it says Sorrento and the arrow is pointing downwards,' one of us commented. 'Perhaps we should follow it.' It was actually a rough wooden sign, hand-painted in red paint. It was also very helpful.

Through the trees from our high vantage point on the Sorrento Peninsula, we had the most breath-taking, fantastic views. Pink-roofed houses nestled among the groves; boats and ferries moved tranquilly through the blue waters of the Gulf of Positano on one side and the Gulf of Naples on the other. The rugged coastline stretched out into the distance.

It was a beautiful day. At one point, as we came upon an olive grove, we saw huge nets strung out beneath the trees. It was harvest time and the nets were ready to catch the olives as they were harvested.

Here and there were wonderful flowering plants in the gardens of houses. Yes, we were walking through farmyards and no one came out to tell us off for walking through their home.

At one point, I stopped and turned to look at Allen, hands on hips in my usual fashion, with a questioning look on my face as I peered over my sunglasses.

'Just keep on going.'

So I did, trusting his judgement. Turning round at another point when we judged it safe to take our eyes off the ground beneath our feet, we could see how walls of tree-covered rock surrounded us. My footwear was not really the appropriate type for a scramble of this kind but I did not fall. (That came later; much, much later when I was wearing sensible shoes.)

Eventually, as the houses in the villages below loomed larger and larger as we came closer to the sea, we felt more confident that we couldn't get lost. So there we were, just trusting our judgement and thanking whomever it was who had daubed a red arrow and a word 'Sorrento' on a boulder on a corner. It was simple but very effective.

Following this sign we eventually, and thankfully but full of excitement at our adventure, reached the road into town.

Adventures in Amalfi and Positano.

The famous Amalfi Drvie was a 'must do'. Amalfi and Positano are on the other (south) side of the Sorrento Peninsula to Sorrento overlooking the Gulf of Positano. The whole stretch of that coastline is known as the Amalfi Drive. The bus journey we knew would be a little uncomfortable due to the twists and turns on the coast road as it made its way to the other side of the Peninsula. However, before we could drive around the coast on the famous Amalfi Drive our bus driver took us over the mountain again, through Sant'Agata, before coming down the mountain on the other side of the Sorrentino Peninsula.

(Some years later, when we had the motorbike, we thought what fun it would be to travel down the back leg of Italy and come across to Sorrento over the mountains. It would have been fun but it was not to be. Perhaps as well. However, on this visit a motorbike was not on the agenda, at least not as far as I knew but it later transpired that someone was harbouring dreams even then.)

On the Amalfi Drive part of the journey, we, along with others, had our hearts in our mouths as the bus driver skilfully negotiated the bends. At one point the front of the bus was hanging over a sheer drop down to the sea rendering two old ladies at the front—deep in conversation—speechless when they looked up and found themselves with a clear unbroken view of the sea.

Reaching the coast road near Grotta Acquata, the driver headed for the famous town of Positano. At every twist and turn in the road we eagerly craned our necks for our first glimpse far below of this famous town. Our first glimpse of the wonderful picture postcard scene of colourfully painted houses cascading down the hillside to the sandy beach and sea far below, and of the famous huge tiled dome of the Church of S.Maria Assunta that dominates the town and surrounding area as it glistens in the sun. We were not disappointed.

With the ever-present sun shining over the sea to our right, towering mountains and walls of rock on our left, and with our skilful driver negotiating many twists and turns, we rounded a headland at Vettica Maggiore and Praiano. Approaching Amalfi, the coast road, not wide at the best of times, became narrow, testing the driver's skill as he dodged and wove around the many scooters parked along its length against a wall.

After a straight piece of road, we rounded another headland at Conca dei Marini and soon reached Amalfi where my husband thankfully staggered off the bus.

Our first stop was the large piazza in front of the famous Cathedral or Duomo that dominates Amalfi. In the piazza, we enjoyed a cool drink while we took in the sights and sounds and got our bearings.

St. Andrew's Cathedral with its stairway of steps rising up to the entrance was a daunting prospect but we were game to climb them. The guidebooks tell us that 'there is a clear reference to Byzantine, Arabic and Norman art'. We thought that the design was not unlike that of the church of S.M. Novello in Florence.

The facade has a variety of geometrical designs in stone; the archways in a black and white design are pointed rather that curved. The bell-tower is rounded. Reaching the top, after admiring the views that lay at our feet, we were thankful for the shade of the atrium.

There appeared to be a lot of people arriving in finery. A wedding was due to take place. Descended the steps we retired to seats at a cafe in the piazza from where we could rest and watch all the goings-on as wedding guests arrived. Tourists lined the steps as if a guard of honour while the bride slowly climbed the steps to greet her future; her long train and veil spreading out on the steps below as they followed their owner.

As we made our way around Amalfi, we were again enchanted. Narrow streets were home to tall tightly-packed buildings whose sheer height shaded the streets; lush vegetation tumbled over balconies while ornate lamps adorned walls.

Back in the main piazza, the bride and groom were descending the steps of the Duomo and, with their families and guests, gathered for a group photo as bells rang out in joy. All watched of course by tourists.

In the Piazza del Duomo is the fountain of Sant'Andrea complete with the usual imposing statuary and flowing water. The sun by now was high in the sky. To cool off, we stopped by a huge fountain where maidens and cherubs poured a constant stream of water into the bowl below. I could not resist. Allen took a photo of me dipping in, grabbing handfuls of water to splash over my neck to cool me down.

We chose to have lunch at a beachside restaurant rather than in town. We chose a delightful restaurant built across the beach as it reached out to sea. It was such a lovely day with a cool breeze lazily drifting off the sea from where the restaurant was built out over the beach. That was the start of our troubles. Or at least, Allen's.

Lunch was simple. The welcome breeze added to the enchantment of this never-dreamed-of experience. As usual, I had good red wine to accompany a simple pizza. Allen chose something else with salad, which in the event proved the wrong choice. (Later, he found that the toilets were right by the kitchen where they washed the lettuce. Ever fastidious, he shivered when he realised the hygiene implications, but more of that later. (No doubt, this arrangement has improved in the intervening years.)

The bus journey back to Sorrento was not without incident. Allen, never a good traveller, became white-faced as he began to feel queasy and quite ill. Near Positano—but he didn't know that we were near a town—he came down the crowded bus to where I was sitting, looking very green & white and said that he had to stop the bus and get off. He didn't care where we were, he had to get off. He indicated that I was to stay on the bus and he would walk back to Sorrento. I was concerned and refused, insisting that I get off as well.

As it happened, the driver was stopping anyway which was just as well as Allen was getting whiter and whiter. Alighting and stepping onto the pavement, we had the sea to our left. Rounding a corner, we realised that we were at Positano. Thankfully, we found a cafe were we headed for a cool seat in the tree-shaded gardens.

Allen revived with a cup of tea and eventually began to feel a bit better. Unable to face another bus journey and not knowing when the next one was due anyway, we enlisted the help of the café staff to call a taxi. Thankfully, we reached our hotel without incident and wondered if something he had eaten had made him feel so ill.

The incident is still so clear in our minds. One bonus was that we did actually get to see a little of the town [Positano] but were thankful to reach our hotel.

Treading the grapes at the festival.

After a quiet day relaxing in the hotel grounds and with Allen fully recovered, we headed into town that was full of a festive air. It was harvest time and a grape crushing festival, where grape treading was a big feature, was in full swing. People, locals, and tourists alike thronged the town with many eager to try their hand, or feet, at the traditional method of crushing grapes to release the juice. Huge trays of luscious grapes were laid out for passers-by to have a go at treading grapes—with their shoes and socks off of course.

Treading the grapes. Sorrento.

Huge trays, built with legs and a spout for juice to escape, were overflowing with luscious, fat, white grapes. There was no shortage of people vying for their turn to 'have-a-go'.

We were interested in the old press on display, along with vats where juice was stored. The press had a huge ratchet screw in the centre. The men placed blocks of wood on top of the grapes and then proceeded to ratchet down the huge screw to press the juice out. This had the effect of crushing the grapes and was much more hygienic. Do you know people were drinking the grape juice that came out of the tap? Perhaps they thought it was wine or was it simply the experience? What of it. They were having fun. On other stalls, grapes were for sale and everywhere was an air of festivity.

In a large vat that contained almost-crushed grapes many people were standing inside up to their ankles in murky grape juice, happily treading away. What a morning! Such fun! I have a photo of Allen drinking some of the grape juice but I don't know from whence it came.

The hordes of schoolchildren milling about the stalls were having fun until, eventually, were gathered together to form a crocodile (an orderly queue) before being taken across the square to their destination. The children were all dressed-up in smocks of times gone by. There must have been some activity on for them somewhere. Obviously it was an important event in Sorrento.

Leaving the festival area, we decided that it would be good to walk out of the bustle of the town along the coast road and meander along the road eastwards, past the railway station into the relative quiet of the S.Agnello district and Piano di Sorrento. Taking time to 'stop and stare', we were treated to some tremendous views across the Bay of Naples and the coastline below and were able to get some good shots of Marina Grande and the whole bay.

A violin serenade.

Sunday, as usual was a quiet day for us. After church, we thought that we would eat out and treat ourselves with a Sunday lunch in a restaurant. Strolling down into the centre of town from church, we heard the sound of a violin playing the famous Sorrento song that urges you to 'come back to Sorrento'. This drew us down one of the side streets. Looking up, there he was. Leaning out of a balcony high above the pavement was an old man playing that wonderful tune on his violin. It drew you into the entrance of the building, which of course was the object of the exercise. What a clever public relations strategy. We couldn't resist.

It was a restaurant and the violinist was enticing people to follow the music and hear more. How Romantic.

Allen pandered to my musings. He was more concerned with feeding the inner man and he does like his Sunday lunch with all the trimmings. In the event, after looking at the menu at the entrance, we climbed up to the first floor to be greeted by a beaming waiter who offered us drinks and a menu as he showed us to our table.

It was a perfect way to spend a Sunday. Especially when followed by a few hours in the shady gardens of your hotel that was only a short stroll away.

Ercolano or Herculaneum.

Today was the day.

We had plans to take the train along the coast to Herculaneum which was another town destroyed by the eruption of Vesuvius all those years ago. While Pompeii (visited two years previously) was not far from Sorrento, Herculaneum was further distant being closer to Naples.

It is pleasant to wander out when the shops open again in the cool evening air. The previous evening, we had been in one shop and chatted to a horrified English shopkeeper about our plans. He was most perturbed that we were considering travelling alone by train into possible danger.

'Do not wear any jewellery,' he advised us. 'Do not take a camera,' and looking at the camcorder hanging around my neck, shook his head. 'Do not take your camcorder. Nothing that can be snatched off you.'

Innocents that we were we thought that he was being over-cautious but he really feared for our safety. Back at the hotel, we chatted to Alfonso, the Bar Manager, as he served us drinks on the moonlit terrace. He too was concerned and thought that we, two tourists travelling alone towards Naples, could be in danger. We heeded all this advice which is why we don't have any firm records of our visit to this excavated seaside town near Naples.

Off we set, bright and early, devoid of any jewellery and cameras as we headed towards the railway station to catch the train. Again, as we were early the town was hardly awake but our strategy—or rather Allen's—had proved itself previously.

Excitedly anticipating the day, we nevertheless had a little corner of apprehension in our minds, wondering what the day would bring.

The journey was much longer that the one to Pompeii which had only taken about half an hour. Passing through this station [Pompeii], the train carried on, stopping at each stop to take on more passengers. These were mainly young people, possibly students, dark, and swarthy looking but in reality were more concerned with their own affairs than two tourists. We kept ourselves to ourselves. Allen had our money safe.

Vico Equense, Castellmare di Stabia, Torre de Greco, and other stations in-between, flashed by until the sign 'Ercolano' flashed into view. This was our stop. (Ercolano is the old spelling.)

The sites of the excavations are well signposted but we did have to walk down some deserted streets. Although these were wide with tall, white, imposing buildings, who knew what dangers lurked. My imagination took flight.

Reaching the excavated site we paid our money, took the map we had either been given or paid for and planned our visit.

Surprisingly, I found Herculaneum (Ercolano) quite interesting. At least, more interesting than Pompeii. The town is by the seaside; in 79AD, it was a port and a resort. Many beautiful and elegant buildings and villas have been discovered; many still in a good state of preservation complete with frescoes on the walls. I felt that I was able to picture how the town used to be and how people lived, before they were overwhelmed by the volcanic eruption in which the town was covered.

This is a record of our experiences which, although delves into the history of where we visited, is not a cultural history book. In order to ensure that you explore Ercolano at your leisure I will leave you to follow your own research via your local library or the Internet.

After such a wonderful morning and completing our tour and exploration we expected the rest of the day to be just as uneventful. We were rudely awakened from our dream as we headed out to look for a restaurant for lunch.

By now, it was out of season and we could only find two restaurants close by. Opting for what appeared to be the better one we went inside. Allen said that he would have the same to eat as I was having as he thought that in Amalfi the salad was the cause of his stomach upset.

We both opted for a simple pizza. Allen had a cold drink— probably his usual Cola Light— while I asked for half a bottle of red wine.

To our astonishment, the waiter brought over a full but dusty bottle of Vesuvius wine, made from grapes grown on the mountain.

'Drink down to here.' He pointed to somewhere about halfway down the bottle and made an imaginary mark.

At this point, I feel that I should point out that this was a laid-back traditional restaurant. The waiter was not dressed in a uniform but in normal everyday clothes. He was though, eager to please.

There was a huge pizza oven at the end of the room from where we could observe the pizzas being cooked; watching in fascination as the pizza man wielded the huge flat metal implement at the end of a very long handle.

A party of six or so asked for a table and, after taking their order, the waiter took them bottles of oil and vinegar as is usual. Actually, these bottles weren't usual. We watched in fascinated horror as he nonchalantly thought it quite normal to ask customers to use oil and vinegar out of bottles heavily encrusted with dried-up deposits from the culmination of many drips. Ugh!

Looking at each other and both thinking that we were glad that we hadn't ordered a salad—the sight of that on our table would have made us feel ill—we pulled a face. [This was many years before writing this but the sight is seared on our memory. Hopefully, things have improved in the ensuing years.]

The journey back from Herculaneum in mid-afternoon was uneventful. With Herculaneum being near to the city of Naples, the train was crowded but station-by-station passengers such as students and workers left the train. By the time we reached Sorrento, it was almost empty.

With a sense of relief, we reached our hotel to be greeted by Alfonso who had been so worried for our safety and who was relieved that we were back safe and sound. We later went into town to show the English shopkeeper that we had arrived back safely. Much to his relief. Isn't it wonderful that people worry and look out for you when abroad?

Then illness struck.

Unfortunately, the rest of the holiday took a turn for the worst as Allen became violently ill. I went to the reception desk to ask for help in finding a doctor. The hotel receptionist located the Citalia Rep who was staying in the hotel. She was very calm and helpful and rang for the doctor who was happy to come out.

He was also happy to examine and give treatment but not before he had been paid lots of lire. We are not in the habit of carrying large amounts of cash as we use other, more secure, methods for payment but fortunately, I was able to scrape, and I mean scrape, together the massive amount of lire he quoted.

Poor Allen thought that he was dying. I went off with a prescription to the chemist where there was an English-speaking member of staff, only thankful that I was able to pay. Allen of course was in no condition to think about getting out of bed never mind dinner; at his insistence, I went down alone. The Restaurant Manager was full of concern when he saw that I was alone and insisted on sending up a tray of light food that went largely untouched.

The following day he [Allen] was still tied to his bed. After tending to his needs I went off into town. The first thing was to draw cash to replenish our reserves. As well as the holiday taking a turn for the worse, so had the weather to match it. We were now well into October and it was drizzling with rain.

I wandered through the streets with tears streaming down my face, tears that mingled with the rain. I really thought that I would be taking him home in a wooden box; I didn't know what we would do if he didn't improve enough to travel; if he did, would he be ill on the plane?; All these thoughts were running through my mind. In my worry, I felt so alone, and yes, scared.

Passing a small craftsman's shop, I paused to admire the inlaid wood [marquetry] objects. With time to kill, I wandered inside to browse further. A picture caught my eye of a man and woman facing each other. He was looking tenderly down at the women he held in his arms as she looked up to him. They appeared to be in a forest. The workmanship was so clever and evocative. (Shh, Rosie, don't cry now.) The owner was a little wizened old man, weather-beaten and lined with age, wearing a beret on his head, who had been carefully observing me from a distance. Catching his eye, I asked the price. I thought it would be a good Christmas present for Allen as a reflection of us. It was also something concrete to hang on to in the depths of my distress.

Thrilled with his sale and carefully wrapping my purchase, the man gave me his card telling me that his name was

Fernando as he pointed to his name and then himself. He truly was an artist and a craftsman. This was a real find.

Arriving back in our room, Allen who had started to improve slightly (thankfully as he would have had to miss the flight home later that week), looked at the parcel which I was carrying.

'Where are you going to put that?' he asked tetchily.

'It will go in my case,' I rejoined. I had tried to sneak it in before he saw it but was determined not to let him see it. Actually when he opened the parcel that Christmas, he was very touched and all was forgiven!

By Thursday, he felt well enough to leave our room and come down, but rested quietly.

Our flight home was due the day after that, Friday, but, as if all this wasn't enough, our big adventure was to come. Yes, there is more!

Arriving at Naples airport, we found that we had a delay. It was an evening flight and the delay was unwelcome. All at once, we heard a commotion in the distance of the airport.

'What on earth is going on?' We looked at each other.

Suddenly, there was a lot of shouting from a man who was protesting loudly at being forcibly escorted into the airport building and away from view. Still we heard nothing about our flight and had no information. All at once, the pilot of the aeroplane that was to take us home came into the Departure Lounge.

Calling us together, he explained that the plane had been damaged. An airport worker, when loading luggage, had somehow managed to damage the plane and there was now a big hole in its side. The pilot pulled a Polaroid photo out of his top pocket to show us. He explained that he had refused to fly the plane back to Manchester. He assured us that we would be given vouchers for a meal; the restaurant would open (by now it was very late) until the replacement plane came out to

Naples from Manchester, but first the new crew had to be gathered.

There was a delay as we waited for the vouchers to be issued. The powers that be however, refused to open the restaurant. The pilot again gathered us and called for attention.

'You need a meal. You need to rest. We have a plane fully stocked with food. We will board you, give you drinks and a meal and you can sleep until the new plane arrives.'

This is what happened until we could transfer to the replacement plane. It really was an emergency plane as it was a very old model. It was however very roomy with lots of leg room and comfy seats. It was also safe to be flown.

Arriving home the following morning, we called to see our daughter who was due to give birth to our second grandchild. In 'full sail', she greeted us.

'Oh, Mum! I *am* glad that you are home!'

She had been having some early signs of impending labour. The following morning the telephone rang very early. While my husband took our grandson to his other grandparents before he went to church, I was privileged to see our granddaughter make her presence known as she very swiftly came into the world.

The following evening, just when my daughter needed me, I broke my leg and spent the next twenty-three nights in hospital. I have a photo of a proud Granny, propped up in bed with an elevated leg, holding her granddaughter.

They do say that things come in three's! But what an ending to our Sorrento adventure.

A Shattered Dream and New Hope

The obvious lakes (or lagos) of northern Italy are Como, Maggiore and Garda. In fact, many smaller ones are not the first ones to come to mind when planning a visit.

Our motorbike travels in 2003 had taken us on an exhilarating ride from the French Riviera, high above the Ligurian Sea (Mare Ligure) on the switchback bends of the coast road. It had been incredible to see the map of Italy come to life, with the contours of the coast laid out below us in the sparkling sunshine.

With the mountains sheltering us on one side and on the other side a sheer drop to the sea far below us, we entered Liguria. Rounding the Gulf of Genoa, we had turned north towards Alessandria and then northeast to Brescia in Lombardy after crossing the mighty River Po at Cremona. It was a short distance then, via Desenzano, to our hotel on the southern shores of Lake Garda. From there we could see the 'spine' of Sirmione as it jutted out into the lake like a finger.

After spending a few days here, we had intended to ride around Lakes Maggiore and Como on our way to Switzerland. It was very hot though—too hot to linger—so we missed them at close quarters.[2]

~~~~~~~~~~~~~

---

[2] *Just Us Two: Ned and Rosie's Gold Wing Discovery. Rosalie Marsh*

Plop! The post dropped onto the mat. Another Saga brochure had arrived. Thumbing through it I once again saw the tantalising picture of the Italian Lakes. My husband laughed and shook his head as off I went to retrieve the map of Italy from the map shelf in the study.

'Do you think that we could do this?'

As we looked at all the detailed information in the brochure, on the website and the map, Allen nodded his head. 'We will be OK.'

It was marked as an easy-paced tour with enough stops and breaks to make it manageable for us. Ten years on from our first adventure, we were no longer able to ride a motorbike and even less able to tour on one; this seemed a great opportunity to visit the places which we had planned to before.

The other enticement was that the tour took us not only to smaller 'hidden' lakes—not always seen on larger maps—but also into the Dolomites which, again due to the intense heat in 2003, we had reluctantly abandoned before reaching Bolzano. Here we were, realising another dream.

The tour description really was very clear even down to the fact that there were some steps to negotiate and a boat ride across to a little island on the first lake, which was Lake Orta. Sitting around the table with maps spread out in front of us, we traced the route with mounting excitement.

Touching down in Milan, we would travel by coach northwest to Lake Orta where we would spend a few days. From here, there were excursions around Lake Orta; into Switzerland as we drove around Lakes Maggiore and Lugano to Lake Como; a trip to explore Lake Maggiore; a stop at Lake Iseo on the way to Lake Molveno and then excursions to Lake Garda and into the Dolomites. As we traced the route given in the brochure, we re-lived our previous aborted visits to these areas.

I was soon searching the Internet for more details of the hotels listed as they were smallish family-run hotels and wanted to check the facilities. They seemed fine but we were a little concerned that some rooms in the first hotel could only be reached by climbing stairs. Checking the Internet I was reassured. There was a lift. All I had to do was to request a room either on the ground floor or near the lift. All rooms had a shower only, which was OK by us.

Because of our various requests, I booked by telephone so that I could check out a few things with the Customer Services Advisor. One thing about Saga holidays is that the price you see is what you pay and that includes health insurance. If you have your own travel insurance, there is a reduction but we have never yet had to pay extra because of medical conditions. The Special Needs department satisfy themselves about cover before confirming the booking. Let's face it, if you are under the doctor you are usually being looked after.

The flights unfortunately only went from Heathrow, which meant that we needed to travel a day earlier from North Wales with an overnight stay near Heathrow. We were able to get an accommodation and parking package with an extra night added on (under a different booking) for the return journey. The flight was an early morning one. This is quite handy as the airport is not usually very busy then. However, as it was too early for breakfast in the hotel we had packed cereal bars to tide us over until we got to the airport.

Booking a taxi from the hotel, we arrived at Terminal 5 where our taxi driver dropped us right by the arrivals door from where we just walked straight in. This was so easy! Unlike our usual regional airport which at the time was often quite stressful to say the least.

As we had hoped, the check-in and security clearance was accomplished without too much trouble. There was a new-fangled check-in procedure that you could use if you wanted to. Our tickets were e-tickets with all the fine breakdown details listed on a large sheet of paper plus the all-important booking code.

I decided that I would be the one to negotiate this new procedure leaving Allen with the luggage. In fact, I think you had to do it all this way but to make sure I asked one of the hovering airport staff for clarification. I punched in the booking number and there we were on the screen. Two little figures sat in the allocated seats. I decided to try and change them to two aisle seats as Allen does not like disturbing anyone if he needs to get up and I like to be able to stretch out my leg [old injury] if I can. I only managed to change one seat as others were blanked out, showing as already taken.

Then I had to scan my passport. That was OK but then the message came on the screen to scan Allen's and, well it was in his pocket. I dashed over to where he was sitting.

'Quick, your passport! Don't get it out of the wallet; just give it all to me.'

I dashed back, scanned it in the machine, and out came our boarding cards. As I was doing this, one of the Saga Holidays 'meet and greet' representatives had come over to Allen to say hello, check who he was and if we had any problems. Not being used to Heathrow Terminal 5, this was re-assuring. The Departures Board clearly showed our flight number together with a time for the earliest bag drop. We still had to go to check-in but at least we had our allocated seats and boarding cards. It was all quite impressive. Security clearance was relatively trouble-free. There was the usual pantomime of taking shoes off and popping them in the tray along with coat, watch, trouser belt. I had put my Net book computer where is was accessible in my hand luggage as computers have to be taken out of their cases and popped into the tray for scanning.

Getting dressed and making ourselves decent again, we made our way through to the departure lounge and shops. Allen wanted a watch battery and I needed to buy eye-pencils and brushes as I had forgotten to pop the contents of my brush and applicator pot into the make-up bag. Although we couldn't find a watch battery, I was able to replenish my eye make-up essentials. Yes, this was a very essential task.

Settling ourselves in a quiet corner with a drink and a snack, we waited for our departure time to come around.

The flight was with British Airways and very comfortable with plenty of legroom. Although we had asked Saga if there would be a meal, they had thought not as the flight was under two hours. The cabin staff, in fact, offered a snack of a bacon and egg roll—on the house so to speak. Very welcome it was too!

Following the progress of the plane on the drop down video screens over the seats, all too soon, we were arriving at Milan Linate airport, which is southeast of Milan. Allen said that there had been a clear view over the Alps but I had missed it as I was asleep.

Exploring the Lakes and Alps of North West Italy

Clearing security and baggage reclaim, we found that Suzie was waiting to gather her lambs, like a shepherdess. Due to parking arrangements, the coach unfortunately had had to park a little way away up a slight incline that was hard going with a trolley. After the driver had packed the luggage away for us into the coach, we were soon off for a drive along the motorway around Milan to the North West and the lakes.

I had my map of the Italian lakes. One that, ever hopeful, I had bought a few years earlier after our aborted motorbike plans when planning if we could make a return trip. Now I traced the route that the coach followed. Milan Malpensa airport is quite a way from Milan to the northwest, and does appear to be a better option for transferring to Lake Orta. In the event however, Milan Linate was a better choice as it was easier for the return journey connection from the Dolomites in the northeast of Italy.

Nearing Lake Maggiore, we turned off the motorway to pick up the road for Lake Orta not far away to the west of Lake Maggiore. It was with great anticipation that we watched the passing scenery until Suzie alerted us that we were near Lake Orta and would soon have our first glimpse of it. We were not disappointed as rounding a corner the scene that greeted us drew gasps of delight from us all. Through the trees, we had glimpses of the peaceful still water lapping at the shore.

A shore surrounded by verdant green trees rising up the hills and sleepy villages.

Lake Orta.

Lake Orta lies to the west of Lake Maggiore in the region of Piemonte; the mountain in-between the two lakes is called Monte Mattarone. The main place of interest is Orta San Giulio (pronounced 'Julio' with a soft 'G') and the island called Isola San Giulio. We however were destined to travel a little way further along the east shore of the lake to the village of Pettenasco where we would spend four nights at the Hotel L'Approdo on the edge of the village and more importantly, on the edge of the lake.

Saga had given us very comprehensive details of the hotel. The smiling staff soon had us checked-in and registered while the porters unloaded our luggage ready to for them to take it for us to our room. We had the requested room on a floor served by a lift. The room was quite spacious with a very large bathroom and excellent shower. As usual, my first port of call was the balcony and was delighted to find that we had a side view of the lake over to its southern end. While we waited for our luggage to arrive, we went to explore the bar and enquire about lunch. Relaxing, we decided that this was 'all right' and that we would be comfortable. The hotel opened onto the lakeside with lovely seating areas dotted around the gardens.

Later during dinner, we met some of our fellow guests and conversation flowed, along with the wine! The waiters were very smart, wearing formal suits. It does encourage you to realise that you are not out of place if you dress up a little.

Pettanasco.

The following morning was free time but Suzie had arranged a lakeside stroll into the village of Pettenasco. Here we hoped to be able to buy a big bottle of water. Before we set off, we booked the optional trip to Lake Garda for later in the week.

Next door to the hotel is a campsite. Making our way through the gate and along the path to the lakeside, we saw that they had a bar and cafe that we thought would be good for lunch. All along the pathway, we could smell the scent of jasmine that grew in abundance. Its white starry flowers grew in profusion everywhere, over walls and even in one place up the trunks of trees. There were so many flowers that you could hardly see the green leaves. While I was busy taking camcorder film, my happy snapper continued to fill the SD card in his camera. And to think that at one time all you could take was about eight frames on a roll of film! Now we come back with about two hundred photos as Allen clicks his way through the holiday. You may think that with both a camera and a camcorder, we have duplicates but, no, we take pictures of different things. Allen captures images of birds, insects, lizards, buildings etc. while I focus on views, flowers, and wonderful displays of goodies such as shoes and dresses in shop windows.

It was a sunny morning and growing very hot. Passing the campsite and crossing the little bridge over the River—or Tio—Pescone we continued along the lakeside walk before turning to go into the village towards the church. Across the lake, the wooded hills rose up above the shore. Lake Orta and the villages around it are in the region of Piemonte, next to Lombardia and quite near the border of Switzerland.

Reaching the church in the village, we came to the cemetery where, unusually in one part, there were plaques set in the wall. We could only surmise that, instead of burying people in the ground, they were placed in a casket that went into a special slot in the wall behind the plaques. Suzie took us around the village, down deserted and quiet lanes where flowers—much Jasmine— and shrubs grew in abundance, escaping over the tops of the walls before cascading down to bask in the sunshine. Eventually, we came into the shade of the old mill where the water wheel was still working.

Up above we could see the viaduct that carried the train down from the Alps in the north, to Novara west of Milan, and onwards through Italy. Suzie left us to wander; after buying water in the Tabaccheria Edicola—the 24hr Supermarket on the Corso Rome in Pettenasco—we rested outside in the sunshine before meandering down to the lakeside again and the shade of the trees at the water's edge. (Actually, looking at the till receipt, I notice that there were two rows of lottery numbers at the bottom. I wonder why?) Later we dropped in to the Camping Pizzeria Verde Lago, the campsite cafe, for an urgent cool drink and then pizza for lunch as we gazed over the tranquil waters of the lake. This gave us the opportunity to chat to fellow guests who had the same idea.

The heat was increasing by now in the afternoon sunshine; we changed into cooler clothes but then a wind came along which brought a cloud over the lake. Then it started to rain.

Water wheel in Pettanasco. Lake Orta.

To Isola San Giulio by boat.

Oh dear! We were due to go on a boat ride on the lake to Isola San Giulio. This promised to be quite an adventure. Now for those who do not know me, I am not the most agile of people, which is an understatement. I was wearing my exercise mules as they moulded to my feet but Suzie had looked askance at them in the morning. I was sure that I would be OK clambering on and off the boat. After all, it would be a good sized one [boat], wouldn't it? Something like the one that we had seen in the morning moving quietly along the lake. No problem!

Shock and horror went through me as I watched a little launch zoom across the lake and moor up. It was so tiny; not at all the larger passenger boat that I and others in the group had expected. There were willing hands to help us so gingerly I stepped off the landing stage onto the top step at the side of the boat and clambered down. Allen was there to catch me and if those with walking sticks could manage, then so could I. There were too many of us for one boat but another one soon followed. In the rain, the boat was cast off [untied from its mooring] and, guided by its skipper, gently ploughed its way into the lake. A mist shrouded the wooded hillside, but we could see enough as we made our way along the water.

Our destination was the Isola San Giulio just off the mainland and the town of Orta San Giulio. By now, the insistent rain drummed on the top of the boat. What a shame after the promise of the morning. All you could do was grin and bear it. Excitedly, we all watched out for the first appearance of the island. It wasn't very big but we had told we would we would be able to walk around it.

With care the skipper moored up at the small landing stage and helped all of us oldies—some more agile than others—off the boat before we all quickly hurried into the shelter of the cathedral entrance.

Isola San Giulio is a very small enchanting island that sits quietly in the lake just off the town of Orta San Giulio. *(http://www.isolasangiulio.it/)*

The great Benedictine Monastery of an enclosed order of nuns dominates it. It is said, that parts of the Basilica date from the fourth century when St Julius arrived on the island, but was re-built between the ninth and twelfth centuries.

Inside the massive porch, steps lead up to the entrance. There was plenty of room for us all to wait until the rest of our group arrived on the second boat and we could all go in together. In spite of clear signs that cameras are forbidden, many people do not understand the reason and think, 'well, I am only taking a few photos'. If you add up all the flashlights that go off it really does amount to a lot and can damage the ancient fabrics on display. In addition, this is not an old ruin, it is actually a living, breathing church, which is still in use at times, and respect must be shown for their requests.

All was silence (apart from those who forgot that they were in the House of God and chatted loudly, disturbing the peace). The Basilica is not actually very big; the main altar was cordoned off but it was possible to spend a few moments in reflection. It was a sobering thought to realise how life must have been in ancient times when this Basilica was built. Who had designed it? Although simple in some ways, it was full of intricate detail in others such as the frescos covering the walls and the pulpit made from black marble. It could not have been an easy task to bring all the materials by boat to this small island in a relatively small lake in the Italian Alps.

Steps led down into the crypt below that was only visible in the gloom by the light of many candles. It was possible to negotiate the steps and look around if you were careful.

Back in the porch we could see from the windows how bad the weather was. It was such a shame as the morning sunshine had promised that the outing would be in fine weather. Did we stay here in the dry porch until everyone returned or did we take the plunge and join the others? We took a chance and braved the rain that was now coming down in torrents and took the planned walk around the outside of the Monastery. The steep path and alleyways were slippy in the rain. As is common with old places like this, there are two lines of paving stones with cobbles in the middle for where the carts would have travelled down. It was so wet; we did not know whether to walk on the smooth flags or the cobbles at either side.

Hopping to one side there was a whoosh! The water came gushing down the drainpipes, escaping through the spouts at the bottom—all over feet and legs. Hopping back and to between the cobbles and flags, at the same time holding up an umbrella and cowering under a rain hood, I had a constant battle to find the best place to go.

Rounding a corner, we found some respite from the rain. A gift shop! Now why was I surprised at this? There always has to be a gift shop hasn't there? I bought a tea towel in the Villa Maria Antonietta for €3. It was souvenir and to add to our collection. It was printed with a map of the island; it would remind us of our brief visit. *I say 'us' as Allen likes to do the pots at home. He banned me years ago from this task, as I was not meeting washing-up standards.*

The gift shop was tucked away in a corner. Gingerly negotiating the slippy steps as we came out, we found that we had left most of the group behind. Do we go down to the right through the covered alleyway? On the other hand, do we go round the corner where the road seemed a bit flatter? Someone commented that people had gone off to the right so off we trooped and we soon found the landing stage. I had actually thought that we would be getting on a coach at some point but I was mistaken. In the teeming rain, we made our way to the two boats moored up. One of them had its steps coming from the side but the other one had its entrance into the cabin through the front windows; you accessed these from the front of the boat. The more agile people went on this one and others on the first one. You can guess which boat I went on! Suzie was concerned at the wet conditions and people slipping but all was well and we zoomed off to Orta San Giulio on the mainland.

The jetty in Orta San Giulio is quite large with many boats moored up. The tree-lined promenade has many seats that then give out onto the piazza and shops. Suzie explained where things were and off we set. The town is very old and very beautiful with narrow streets and ancient buildings adorned with balconies over which flowers tumbled in riotous abandon.

We had the opportunity if we wished to visit the complex of the Sacre Monte di Orta (Sacred Mount of Orta). Its twenty chapels are dedicated to St Francis of Assisi. On a hilltop overlooking the lake it is four hundred and one metres high it overlooks the lake.

From San Giulio Piazza on the waterfront we came to the cobbled streets of the town proper and the shops. Looking to our right we could see a narrow street with many cobbled steps climbing up to a pastel coloured church at the top. Huge flower-filled troughs strategically placed no doubt to deter vehicles from using it. At first, we thought that this was the Sacre Monte di Orta but no, this was the fifteenth century church of Santa Maria Assunta. Facing the lake from its lofty height, there must have been a wonderful view from its entrance of the lakeside town, the Isola San Giulio, backed by the densely wooded mountains.

In any event, quailing at the thought of climbing all those steps reaching high into the sky, we decided to give this a miss and carried on to explore the enchanting mix of old buildings, cafes, and shops where their wares spilled out onto the pavement.

The rain was still coming down relentlessly; it was time for a cuppa. We strolled back to the Piazza Motta and found a cafe under the arches. This proved to be an arcade of cafes and shops where we soon found a little seat near an archway overlooking the almost deserted square. At this small but lovely Ristorante Ai Du Santi, a pot of tea and cold drink came to only €5.50. Allen decided that he would go off and buy a plastic poncho to cover him from the rain. I had forgotten my fold-up bag for day-to-day things and wanted something to hold umbrella etc. The shops in the covered archway were full of all manner of goodies and I could see a selection of little fold-up bags in Cose di Zoe. You know how we have fridge magnets and mugs with names and their meanings. Well, the bags were just the same but they were patterned with flowers. I chose one called Rosella (Romantica e Creativa) which I thought was rather apt. Although appearing to be Italian it is actually made in China.

While we chatted to each other, watching the world go by, we noticed that people were walking past with umbrellas down and waitresses wiping the pools of water off the outside tables and chairs. The rain had eased off and had now stopped; it was time to stroll again. Eventually making our way down to the waterfront, we found a seat to wait for the rest of the group to gather. Meanwhile we were entertained by the big discussion going on among the boatmen. Actually, it sounded like an argument but this was Italy and everyone gets very excited and voluble. By now, the sun was shining, lighting up the Isola di San Giulio and casting dappled shadows on the water.

The journey back to Pettenasco was enchanting; in the sunshine, we ploughed across the smooth water of the lake between the island and lakeshore. The full beauty was evident as the mist rose and the clouds cleared to reveal a blue sky. The newly washed trees and plants lifted up their heads once again to dry out in the warmth of the sun's rays. High on a rocky outcrop was a church. We had a discussion later as to the exact position of this as Allen was convinced that it was further down the lake.

'Wait for the camcorder film. That will sort it out.' I urged, brooking no argument.

Stepping off the boat at the landing stage in the, by now, sunshine we opted for a seat in the garden to enjoy a cool drink and relax. A perfect ending to a perfect day, well almost the end as dinner was still to come.

Dinner again, was in the area of restaurant reserved for us. With round tables, we found that conversation was easy and we had the same company as the previous evening. The menu was in Italian and English with a good choice. Allen had cream of pea soup, which I did *not* want. It is my least favourite as I had been given this after an operation when I was in my teens. Let's say it did not go down very well and forever after its association is with hospitals! I opted for sedani pasta with fresh tomato, buffalo cheese, and aubergines. Allen as I expected followed with roast lamb with thyme and rosemary while I settled for an omelette with aromatic herbs. After our sweet, delicious wine and good conversation we went to the bar for coffee followed by an early night.

The 'Three Lakes' Tour of Maggiore, Lugano, and Como.

Tuesday dawned with an overcast sky that soon turned to drizzle. It was such a shame but you have to remember that we were high in the mountains and often in the clouds. We were off today for the 'Three Lakes' excursion. Suzie had thoughtfully provided us with a map of the lakes so that we could follow the route.

(Looking at the map to check my facts, I see that we were now not far from Domodossola where we stopped for lunch in 2003 as we headed through the mountains to the Simplon Pass and Switzerland on our motorbike.)

On this visit to Italy, our route would take us from Pettenasco on the eastern shore of Lake Orta north towards Gravellona Toce near where a tributary of the River Toce—the Strona—flows into the Toce which in turn, flows south into

Lake Maggiore. At Gravellona Toce we would turn right (northeast) between Lake Mergozzo—a small lake at the mouth of Val d'Ossola on our left—and the western tip of Lake Maggiore on our right to Verbania. From here, we would proceed northwards along the western side of Lake Maggiore, through Ghiffa and Cannobio, in the shelter of the Val de Cannobina to Locarno at the northern end of the lake. The River Ticino feed this as it flows down the mighty mountains. Locarno is actually in Switzerland as is the top part of the Lake Maggiore, which is sixty-five kilometres long (about forty miles).

At Gravellona Toce, the sky was heavy with unrelenting rain as the mighty mountains poked their heads above the clouds, clouds that were on a level with us in the coach. It was a shame as they [clouds and rain] obscured the much of the view. At one point, so low were the clouds that they appeared as a huge blanket of cotton wool protecting the valley below. It was a fantastic view.

I may have mentioned it before but Lake Maggiore has one shore in the region of Piemonte and one in Lombardia.

Near Verbania, the road hugged the western shore of Lake Maggiore. The clouds, although still black and heavy, did appear to be rising a little. A number of boats were dotted here and there on the water but many were moored up at the lakeside. Across the water, mountains protected the eastern shore. At Oggebio, signs warning of rock fall from the mountains on our left flashed past as we travelled on. Only trees came between the water and us.

Negotiating the traffic in one town I remarked, 'Fancy coming down here on the bike!' There were a lot of cobbles and it would have been hair-raising in the rain with a heavily laden heavy motorbike.

Near Brissago we came to the Swiss Border. Suzie had earlier warned us to bring our passports in case the Border Guards asked for them. As it happened, the Border Guards were happy to wave us through after checking our coach. The large SAGA sign in the window must have been our passport for a smooth entry to Switzerland. Leaving Italy, our mobile phones started to 'ping' like mad, as they picked up the Swiss mobile signals.

As we drove into Locarno on the edge of the lake, Suzie explained that we wouldn't be stopping here but in Lugano on the edge of Lake Lugano. She helpfully advised us to take Euros everywhere and gave us an approximate exchange rate of Euros for Swiss Francs to make calculations easier when we stopped later.

We joined the motorway at Bellinzona to head south, through the mountains, to Lugano on the edge of Lake Lugano in southern Switzerland.

Lake Lugano.
Our driver parked up in Lugano by the lakeside. The mountains and everything around were shrouded in mist and dripping wet as it was still raining. This was a shame. Trooping along behind our leader, we soon found ourselves in the town in front of arcades of shops under stone arches, which seemed to go on forever. The sides, supported by fat stone pillars, were open to the cobbled street, which in turn, joined others in a large cobbled square. They had the right idea in those days—building shops under cover. As well as being practical, they add to the charm of the town.

The first stop was a watering and comfort one. We found a nice café/confectioner shop and looking through the window saw a few of our party. That was good enough for us. Banquettes and tables lined the outer edge of the cafe area with the middle of the floor having normal tables and chairs. On one side of the counter, there were two beautiful, contemporary sculptures. Pictures, framed mirrors, and wall lights lined the wood-panelled walls. It all made for a welcoming and friendly ambience.

Being now in Switzerland, we were dealing with Swiss Francs. Suzie had also advised us not to risk paying for a cup of coffee with a large Euro note as the change would be in Swiss Francs and after leaving Lugano, we would be back in Italy and unable to spend them. We would have either to spend in Switzerland or take home and exchange there.

Having a good spend seemed like a good idea and one of our group did in fact forget the advice and use a large note instead of a small one. As it was, there were two figures on the till receipt and we thought that the 7.50 was in fact Euros and the other figure of 10:25 was Swiss Francs. To make things easier, Allen put €7 with the till receipt which, as it turned out included a very good tip. On talking to friends later who had been in the cafe just before us the 10:25 was the time and the other figure was Swiss Francs which actually equated to approx €5.82! How stupid can you get?

Peering into shops as be made our way along the arched walkway, we stopped at first one and then another watch shop. Wouldn't it be nice to go in and buy? We could only window-shop. But wait! Allen was in another one and having a conversation. Actually, Allen had been having a problem with his watch battery, which kept stopping, and we hoped to find a watch shop in Switzerland that could fit a new one for him. After all, Switzerland was noted for its watch making wasn't it?

At the third try, he was successful and they said they could fit it in ten minutes. Brilliant news! However, I still had my nose pressed to the window; dropping seeds into the puddle of hope didn't yield any results.

Walking along the shops under the stone arches that formed a covered walkway, we soon returned to the shop named CHRIST-Orologi & Gioielli, on the Latgo Zorzi 14 to collect the watch. We were impressed that they were able to do this small task as in general, many shops simply have sales people and not a watchmaker. When told that it was CHF20 I asked what that was in Euros. After a lot of punching of numbers and huffs and puffs, the assistant gave a figure that seemed a lot. A lot to break into our small store of Euros allowance for running expenses anyway, and decided to pay by credit card. When paying by credit card abroad, you often have the option of paying in local currency or paying a converted rate. A newspaper article had once advised that it was best to pay in local currency e.g. Euros, as the rate given by the shop may differ from the ones used when the credit card company converts the transaction.

With more punching of numbers on the screen, more huffs and puffs, the assistance finally came to a figure and turned the card terminal towards us. This showed both Swiss Francs (CHF) and Great Britain Pounds (GBP) about £13.37 or something. We opted for the CHF figure but on calculating later at home, I think they actually used a very good rate, as the figure that I have just arrived at was not much different. In any event, we paid a lot of money for a watch battery and I had a glimpse of some very beautiful and unusual watches and jewellery.

The clouds were lifting as we made our way back to the meeting point. The steam, not mist, coming off the mountains revealed the tops to be covered in snow. Before all the party re-grouped, we had found a few minutes to pop into the cable-car station from where the cable cars left for Orselina, Cardada, and Cimetta even higher in the mountains at one thousand, six hundred and seventy-one metres. High up above the street we could see a cable car moving slowly. The views must have been spectacular in spite of the weather. Across the road was a small park surrounded by many colourful flags. A sign told us that we were in the Muralto area of Locarno.

Re-joining the coach that was parked a little way along the lakeside; we anticipated the next part of our journey. The whole area is surrounded by mountains some of which reach a height of over two thousand metres or six thousand, six hundred feet.

The rain had eased off by now. The mountains were dark and dramatic with huge swathes of mist rising out of the deep crevices and folds of the contours. At one point, what appeared to be a view of the sea below was actually a large white cloud, which is a good indication of the height of this mountain road. When we did have a clear view of the valley, we could see well-cultivated green fields and farms. We really were on top of the world at this point.

Traversing the road bridge at Melide, the mountains came down from each shore appearing to meet almost in the middle.

Near Chiasso, we again crossed the border and found ourselves back in Italy. From here, it was but a short way to the town of Como on Lake Como.

Lake Como.
Our driver, apart from being a very steady and safe driver, was also very considerate in that he dropped us off as near to our starting point as he could. In Como ,he found a handy parking spot and the coach disgorged us near the cathedral.

Taking some time to look at this wonderfully ornate building and take photographs, our mission was to find food.
After a stroll around, we needed to find some lunch.

Some of our party had ploughed on ahead to do a short circular tour of the area but we decided to abandon this as we found ourselves going out of the restaurant area. I was concerned that the cafe's, like many of the shops, would be closing for siesta due to the rain. Due to the wet weather, most of the outside tables were empty so it was hard to judge which the was best café to choose. With the rain, many were not serving outside.

Cutting through a few narrow side streets and coming back in a circle towards the cathedral, we eventually found a small bar called Bar San Fedele that looked very small inside but we opted for this. The young waiter was busy wiping down the tables outside and re-setting them with clean tablecloths. The hot welcome food was fairly good but simple. We had chosen lasagne and Allen's Cola Light was expensive to say the least. Wine proved a better bargain! It all came to €20. I think the owner had rounded up a little. By now, it was nearing 2:00pm and time to meet up with the group.

You may be wondering how I can remember all this detail. I will let you into a secret. In Italy it is (or was), an offence not to be given a receipt and actually an offence I think to leave the establishment without one. I keep them all and refer back to them as I sort out all my memories.

With appetites satisfied, there was time on our way back to the meeting point to take a few photographs of the area around the cafe.

The bar was in the Piazza San Fedele and quite near to a basilica of the same name. The huddle of buildings was old and of varying heights; smaller ones, which looked older, were tucked in-between taller, narrower, pastel-coloured ones. The ochre and terracotta colours of these contrasted yet complimented the brown walls of the older buildings that had over-hanging eaves.

Stopping outside the cathedral I recorded some commentary.

'Restored now by lasagne and red wine, the rain has stopped and we are just going to do a quick tour now of the square before we get on the boat to go around Lake Como.'

Although I only took a little film, being more concerned with capturing the wonderful display of colourful fabrics and fashions in nearby shop windows, Allen clicked away happily on his camera.

Como Cathedral is not in its own grounds as are many in the UK, but simply part of the street like any ordinary church. One feature, which took our eye, was the number of carved, stone figures set above the door and vertically down each side. On each corner, a massive column of these rose high into the sky.

Our photograph taken from a side street, shows this to great effect.

From our limited time here, we were not able to see much. The huge doors of one building had a ring in the middle to turn the latch. Allen filmed me stretching up to reach this.

Arched walkways protected many of the elegant shops surrounding the piazza from the weather. It was pleasant to walk around the cobbled central courtyards.

Flowering plants spilled over the ornate balconies that graced many buildings. Huge tubs of greenery played sentry at the doorways of many shops. One florist had spilled her flower displays onto the cobbled street.

Playing the film back now, I can see that I have inadvertently caught my better half on film as he trudged back up the narrow street [in the photograph].

A peep at Como Cathedral from a narrow side street.

The tour itinerary had said that we would have a lakeside drive. Suzie had suggested that, if we wanted to, we could go on a boat on the lake to see the lakeside villas, as you couldn't see much from the road. We thought that this was an excellent idea and made our way to the landing stage. The square or piazza in front of the harbour is quite low and when the water is high, it can come right into the square. It wasn't far off today. The boat once again was not a big one but held us all. Gingerly we all clambered aboard. Allen sat inside but I made a beeline for the back of the boat outside. There was no cover but the rain had stopped so that was OK. The skipper gave an excellent commentary as he explained about all the magnificent villas along the lakeside. From time to time, he stopped the boat to allow us to take photographs.

Lake Como is shaped like a long stick with two branches coming from it at the bottom end. Como lies at the bottom left or east branch facing the mountains. As the boat went north the mountains of the Italian Alps rose higher and nearer. It was all very dramatic. Some of the villas dated back hundreds of years; some of them were being re-furbished. At one point, after a brief stop, the skipper opened the throttle and shot off. Water flew up in the air and landed on the seat, giving all of us outside wet behinds. It was all exhilarating and wonderful!

Our journey today had brought us quite a way east into Lombardia; we now needed to head across country to Lake Orta in Piemonte. Our route therefore was to head south on the motorway before turning northwest towards Lake Maggiore. Skirting the bottom of this lake, we turned near Arona to cut across to Lake Orta and north to Pettenasco. It was a long but thrilling day with many memories. Moreover, Allen had a fully functioning watch!

Over dinner that evening, we had much to talk about and discuss. We had the same company, which was nice although we didn't have to keep to the same table if we didn't want to. For starters, there was a choice of Buffalo caprese salad with tomato (I think that meant Buffalo cheese), vegetable soup, or little dumplings with meat ragout and parmesan cheese. The main course was a little more challenging with a choice of rabbit with olives, fillet of suckling pig with honey and chilli pepper, Greek tomatoes or, much to my delight once I had confirmed that it was cooked, salmon slice with aromatic bread. After puddings, we again retired to the bar for the included coffee. I think I opted for a G&T instead!

A countryside tour.

Wednesday dawned bright and sunny. Hooray! Summer has arrived! Shorts and short sleeves were the order of the day. Our day would see more of Lake Maggiore before ending with lunch at Omegna at the top end of Lake Orta. Little did we know it, but there were some treats in store for us.

Firstly, we were to visit an umbrella factory at Gignese in the mountains between the two lakes. The road northwards out of Pettenasco took us up the east side of Lake Orta before joining the motorway at Gravellona Toce.

This would take us south to near Stresa from where we would hit the mountain roads. Making good time, we arrived in Gignese before anywhere, apart from a cafe, was open so we wandered in the sunshine or sat on a bench.

A signpost showing leaving one town and entering another.

Museo Dell'Ombrello e Del Parasole at Gignese.

The museum or Museo Dell'Ombrello e Del Parasole didn't open until 10:00am. Neither did the little church. At ten o'clock, we wandered back towards the museum, stopping to look inside the little church that was now open. Again, there were some loud conversations. Very disrespectful! It wasn't a ruin or disused church.

The village was very sleepy as it lay in the sunshine in the shadow of the towering mountains with only trees to give shade. The umbrella museum was housed in a modern building. We were still in the Piemonte region but in the Province of Verbana Cuso Ossola. This museum is the only one of its kind with exhibits dating from the year one thousand, eight hundred to the present day; it is a lasting memorial to the umbrella makers of Vergante. The umbrellas and parasols, some of which are very rare, are displayed in glass cases and grouped into different periods and styles e.g., mourning styles, together with luxurious feather fans. The pictures of ladies with nipped in waists, wearing long flowing dresses topped by huge hats and twirling a parasol reminded me of my Granny in her wedding photograph of the year 1900 (one hundred and fourteen years ago—another time altogether). She always wore a big hat when she was dressed up. I believe that hats were her weakness.

The exhibits on display were not only of the finished product but also of the parts that went into the making of the umbrella frame such as the spokes, handles, and all the little connections. Allen said that there was nothing new really, as he pointed out a folding umbrella and one that fitted into the bottom of a bag. On display also were a selection of sewing machines and other implements for making the parasols and umbrellas. There were some fascinating samples on display.

The shop downstairs had replicas of some of the umbrellas. I was intrigued with those which sported a double layer and the bright colours of the inside fabric. One of our new friends told me how she had visited many years ago as a young girl and fallen in love with an umbrella. She was thrilled to come away with one that her husband bought for her.

Arona.

This trip was meant to be a half day one but there was no way that was possible. A three-quarter day trip was more enjoyable and sensible. Leaving Gignese we headed towards Stresa. I think that the original intention was to go to Raveno a bit further up the lakeside but Suzie offered us yet another boat trip. A ride around the Borromean Islands on Lake Maggiore.

Heading towards Stresa we stopped in a small car park in Arona where there was a very unusual statue. It was colossal; it was huge; it was amazing; it was of St Charles Borromea who was born in 1538 in the family castle in Arona into the aristocratic Borromea family. His statue stands on a plinth that is twelve metres in height. The statue is twenty-three metres tall; it is possible to climb the steps inside right to the top where you could 'pop' out of the eyes to survey the scene below. Such is the scale of the statue.

Across the road was a church and one of our party said they had found an excellent view of the lake from the far end. Off I went to cross the road. Climbing the many steps to the church door, I was high above the road. The view across to the lake was astounding. Entering, I made my way right to the back of the church. The windows in the display area behind the Sanctuary afforded unsurpassed views of Lake Maggiore. With the brilliant blue water surrounded by trees and colourful buildings against a backdrop of distant mountains and blue sky, it was breathtaking.

Reluctantly making my way out of the church and back to the road I could see Allen and others in the group seeking shade under the awnings of the gift stalls that had been set up in the open area in front of the statue.

The Borromean Islands in Lake Maggiore.
Reaching Stresa just down the road, we decided whether or not we wanted to go on a boat ride. The Borromean Islands consist of three small islands and two small islets just off the lakeside. I was thrilled to be able to have a ride around these islands.

Sometime ago I read a story which was set on the Isola dei Pescatori and was quite sad. *An Italian family—ice cream makers—went back to the islands from the East End of London every winter. A young girl who was left behind eventually married into one of the families and left England to live here with her husband. She found it very strange and fell in love with a stranger. Her husband realised his dream of having a fishing boat but was drowned in the lake during a storm. Eventually there was a happy ending but the story remained in my mind.*

The Isola dei Pescatori or Fisherman's Island is the only one that is inhabited today. The other two are Isola Madre, which houses a palace and botanical gardens, and Isola Bella, noted for the many terraces cascading down to the water's edge with many statues on the ornate walls of the terraces.

Allen decided that he had had enough of water and waves and elected to stay on terra firma. Ever excited, I clutched my ten-euro note in my hand and clambered aboard. The back of the boat was covered-in to provide a sunshade and it was crowded. Off we shot and circled one island after another only just keeping our balance as we all hopped from one side to the other of the boat to get a better view and shots for the album. The skipper gave an excellent commentary and at one point played some romantic music. In the lake was tiny mound of land with about three trees, and what appeared to be a lot of sand. He said that that was the Island of Love. Not much shade there!

Using the zoom facility on the camera Allen had taken some photos of the boat leaving, plus some of the islands. I had taken a good bit of camcorder film but commented later that he might feel queasy when he watched it due to all the motion, but between us, we had a good account to jog our memories.

Omegna.

It was now time for lunch. Much more than time. We left Stresa on Lake Maggiore, heading to the top of Lake Orta to Omegna where there was a good selection of bars and cafes. Being very hungry as it was late for us to have lunch; we stopped at the first decent one we saw, forgoing the chance to explore further. The outside tables were full of noisy teenagers who had apparently finished school for the day. It was 2:00pm; they of course start early and finish early. After a bit of slow service, we had a wonderful pizza each that filled a big plate. At €5.50 each (approx £4.75) it was excellent value. We only managed to finish them in time before making our way up the road to re-join the coach.

Soon we were back in the hotel with time to chill-out. Tomorrow we were due to move to our next hotel on Lake Molveno. Packing could wait. Tonight we had a gala dinner with live music in that wonderful restaurant which overlooked the lake. Again, there was a good selection of food. We chose the veal in monferrina sauce, the beef dish, and the sweet. After a relaxing drink in the lounge and chat to friends, we reflected that the whole trip could not have been bettered—up to now that is.

To the Dolomites and Hidden Lakes of North East Italy

Our very first glimpse of the Dolomites had occurred a number of years previously when we flew into Venice on our second visit in 1994. Looking out of the window, I had been so excited and thrilled that the break in the clouds afforded a view of the soaring snow-covered mountains. There they lay, dark and forbidding as they sheltered the deep lakes below. It was another world. In my excitement I had grabbed our very new camcorder and started to capture this unexpected aerial view until suddenly a voice came over the tannoy.

'Passengers are reminded that it is an offence to take photographs while flying over Italy.'

I had looked up to see a member of the cabin crew at the door of the cockpit, looking pointedly at me down the length of the plane. Sheepishly I had put away my toy.

Eighteen years later, here we were again on this last leg of our Saga Holidays *Hidden Lakes Escorted Tour*. Once again, the sun was shining brightly in a clear blue sky. Today, Thursday, we were packed and ready for our long journey to Lake Molveno in the Dolomites.

The mighty range of mountains knows as the Dolomites, on the eastern side of Northern Italy lie in the region of Trentino Alto Adige. They are roughly bounded by four rivers: the Rienza in the north, the Piave in the east, the Brenta in the south, and the Adige in the west that has its source in the South Tyrol near the Italian Border.

Other rivers flow into the Adige in addition to its tributary, River Isarco. Flowing southwards down the mountains through Bolzano, Trento and Roverto, the Adige swings east past Verona to escape into the Adriatic. On the western side of the Dolomites, the Adige more or less follows the route of the motorway (to the east of Lake Garda).

The part of the mountains to which we were bound as our base on this tour however, were not to the east of Bolzano where the Great Dolomite Road takes you to the heart of the Dolomites and into Austria. We were bound for the west of the River Adige in what is known as the Brenta Group or Dolomiti di Brenta, also in the region of Trentino Alto Adige. We were informed that the Brenta Massif has the same rock formation as the Dolomites in the east. We knew that the main route in the Dolomites was the Great Dolomite Road. Completely encircled by the mountains, it goes from Bolzano to Cortina D'Ampezzo.

In 2003 when we were planning our Italy trip on the Gold Wing motorbike, we had planned to explore this route and indeed set off early one morning but had to turn back at Trento due to the intense heat with temperatures at forty degrees[3]

We thought that the trip into the Dolomites on this tour would be into this specific area and were just a little disappointed to find that it wasn't. On reflection though it would be difficult and a hard journey if not hazardous to take a coach from Molveno, so far east into the mountains and back again in one day on what was planned as an easy paced tour.

Actually, as soon as we arrived home at the end of this current trip, I took out all the maps of Austria, Switzerland, and Germany, which we had bought in 2008 when we were planning to make the trip again. We subsequently had to abort these plans when 'Ned' [Allen] was forced to give up riding and we had to sell the Gold Wing. I

---

3 *Just Us Two: Ned and Rosie's Gold Wing Discovery. Rosalie Marsh*

just had to check out the possibility and feasibility of going in the car—one more dream still to chase!

The journey from Orta to Molveno was a long one; we needed a comfort stop along the way as well as ensuring that we did not arrive at the hotel in Molveno too early. We were excited to find that we would stop for lunch at yet another lake. From Lake Orta, our driver took the motorway roads, making good time as we passed Milan. Stopping at the service station at Brianza at about 10:59 am for a comfort stop, Allen & I stocked up on water, cool drinks and mints to chew on the journey—and a chewy chocolate biscuit bar to fill a hole! Shortly afterwards, we turned off to cover the short distance to Iseo on the lake.

Lake Iseo.

The town of Iseo sits at the southern end of the lake. It nestles in the mountains surrounding three sides with the Po plain to the south. It sits slightly to the west of Lake Garda in the Lombardy region of Italy.

Most of this part of the journey was on the motorway but afforded some spectacular views. It was quite a contrast to one minute see a very old church tower on a church belonging to one of the oldest families (who no longer exist), followed by very modern car showrooms a short while later.

Arriving in the heat of the late morning sunshine, after disembarking from the coach, we all walked the short way up the road into the town. Suzie was mindful that some could not walk as fast as others could and managed to keep us all together.

Everywhere was a profusion of flowers, with the street leading to the water's edge perfumed by the many white, starry jasmine flowers that, growing in abundance, tumbled and cascaded over the walls of the buildings that provided welcome shade.

Suzie took us to the edge of the lake where there was a walkway to give us a wonderful view of the lake and mountains beyond. As we neared the harbour, I could not help but look into the shops that lined the waterfront. One in particular had a very simple but effective display of pure white dresses, each with a deep border of lace cutwork around the lower part of the long skirt.

As we continued along the walkway that ran along the side of the lake at this point, we could see the large ferry crossing the water.

In the middle of the lake is a small mountain called Monte Isola on which is a town of the same name. Monte Isola at five hundred metres high is covered with lush vegetation and is lived on; hence the need for a ferry. It was quite strange to see a mountain in the middle of a lake.

Reaching the main square—Piazza Garibaldi—it was by now 11:30 am. Suzie checked her watch, arranging a meet-up time before we all dispersed to explore at will. Most of us elected to find a shady spot under one of the umbrellas that abounded among the many café's and shops. After settling ourselves in a shady spot and ordering cool drinks, we decided to waste no time in ordering lunch as well, settling for brushetta. It had been an early start and hunger pangs were setting in after an early breakfast. This simple meal all came to €13.50. Our new friends joined us at the next table. This was pleasant. On searching for the facilities we found that, it was actually a 'hole in the ground' type. Thankfully, there was a perfectly clean and modern Public Convenience building nearby through the archway that led to the lakeside. However, you had to ask for them to be opened up for you.

View from Piazza Garibaldi in Iseo. Lake Iseo.

Everywhere was so pretty. The traditional mellow buildings around the cobbled square of ochre, white, and rust seemed timeless; an old man serenely rode his bike through the throng. Pigeons pecked at food crumbs on the ground.

The Piazza Garibaldi is graced with a huge statue of an imposing man in the centre.

'Is that Garibaldi?' I hazarded a guess.

'Correct.'

'Wow! I got it right and it was a guess.'

From where we sat at the cafe tables, we could see, through the archway, flowers tumbling on the wall of a pink-hued building, a deep blue sky and a tantalising glimpse of water with the mountains rising up behind. It was such a long way from the hustle and bustle of daily life at home. Well, our daily life; here, everyone appeared to take life as it came. Is that their secret of a long life in these Mediterranean countries?

On our way back to the coach, we once again walked by the lakeside.

'Have you seen that crocodile they have just fished out of the water?' Allen sounded quite serious.

'It is not a real crocodile.' My protests were met by a chuckle from one of life's big teasers.

Facing the water, there is a statue or monument surrounded by flowers. Looking up at this huge, stone, pillar with figures carved into each side, I craned my neck to see a huge bust of a man with curly hair and an enormous beard was on top; I queried this from my other half who is usually a fount of knowledge.

'Who is this chap then?'

'I don't know. You would have to have a look. (I have, and we were in Piazza Gabriele Rosa named after Gabriele Rosa who was a politician and a man of letters.)

Stopping to look at the ducks in the water, we were enchanted to see that one little baby duckling was having a ride on its mother's back. This duck was unusual in that it had a little cone of feathers on its head.

'Oh, look at that one.' I laughed delightedly. 'It is trying to climb up onto the big duck's back'.

Try as this little one might, it could not summon enough strength to climb up and big duck wasn't having any of it; it was constantly shaking the little duck off so that it had to swim. Allen laughed at me but he took photos nevertheless while I continued to film around the very pretty lakeside.

Lake Molveno.

Leaving Iseo I commented that the countryside was very lush everywhere. I filmed the map of the next stage of our journey which would see us travel some more on the motorway as we headed towards Brescia, past the southern end of Lake Garda towards Verona before turning northwards.

Leaving the Po plain behind us, we entered a more mountainous and interesting area. Passing through the Toll Station, we took the A22 Brennero road north to Trento, Bolzano and beyond We learned about the area to which we were heading including that the Alto Adige (Upper Adige) is in the south Tyrol. In the First World War, this part became part of Italy. We passed a solar energy farm where rows and rows of solar energy panels were in a field by the side of the road.

One more stop at the Brentino Belluno Service Station gave us the opportunity to buy ice cream, which we ate outside as our driver did not allow ice cream to be eaten in his coach. And rightly so, as he had to clean it and some people are inconsiderate and wipe their sticky fingers on the seat out of habit.

The mountains facing us in the distance towered high towards the clouds, the grey of the granite rock stark against the blue sky. The houses were chalet style which reminded us that we were in a different area altogether. There were many fir and pine trees; traffic was heavy with lorries that transported good over the treacherous mountains from country to country. Up on a hillside was a church nestling among the huddle of houses that formed the village; the timeless bell tower that stood high and proud was clearly visible from the surrounding countryside.

In the wine-growing area, there were many vineyards with vines growing up stakes to lift the precious plants off the ground.

We were now in the Trentino-Alto Adige region. Carefully, the driver coaxed the coach around the hairpin bends. You can tell how smooth and skilful our driver was as Allen is not a good traveller and he was OK. There were no fierce stops due to sudden braking. Everything was smooth and controlled.

Molveno is at the northern tip of Lake Molveno. We did not turn off at Trento as I had imagined we would. (I was following the route on my Italian Lakes FlexiMap.) Thus we had a wonderful drive through the stark mountains as our driver drove north of Trento until eventually we went through a Toll Station to take the Cles Road before dropping down at around Mezzolombardo on a very scenic and dramatic route south to Molveno.

Passing through alpine towns sheltered by towering granite, mountains our driver negotiated narrow roads from where we could see deep valleys and glimpses of the lake from the road high above.

Making our way through the town of Andalo the lake came nearer; houses cascaded down to the water's edge. Negotiating the narrow, winding streets of Molveno we soon reached our Hotel Du Lac. It was built, as were all the houses in the area, in chalet style. Dominated by rich golden wooden structure the walls above held balconies that rose up to the roof. They were painted a lovely light colour; some balconies on the first floor were sweetly curved and faced with pink and cream tiles. It was all so pretty. Inside we were not disappointed. Check-in was smooth and, again after dropping our hand luggage in our room we made for the bar. All the rooms had a name painted on the wall beside the door. The facilities of the hotel were very modern with a spa and pool. The key for the room door was like the high tech. one we had had in Alberobello the previous September. (More on that later.)You just swiped it across the door sensor.

Our room was beautiful with French windows opening onto a balcony overlooking the lake. We could see porter and driver emptying the suitcases from the coach and knew that they would be brought up shortly.

Suzie said that she would wait by the door at 5:00 pm to take those who wished to on a small tour of the town that was just at the back of the hotel. We declined. Allen actually had a lie down in the room while I took myself off for a short stroll down to the lakeside that was just across the road from the hotel.

Turning left out of the hotel, I came to a little bridge. There were paths down to a shingle beach but I was content to stay on the bridge and drink in the view.

Lake Molveno is not very large. When I say not very large, I mean that at only four and a half kilometres long and one and a half kilometres wide it really is quite small. It is however, very beautiful.

Lake Molveno is an alpine lake with many rivers flowing into it. At times, it looks green but that is due to reflections in the crystal clear waters from the forest-covered mountains surrounding it. Dating back to the post-ice age, it has,

'a depth of about 130m; it is second only to the Lake of Garda and its waters hide an entire prehistoric forest, with evidence of settlements dating back to the Bronze Age.'

http://www.alledolomiti.com/en/Molveno-and-surroundings/The-Molveno-lake. (sourced 09.07.2014)

Dinner that night was a lively affair. After choosing our meal, we then had to choose for the following evening. This seems to be the normal practice in family run hotels. It does seem economically sensible as food can be bought fresh and more or less be cooked to order without too much delay. I have to say that, apart from local/regional delicacies such as rabbit, some things got lost on the translation. One night it was pork in *bear* sauce. They actually meant *beer*!

The itinerary had promised a half-day afternoon trip into the Dolomites the following day with the optional full day trip to Lake Garda on the Saturday. Sensibly, after discussion, this was changed to the Garda trip the following day and a morning half-day mountain trip on the Saturday, which actually gave us time to unwind afterwards and perhaps explore the town a little. It also avoided a very long day just before a long travelling day on the Sunday.

Checking the temperature forecast on my Net book (yes, free Wi-Fi in this mountain hotel) I found that the temperatures on Friday in Lake Garda were due to be in the high twenties centigrade. A strappy top it was for me and shorts for Allen!

Exploring Lake Garda.

We were so excited to return to Lake Garda and see more of the towns along the extensive shoreline. We had ridden around Lake Garda in 2003 when on the motorbike.

The reason for this was quite simple—because the cost of a boat ride from Sirmione was so expensive. From where we were staying then, in the Yachting Hotel Mistral on the lakeshore at its southern end, we had just walked to Sirmione and had no idea of the scale or size of the lake. Sirmione is on that finger of land or peninsula that juts out from the southern shore and cuts the lake in two at this point. We could in fact see our hotel from there and it was here that we had found a laundry for our washing. Thus, we thought the boat ride was expensive. (Well it was but probably better value than we had initially thought.) We had therefore decided to ride right round the whole lake.

Today, another treat was in store for us on this current adventure. Gathering outside the hotel in anticipation of what the day ahead held, we enjoyed the early morning sounds of birds twittering and the contrast of the lush vegetation and trees against the brilliant blue sky in the crisp mountain air.

As the coach turned left out of the hotel and crossed the bridge over the northern end of the lake, our tour guide Suzie explained where the route would take us. We soon found that our journey would not take us quickly back along the motorway to the southern end of Lake Garda from where there are easy connections to various points, but along the eastern side of Lake Molveno heading south into the high mountains with their massive rock formations, deep gorges, tumbling rivers and spectacular views. About six kilometres from the southern end of Lake Molveno, almost hidden from view, we had a glimpse of tiny Lake Nembia—truly a hidden lake. More of a puddle really.

This tour was billed as the 'Hidden Lakes'; Suzie therefore encouraged us to take note of how many lakes we had seen on this trip so far. I worked out that Lake Nembia would be our seventh lake: Orta, Maggiore, Lugano, Como, Iseo, Molveno, Nembia, and with more to come. (This not counting the sub-alpine Lake Mergozzo near Lake Maggiore. I am not sure if we actually saw anything in the rain.)

South of Lake Molveno we came to Sarca Schlecht in the Sarca valley, which marked on the map as a viewing point. The road wound in switchback curves. As Suzie was explaining how many bikers used this road, some of them 'more mature' or silver tops as we call them, and others who liked speed, we saw coming towards us a group of bikers.

'That's a Gold Wing!'

I was so excited, and Allen quietly so, to see this beautiful machine effortlessly make its stately progress with ease along the mountain road. Rounding a bend, we were now on the high viaduct over the gorge far below us. The bikers were lost to view, hidden as they were by the trees that covered the mountains. Then we had a glimpse of Lake Toblino.

'Toblino is considered to be one of the most romantic lakes throughout the Trentino. What is most impressive is its location amidst soft hills, dense forests, vineyards, fruit trees, cypress alleys and Piccolo Dain rock face (971 m).'

(Source http://www.tr3ntino.it/en/nature-and-landscape/lakes/lake-toblino.html 12.2011)

In the Valle dei Larghi we went through the towns of Dro and Arco, craning our necks to see the tops of the mountains one minute and down into the gorges the next. The pretty town of Arco is just north of Riva del Garda. We learned that the Moto Cross comes here with hundreds of bikers. Turning onto the bridge over the river a little boy wearing a helmet rode his little bike over the bridge ahead of the adults. The river here is wide; the sheer walls of rock rearing into the sky watched over it.

Riva del Garda.

Our adventure on the lake started as we came to the town of Riva del Garda on the lake's northern shore. There are old houses, with hanging eaves and strange chimney pots, which were built under the Austrians (when this part of the Alto Adige was in Austria). Palm trees shading the pavements were covered in Jasmine that gave an effect of a tree trunk surrounded by white starry flowers. The perfume as you walked past must be delightful.

Pulling up by the lakeside, I was surprised at how small was the town; although it seemed to have everything that you could want.

We watched a ferry unloading its passengers. Gathering around our guide, she explained that we had free time to wander off before meeting again at the hotel with the green shutters where lunch had been prepared. It was set back, on the edge of the square facing the water.

In the huge square that ran down to the shore, market stalls lined the waterfront while a good selection of café's abounded, mingling with the shops that aired their wares outside. People mingled with families on bicycles crossing the square. The many shops were shaded by the arch-covered walkways. We found a shady cafe for a cool drink and commented on how quiet it was. Our cold drinks came to €4.80 so you can see where the money goes without even buying trinkets and souvenirs. Wandering around the streets leading off the square and not straying too far, we found wonderful displays of lemon sweets, liqueurs and other goods in the shops. It was all so delightful with the mountains forming a constant backdrop.

Eventually coming back to the harbour we saw what appeared to be a statue of a man dressed all in white with a white face, suit, hat, gloves, and boots.

This statue was so still; in fact it was one of these people who dress up and stand motionless hoping that tourists would throw some coins in the hat. It was pleasant to sit in the shade of a tree and watch the world go by on the water. Ducks and their families of ducklings swam about; the little feet of the baby ducklings working furiously as they tried to keep up with each other but not too far away from Mum and Dad. Some ducks were brown but one had a head of jewel-like green and blue feathers.

Lake Garda is thirty miles long and ten miles wide, almost like a sea in places. Mountains on both sides of the lake, with the ones on the west side coming right down to the water, make a wonderful frame for the view down the lake.

The town of Riva del Garda at the northern tip of the lake must not be confused by the town of a similar name—Garda—which is on the lower eastern shore where the lake widens out and near to Bardolino. You wine lovers reading this may not have realised just where your red Bardolino wine came from.

Ready for lunch, we all gradually met up in the middle of the square so that we could all go in to the restaurant together. We easily identified the Hotel Central by its green shutters and its prestigious position overlooking the lake. They had long tables laid out ready for us with wine and water. The first course passed off uneventfully. However, the second course was a little different. The meat was not just pink but running red. Asking for it to be a little more cooked, the waiter was surprised and curled his lip in disgust and horror. The meat was a long time coming.

'Perhaps he is blackening it', suggested one.

This prompted the tale of when we were with my mother in a small Auberge in northern France, and the meat at dinner was decidedly uncooked.

' *"Could we have this well cooked, please? Rare."*

In disgust, he took both my mother's plate and mine away. Eventually coming back, he presented them with a flourish. We took one look. My mother's was OK but mine, well . . .

"No. Rare s'il vous plaît." I was emphatic.

The waiter bristled and stomped off carrying the offending plate. Waiting patiently, we started to chuckle. Once again, the waiter came back and with a flourish and a bow, he presented my steak.

"You wanted 'well done' Madame?"

Allen and my mother were managing to hide their mirth. I joined in as Allen commented that, "I think he poured petrol on it."

It was certainly well done. It was black!'

We had just finished our tale amid gales of laughter when the two offending plates came back in a much better condition and we were able to finish our meal.

Malcesine.

We were now ready for our short ride around the northern tip of the lake to go down the east side to Malcesine. Piling into the coach, we set off along the busy northern shore. Rounding the corner at Torbole onto the eastern shore, we found that the whole area was extremely busy. We learned that the many oleander trees planted here were because they have the ability to absorb fumes from traffic. The masts of many boats and yachts pointed high into the sky and contrasted with the elegant buildings. Travelling along the east shore there is a fantastic view of the west shore. The road that runs along the west shore is the Occidental road with many tunnels and galleries from where you can look out over the lake if you are a cyclist or motor biker and able to stop.

Windsurfing boats plied back and forth; hang-gliders floated effortlessly over the lake—we watched as one carefully judged a safe landing onto a small patch of land on the shore, just missing the trees. Malcesine castle stood out from its position on the lakeside.

We remembered Malcesine as an ice-cream stop in 2003 where we just pulled into the side of the road and sat by the water's edge.

Now, our driver took us into the centre to the harbour area where there were boats of all kinds including small fishing boats and long boat, more like a gondola, with a crew of about five or six men.

I haven't a clue what *they* were about!

A large clipper-like boat was tied up in the water but, in addition, there were two smaller boats, the kind with seats on top as well as inside. One chugged off and our tour guide said that she was not sure if it would be that one or the one still moored up but to be there waiting at 2.15pm so that we could all go on together and be counted on. What a nightmare for her as other passengers mingled in. Not wanting to stray too far we opted to sit at one of the cafés just in front of the water's edge to share a cool drink. Yes, another one but you can't sit and not buy.

All at once, a bride in a beautiful, strapless dress, exquisite in its detail, and carrying a round bouquet arrangement of creamy flowers arrived with her groom whom himself was wearing formal dress complete with tailcoat. The groom had the back of his new wife's dress bunched up in his hand to keep it off the ground as she proceeded to climb onto the boat. (I dread to think how many creases she ended up with.)

Handing her bouquet to an assistant, she made her way to the top deck, which was open to the elements, followed by the rest of the wedding party. The bridesmaids were wearing long strapless dresses of a red grape colour with a cream under-bust sash. Other gentlemen of the wedding party had shed their jackets in the heat. Most of the lady guests had dressed for the hot weather. After a few photographs, the boat zoomed off in the direction of Sirmione to the south of the lake. What a way to transport the wedding party and guests to your wedding reception! It certainly has one up on a coach—horse-drawn or other type.

The side of the gangway sported a colourful sign. 'Boat Tickets. FAHRT NACH LIMONE' 9.00€Ticket,' it proclaimed. Translated this mean 'Journey to Limone' but interestingly the word 'Ticket' was in many languages and the other part of the message was in German.

The huge clipper ship, packed with tourists, sailed off majestically. Swans and ducks vied for space as they watched the action in the harbour.

Patiently waiting in the queue, Allen turned to me.

'I know which part you will be going on.'

'Well, I can get some good shots from the top. That is if I can get near the front.' I returned.' Will you be inside or, what about the seats at the back outside?'

'I might just sit outside, quietly.'

As the boat came in, some of the top-deck passengers appeared reluctant to move and I thought that they were staying on, in which case the best seats would not be available. But no. The last one off wanted to pose for a photograph as she came down the steps.

Malcesine and the castle from Lake Garda.

Suzie counted us all on board and then came on top to do another count. Worriedly, she said that she was four people missing. They had to catch the boat or they would be stranded, as the coach was to go around the lake and meet us in Limone on the other side. Counting again, she was still short and managed to hold the boat. Leaning right over the side of the railings, I could see Allen sitting outside at the back of the boat. A big clipper ship slipped its moorings and edged its way out of the harbour to go to the southern end of the lake. I could see swans and ducks with their babies floating in the water but keeping to the shelter of the harbour wall. Then someone commented that two couples had gone right inside and out to the front of the cabin out of sight. So all was well and the skipper cast off.

Limone.

What a wonderful experience! As the Garda Express, left Malcesine behind it entered the open water of this huge lake giving us a wonderful view of the villas on the lakeside. We passed the castle that, from the lake was framed with another but different mountainous backdrop. Such wonderful, ornate, pastel-coloured villas sitting timelessly in the hot afternoon sunshine, that Allen, from his seat outside on the bottom deck at the back of the boat, was busy capturing as he snapped and clicked with his camera.

Dark, forbidding walls of rock, rearing up into the sky, sheltered the lake. Boats plied back and to across the lake as we came nearer and nearer to Limone. The church with its wonderful bell tower—its top elegantly shaped— came into view, as did the huddle of buildings against the mountains. Café's lining the shore loomed larger and larger. The harbour was chaotic!

Mooring was also a bit chaotic to say the least. I couldn't see where we were to tie up as there were already boats filling the confined space.

In 2003, we had simply pulled off the road into the car park at the water's edge and bought ice cream to eat while we cooled off. We did see a sign for the town but thought that it was up a hill so we didn't venture and, to be truthful, I don't think we wanted to leave the bike—it was all new for us.

This time we had the full experience.

'I don't know where we are going to moor but. . .,' I commented.

The harbour was full of small boats bobbing about on their moorings. The small jetty was crowded with tourists waiting for the next boat. The one tied up was full and there was another one nearby tied up. Somehow, one of the boats cast off and moved a little way down. Our boat turned around and managed to tie up at the end of the landing stage. This however meant that we disembarked, not from the back where we had got on, but through the front of the boat. You know the narrow part with not much room.

Those waiting looked as if they were eager to get on even before we had got off, so eager were they not to lose their place in the queue. Some had rucksacks. What *do* people put in them especially in this heat? Allen only wears his waist bag. I actually thought that in the crush, we would be knocked over into the water, but people did move enough to let us past them.

Coming onto dry land so to speak, right in front of us in a warren of old, arched buildings were shops. Gorgeous shops with wonderful wares. The first one to hold my gaze was selling Murano glass. I had to have a look. In Venice on that 1994 trip, we had bought hand-made glass sweets but two had smashed recently when a photograph had slipped and sent the brass sweet dish crashing to the floor, smashing the sweets in the process. (The toffee trays were also hand-made but by Allen in his apprentice training days many moons previously.) In this delightful shop built into the rock face, there were also some wonderful paperweights and other items of beautifully crafted Murano glass.

'Don't you have enough paperweights?' I was being cautioned gently not to buy.

Sadly, I pulled back from impulse buying. He was right. The next shop, another cave-like place, had a rack of beautiful float dresses hanging outside. Quite loose and short they were and I drooled. Then I saw another one. Suzie had come past and stopped.

'Those are just your colours.'

'It is too small, but look how it swirls around my legs.'

'They might have another size inside,' she said and wandered on.

Reluctantly, I shook my head and left the gorgeous dresses on the rail where they *didn't* belong.

Meandering along, past the shops with arched, covered walkways festooned with colourful flowers, we came to a small piazza overlooking the water. Tourists lazily enjoyed the lake-view sheltered by large umbrellas and yes, music. A small band was playing.

Finding a shady seat, I could not resist an ice cream and I certainly could not resist a big fancy one. An Amaretto one in a big glass dish. What a concoction! Ice cream, Amaretto in the bottom so that there was a tantalising fleeting taste when you scooped up the ice cream, lots of cream swirled on top and dotted about with the tiniest little biscuits. What better way to relax in the sun?

Back to Lake Molveno.
Making our way to the coach park, we recognised this area as where we had parked up on our last fleeting visit.

I make no apologies but it was memory time all the way that day!

Boarding the coach, we settled down for the reverse trip through the mountains. The road took us on the familiar dark road that ran through tunnel in the mountains on the west side of the lake.

At this point, we were actually back in Lombardy as the boundaries slice through the lake with Riva del Garda being in the Alto Adige, Malcesine being in the Veneto region and Limone being in the Lombardy region.

The driver negotiated the dark, lakeside road through the mountain tunnels with care. To provide some light, there were cutouts in the walls of these mountain tunnels. These were still the same as we had ridden along before but there was one slight improvement; a few lights had been installed in the roof. This did afford a bit more light than we experienced in 2003 when, apart from the light coming from the galleries and lookout points in the rocks, it was pitch black. It is however, an experience never to be forgotten whichever way you do it.

It was interesting to see the scenery in reverse so to speak but most of us were tired and fell asleep. In the mountains, we were taken to a cafe where they served a special cake and sweet wine that we were able to sample and savour from the terrace overlooking a lake, if we wished.

Into the Dolomites.

Although our stay in this part of Italy was short, we did manage to pack a lot into the time allowed. After our transfer from the North West and our wonderful day exploring Lake Garda, we were more than ready to find what delights the mountains had in store for us. We looked forward to a circular tour through the Brenta Dolomiti.

As I said earlier, I had mistakenly thought that the tour would take us in what I understood to be the very heart of the Dolomites. However, there is another group of mountains apparently regarded as part of the Dolomites; the Brenta Dolomiti that are to the west of the Adige. They have the same rock formation and are very impressive. When considering the feasibility of a coach tour, many aspects must be taken into consideration with safety and access at the forefront. Pushing a little niggle of disappointment at one side, we eagerly awaited the experiences and adventures of the day as we left the hotel and the wonder of the view of the lake as it nestled amidst sunshine-bathed mountains.

Suzie had thoughtfully prepared maps for us that clearly showed that we would be doing a circular tour. She pointed out some of the main towns which we would go through as we circled the Gruppo di Brenta: Andalo, Cavedago, the man-made lake at Sanzeno, Cles, Cic, Malè in the Val de Sole or Sunshine Valley, Madonna di Campiglio near where we would stop for lunch at Campo Carlo Magno, Pinzolo, Sténico on the southern part of the circle, and finally Dorsino before passing Lake Nembia to reach our hotel on the northern tip of Lake Molveno at the end of what promised to be a wonderful day out.

Heading north towards Andalo we almost didn't make it at all as an impatient car driver almost crashed into our coach on the narrow roads of the town. He gave way as he backed up to let the coach through.

Vineyards here are prolific as they nestle in the shelter of the mountains; all available land is used, even to the edge of the road. Our driver navigated round unceasing tight bends as the road traversed deep gorges. The houses had chimneys with little roofs and polished balconies.

Soon we were passing many electricity pylons that looked at odds with the mountains. It all looked quite industrial here in the midst of beautiful countryside. They were however, essential as they brought electricity generated in the electricity generation station from the waters of the River Noce. These waters are collected in the huge man-made lake (reservoir) of Santa Giustina at Dermulo and Cles. The lake is seven and a half kilometres long and very deep. The town of Sanzeno lies on the other side. Across the valley marches the imposing Trento-Male railway.

Our view of this deep blue lake brought forth a spate of, 'It's gorgeous!' exclamations.

Coffee in Cles.

Soon it was time for the all-important coffee stop and an opportunity to stretch our legs. Cles was busy. The church clock showed 10:00am but I am not sure if the clock had been altered for summertime. We soon found a nice cafe and settled under the umbrellas at an outside table. From our vantage point, we admired a sculpture on the roundabout. The lifelike bronze figures of two dancers leaning backwards in a graceful movement, hair flowing backwards over her partners body as he wrapped his foot around her leg, was such a contrast to the alpine architecture and Q8 Petrol Station.

The bells of Saint Roch Church sonorously clanged out, telling the time. Nearby was a map of the town that allowed us to have a good impression of the area.

Time seemed to stand still. I have a lovely photo of a relaxed hubby in a lemon-coloured shirt smiling that sweet smile of his as he relaxed in the clear air; no doubt also recovering from the first part of the trip!

We were now well into the Adamello-Brenta National Park. We continued on to Malè crossing deep gorges and a river that flowed over its stony bed. Everywhere was a backdrop of mountains. By the sides of the road were huge stacks of trimmed tree trunks, piled high in readiness for winter.

There was snow on the mountains when we stopped at Madonna di Campiglio at 11:43am. This was a great photo opportunity as we were a little early for lunch. The view across the valley from the roadside was out of this world. In front of us was a golf course backed by rows and rows of dark green pine trees. The mountains behind has snow on the tops. Everyone was busy with cameras and camcorders as we strove to capture this wonderful view.

'Just to get the view,' I commented to Allen. 'It is part of artistic composition. It is all so huge and I am trying to get it all in.'

'I know.' I heard a laugh.

'Stop skitting,' [making fun] I chastised.

Flowering trees, plants, and leaves of all colours lined the roadside.

'A photo wouldn't do it justice.' Allen was sceptical.

'Yes, but a picture speaks a thousand words,' I soothed.

'The green there, in between the trees, they have put pistes for the ski season.' (There were smooth green swathes of land down the mountains that in winter would provide a clear path for skiing.) The sky was a brilliant blue.

'You forget how high up we are,' I commented.

'Helmets on' Allen said suddenly as a group of motorcyclists came past. There was a bus stop for the Ski Bus. The golf course was in an unlikely spot; in front were pretty purple alpine flowers.

Madonna di Campiglio. Brenta Dolomites.

Lunch.

From my notes, I think that we headed for lunch to Campo Carlo Magno but the hotel wasn't far away. Suzie explained that a family who had great foresight built the hotel in 1870.

Everywhere was so beautiful and the views faced the Brenta Mountain that is three thousand, one hundred and fifty metres high. Approaching the restaurant, we were enchanted to see on display a sleigh. The sleigh was quite big and sturdy with room for two rows of passengers. It was like a huge box on skis; all beautifully carved and decorated of course.

After lunch, some of us strolled through the village.

'Where are we?' I wondered. A voice behind me answered what sounded like,

'Campione!'

'Louder,' I called.

'Campione,' shouted the laughing voice.

To be truthful, looking at the map, I am not sure if we weren't in San Antonio di Mavignola which is a little further along the road from Madonna di Campiglio. Perhaps I shall have to return and do it all again—just to clarify my impressions.

The river was noisy as the water rushed down a small weir and over large, flat stones as it escaped down the mountainside. It was quite a walk back up from the riverside to the road. Allen sensibly didn't try but contented himself with filming me huffing and puffing up the steep slope.

'Gosh, those trees are very tall,' I commented as I paused for breath when I joined him and we surveyed the view.

It was now 1:15pm and time to go back to the coach and continue our journey through the Carisolo / Pinzolo area.

When the cyclists held us up.

Coming to a tunnel shortly after we had set off, our driver had to wait while the Police stopped the traffic and held us back.

'What is it?' We all wondered, craning our necks to see if there had been an accident.

But no. A car carrying a number of bicycles on its roof eventually came through followed shortly afterwards by a group of cyclists pedalling furiously, legs going like pistons, as they tackled the mountain road. Other cars followed including police cars. It only took about five minutes for the whole procession to pass through.

Back to Molveno.

Continuing on this scenic route on the west side of the Adamello Brenta National Park, the peaks of the Gruppo di Brenta Mountains soared high into the clouds. Mile after mile they flashed by as we glimpsed them through the trees by the roadside. The lower slopes formed a green, carpeted landscape to the more majestic, towering, limestone rocks. A lone paraglider soared like a bird across the valley, floating high in the sky; his colourful canopy a stark contrast to the scene below. Sténico on the southeastern part of the circle took us up to Dorsino.

We had one further comfort stop as promised before, passing by tiny Lake Nembia, we drove along the eastern shore of Lake Molveno back to our hotel.

Exploring Molveno.

As promised, today's trip was not be a full day. Arriving back at our hotel in the mid-afternoon we decided that it would be a pity not to explore Molveno itself.

After freshening up in our room and grabbing a cool drink from the bar we relaxed and chatted.

'Come to look at the souvenir shops—just to look,' I entreated. 'We have had such a wonderful day in the Dolomites. We arrived back quite early so once the shops open at 4:00pm well . . . perhaps we can give the credit card some exercise. Poor Allen is laughing at that.'

'He's not laughing.'

'Well, we might not,' I corrected hastily not wanting to spoil a perfect day.

Wandering from the hotel, we set out to stretch our legs and have a final stroll before dinner and explore when the shops re-opened. We quickly came to the church with its square bell tower, its walls painted white between the grey slabs if stone. All around were mountains, sleeping like the town in the heat of the afternoon.

'It is a beautiful, beautiful spot,' I breathed. 'We are surrounded by heights.' A child rode its bike on the open space outside the church.

Finding an ice-cream shop, I went inside to order. It appeared that younger members of the family were holding fort (manning the shop). After all, siesta time was not quite over. Friends of the young person serving came along and they sat chatting in a group.

Rested, we strolled through the narrow, winding, still deserted street to look at the small selection of shops glad of the shade that they cast.

Coming across an information board with a relief map of the area, we were able to trace where we had been and where the other parts of the Dolomites and the Austrian border were.

'Today, we have explored the western part of the Dolomites,' I recorded for the camera.

It was now 4:30pm although the clock was an hour slow for summertime. I filmed the narrow streets, the colourful wares outside the shops, and the wonderful, colourful alpine chalet houses and hotels with their overhanging eaves, and flower-filled balconies. I captured the many flags flying from some of the buildings.

And there he was. Another paraglider was soaring down the mountain towards the lake, just missing the rooftops. All the while, birds twittered and tweeted their little hearts out as they sang out their joy of the day.

Meanwhile, Allen panned around with the video camera to capture a lasting memento of this beautiful piece of paradise.

'You can get me in if you like,' I offered as he caught a shot of me.

'You were posing!'

'Posing?' I laughed. 'I will cut that out when I edit it.'

He is always the teaser!

Tasting the Delights of Southern Italy

As you will have gathered by now, pouring over holiday brochures is one of my pleasures in life; to read about other countries and their way of life sets me dreaming and thinking 'what if'.

Riding down the back of the long leg of Italy across to Sorrento on our Honda Gold Wing was an unfulfilled and now impossible dream. Further mad plans to ride through the south of Italy down to the toe and across to Sicily on the converted trike were also unfulfilled. On our visit to Sicily in 2005, we actually took the train to Messina to find out how the ferries operated; such was our optimism. However, it was not to be for reasons I have said earlier.

When I read about a new escorted tour with one of our favourite holiday operators who cater for the more mature person, I rushed to the map shelf in the study. Looking for the towns named in the brochure, I resorted to the Italian map of Italy which we had bought in Sicily some years previously. It was a large-scale map and the only one with all the information; the locations were so remote and small they did not appear on our smaller scale maps. With rising excitement and heads close together, we found Puglia, Alberobello, Ostuni, Martina Franca, Basilicata, Calabria, Altomonte, the Apennines—all these jumped out at me as we traced them on the map.

Laying the maps out on the dining-room table, we pored over them. On our last trip to Sicily, I had bought an Italian map of Italy when in Syracuse where I espied a Tabaco

(Tobacco shop) which sold maps. I had been having withdrawal symptoms you see and could not get properly orientated without a map. I now brought this out, as it was the most up-to-date one that we had.

Deep discussions followed. Could we? Couldn't we? Would it be too hard? The detailed descriptions of the trips helped and hope flared. What had been seemingly impossible now became possible—albeit under different circumstances—and, to follow our mantra of not saying 'if only', we focussed on the more positive 'what if. . . .'

Google Maps is a good resource for seeing and examining the terrain around the hotels. A search on Google Maps was by now mandatory as was a quick search of each hotel name in a search engine, which soon identified its location. We then did a search of each hotel on the Internet so that we could get a clearer picture of hotel facilities and the logistics than is possible in a brochure, even one as comprehensive as this [Saga] one. The hotels' Web pages were of course in Italian; we needed a lot of guesswork, reference to my limited language knowledge, and my Italian phrase book.

By matching up this information with that on the relevant page on the operator's website we were able to get as much information as we needed.

The proposed tour offered a good mix of included and optional excursions, which provided a little flexibility according to an individual's needs. After reading a brief overview of each we decided that the 'what if' could and would become a reality. Saga has started to grade their tours into different levels of pace. An easy one was what we wanted and this one fit the bill. The hotels all had easy access and lifts and mainly a level location around the hotel. As they were set in the countryside there would be no need to venture out on foot too far as a shuttle bus was provided if needed and the coach was outside the hotel. (Not like some holiday resorts where you have a steep hill, or the nearest pick-up point is about four hundred metres away.)

Unfortunately, departure was from London Gatwick only. As flight shuttle times from Manchester did not tie in with the Gatwick flight and were expensive, we decided to make the two hundred-and-fifty mile drive down and stay overnight at an Airport Hotel. Good move! The flight home was changed twice in the event, landing just after midnight.

With all that was going on in our lives there wasn't much time in the weeks leading up to departure, to plan. I had marked out the routes on my Italian map of Italy, put it to one side, and then promptly forgot to pack it. And, yes, that was a sacrifice. To absorb what we are seeing, we like to follow where we are on a map.

We were both keen to see southern Italy for different reasons. Allen is really into the history of the area and who conquered whom. He is fascinated by the connection of our history and that of Europe and what happened there when such and such was going on here.

I am more into the things on the surface, where I can see the here and now; like how the grapes grow on the vine and seeing the sea in the distance. For me, all these bring the map alive. We are chalk and cheese really but, like salt and pepper where each brings out different aspects and flavours of the food, we complement one another so that we can both enjoy.

One bright day in September, we found ourselves at our Gatwick hotel. The telephone rang. My husband listened carefully.

'We are in Gatwick actually,' he laughed as he listened carefully and put the phone down.

'That was Saga,' he called to me where I was exploring the spacious bathroom in the hotel. 'They don't have a room in Sicily.'

'Oh no,' was my first thought, 'Sicily was the reason for the trip.'

As I kept calm and looked disbelievingly at him, he ventured warily,

'The hotel is full and we are now staying at a sister hotel about thirty kilometres nearer to the coast!' Oh, he is naughty!

That was OK then. Perhaps it was as well that I had forgotten to leave details with our children of where we were staying etc. There had been so many changes, that I thought Saga must be dizzy, never mind embarrassed, even though the changes were not of their making. The thoughts of being nearer to the coast instead of halfway up Mount Etna were, I confess, appealing. I tried to picture from memory all I had absorbed from the maps. The one I had forgotten.

On our last stay in Italy, we were based in Giardini Naxos, a delightful town with a sweeping bay looking across to Castel Mola in the hills above Taormina and where the church bells rang out their Aves every morning bidding you to join in the day.[i]

For this trip, we had arranged a parking package with the hotel and booked a taxi transfer to the terminal. This way our luggage was manhandled for us. Although a bus runs frequently from the hotels to the airport, we had found to our cost on another trip that this usually involved heaving heavy suitcases onto the luggage rack. It was an experience that neither of us wanted to repeat.

With an early morning start, as we waited in the hotel reception, I managed to grab a few minutes before the taxi arrived to log onto the free Internet (wonderful) and send a quick e-mail to the [grown-up] children with brief details of our itinerary. The details we knew anyway.

The taxi driver dropped us at Departures entrance and explained where we had to go. This was unfamiliar territory and we were pleasantly surprised to find a moving walkway to take us up one floor. Then there was a choice of either an escalator or lift to the next floor and check-in desk. (I chose the lift, as I am not good on escalators and especially not with a suitcase!)

Check-in was unbelievably smooth—how things have improved—possibly due to the very early hour. Allen passed through security without a hitch but as I went through the scanner—ping! I had to submit to a full body search and 'shoes off' was the order of the day.

While you are being searched, your tray with loose things and hand luggage containing your passport is trundling through the bag scanner and being left unattended for a short time. Anything could happen if someone behind you gets to it first. Perhaps this should be looked at by the powers that be. Well, as the security guard did her stuff, my sleeve moved to reveal my decorative, metal, cuff bracelet.

'What a—, too late now', chided the security lady.

Passing through the Departure Lounge, we settled ourselves in one of the coffee / lounge areas, to watch the world go by as we waited for our boarding call on the departure screens. Our flight was uneventful. It was a scheduled flight and I was struck by the lack of commercialism, which you get on dedicated holiday charter flights from some operators. No scratch cards! No duty free sales! No drinks trolley sales! Quite simply good service with a free drink offered with our meal.

Puglia.

Bari airport in southern Italy was surprisingly modern. You hear such tales of the cultural differences in the north and south—the north being more cosmopolitan—we hadn't really known what to expect. But, hey! We were on an adventure.

As it happened, security clearance was quick with baggage reclaim swift; facilities, although limited were clean and modern. We had been advised that we would need a €2 coin for a trolley but had been unable to find one. Our new compact suitcases were easy to handle so we decided to forget the trolley and just trundle them out to meet our Saga Rep.

Passing into the Arrivals Hall, we scanned the milling passengers and greeters for the familiar Saga board. There it was and above it, the smiling, friendly face of Serena, our Tour Manager for the trip who directed us out to the coach area.

Renzo our driver stored away our baggage into the deep luggage cavern of the most beautiful coach I have ever seen. It was a lovely relaxing pale green with very little signage on it which made it seem a bit more special and private. We would next see our luggage in our hotel room, such is the smooth check-in, and porterage of luggage provided.

This being our first organised tour—at least, one not organised by ourselves—we were not sure what was in store. There were no doubts about being well looked-after as this was our thirteenth holiday with this holiday company. Would we be herded around like schoolchildren though? Would we be regimented with no time for ourselves? These questions had been considered and cast aside as, on balance, passing up an opportunity to see the countryside and life of southern Italy and then to return to Sicily was not an option.

Serena soon dispelled our niggling fears: optional trips were optional. Following the guide around towns and villages was optional if any of us wanted to wander and explore, as long as we met the coach at the prescribed time.

For instance, as I write this on a glorious hot Sunday in Italy, I reflect that the day before, I declined to go right up to Castel del Monte on the shuttle bus, electing to find a seat in the shade in the bus/car park. In fact, having declined to go to Lecce—said to be the Florence of the south—we are settled with a cool drink (of course!) in a shady nook in the gardens of La Chiusa di Chietri, our first hotel in Alberobello. We are listening to a gentle breeze rustle through the trees; revelling in the peace and quiet; watching the sun casting dappled shadows across the tubs of flowers, crazy paving paths, and stepping stones in the grass. The umbrellas in the eating area are at rest, no doubt well earned after the wedding party the previous night. The huge, deep settees and chairs are without cushions, they being locked away if there is no function taking place. But, no matter, we are comfortable.

However, I digress.

Back in Bari Airport, Serena introduced herself and counted all her lambs. A feature of this holiday company is that the Reps are usually more mature. They have seen something of life. They are dedicated to the tour or hotel in which you are staying and live in the hotel. This is re-assuring in case of emergency, at which they lose no time in summoning help. They are tuned in to the diverse nature of the clientele. Serena was no exception. In fact, she exceeded all expectations. A wonderfully warm, firm, but emphatic lady of mature years, she had masses of energy combined with an unrivalled knowledge of Italy, its history, customs, and language.

The journey to the hotel took about an hour during which Serena took the opportunity to share some facts about the hotel and life in this part of Italy, which is Puglia. Laughingly, she explained that we had to choose our meal for the night as it was waiter service and they needed to know what to cook for each. It saves waste at least and in the long run keeps the cost down.

La Chiusa di Chietri is set in the countryside just outside Alberobello. This type of hotel is used for touring, conferences, functions, and has the land surrounding it that you would not get in town, which in fact is very old. The brochure stated that the hotel offered a free shuttle bus, which counteracted the isolation, was very welcome, and overcame doubts as to location. Arriving in the middle of the afternoon after an early morning start, threw our mealtimes out somewhat. However, we were able to buy sandwiches at the bar; we devoured these with a cool drink in a shady area outside, once we had seen our luggage safely deposited in our room.

The outdoor lounge area was shaded with huge umbrellas. The walkway, between 'arms' of the hotel, led down to the pool area below. Here were stunning views across the Puglia countryside and hills beyond.

Gathering in the lounge area in the evening for the usual 'welcome' drink which Saga often provide, we settled ourselves in the cavernous settees to meet our fellow guests and began to break down our barriers of reserve. Serena gathered us all together while she further expanded on the hotel's various facilities and the trips scheduled for the next few days.

The drill was to keep to the same table for the next few days for meals, with the expectation of changing round at the next hotel. This was a good idea, designed to give us time to get to know our fellow guests. The restaurant was beautiful with large round tables in our area. Our tour group appeared to have a few extras as somehow we had a table set aside for tea and coffee, a salad course, and in the morning our own buffet breakfast area. All designed to make you feel special.

Typical Apulian towns.

The towns that we were destined to explore were difficult to see on a map of all-Italy, appearing as little dots. In fact, if you didn't know anything about them, as we didn't, you probably wouldn't bother. This is where a knowledgeable tour guide comes in. Ostuni, Martina Franca, and the Trulli houses of Alberobello to the southeast were our destination the following day, Thursday September 15th 2011. After relaxing in the lounge after dinner that first evening and a good night's sleep, we were ready for our first foray into the Puglia region where we were staying.

Ostuni.

We were all up bright and early for our day of exploration in the hitherto unchartered [for us] territory of these small towns and villages of the south. In geographical terms, we were in the back of the heel of Italy. On the map, everything looks sparse with not much habitation. Our perceptions were soon dispelled.

Setting off in bright sunshine, the tinted windows of our luxurious coach were welcome—as was the air-conditioning. Serena made the usual introductions and head count. Bidding us to greet our driver Renzo, we had our first Italian lesson.

'Buongiorno, Renzo,' instructed Serena.

'A great chant of 'Buongiorno Renzo,' went up.

'Come sta?' continued Serena.

'Come sta?' we obeyed like children. We all laughed at the incongruity of it. Renzo was appreciative and laughed with us. This set the tone for the whole trip. We were together for eleven days and needed to gel [become comfortable] together and make friends.

We were sitting on the right-hand side of the coach and, as suggested the day before, we moved back two seats each day so that others could have the benefit of better views. Excitedly, I captured what I could on the camcorder. I also found this a useful tactic for capturing all that Serena was telling us about the region. Her knowledge really was second to none. I am sure that she eats, breathes, and sleeps Italy, its culture, customs, and way of life. This was a real bonus.

Serena explained that some vines were covered with plastic to protect them from the rain and damage to their skins. These were eating grapes and needed to be blemish free. Other vines were for making wine. The area was prolific with olive groves and vines. I had expected that the olive groves would be just like woodland with all the olive trees huddles together. I was astounded to see how cultivated was the ground beneath and how the trees were set apart in a regimented order. This was fascinating.

Travelling out of Alberobello, we headed towards the coast road, which would take us to Ostuni.

Parking up in Ostuni, we arranged a meeting-up time and followed Serena out of the car park into the town. The car park you understand is not the kind that you probably have in your mind's eye, as they are in Britain. Noooo, noooo. Here, it was quite simply a small, designated area for coaches and cars to pull in.

Reaching the main road we crossed over, turned a corner and wow! What a delightful sight. The main street was lined either side with brightly flowering trees. I have checked in my very comprehensive full-colour gardening book and I think they were possibly Oleander. Whatever, they provided welcome shade in the increasingly hot sun as it rose in the sky.

A local man raced past us and ahead, stepped in front of a side street and indicated that we should take photos. He did not want us to miss anything. Following Serena, we reached the main square with its towering monument of golden stone standing proud, before coming upon the ancient cathedral. This was an absolute gem.

Outside, there was a florist's van with its doors open to give us a peep of the most beautiful arrangements of white and pink flowers with a number of fat candles set among them. The driver carried one arrangement in each hand and suddenly, horrors of horrors, one of the candles toppled and fell. He couldn't try to save it, as he would have dropped the lot. Evidently, these arrangements were just the norm, not a special occasion at all.

Turning, we were in front of an ornate, covered bridge that linked the Bishop's House on the left, to another building on the right that housed offices. The bridge looked like the Bridge of Sighs in Venice. Having been there, our minds winged back years to our visit there.

Strolling along while Allen took photos of the carvings and such like, I turned into a narrow street. I could see the sea beyond. Eventually—it was steep and rough—I joined others who had the same idea. Arriving at a sea wall, we were treated to the most fantastic view across the plains, which stretched out to the coast below. It was truly amazing and breathtaking. One hardy and confident guest actually stood on the wall to get the best shot he could on his camera, oblivious to the sheer drop below.

Retracing our steps through the town to the meeting point for the coach, I bemoaned the fact that I had forgotten the map on which I had painstakingly marked out our routes. Passing a small shop, we stopped to look in the window.

'Maps! Maps!' I shot into the shop and asked for a map of Italy. It was large and more like a road map. Really, we wanted the south. The Signora understood and reached for a map of southern Italy. Just the ticket.

Paying our Euros, smiling and nodding, I bounded out of the shop clutching my purchase. I was now complete with my map and could see where we were. It all becomes more real and in perspective when you can trace where you are on a map.

Well, as I spread out the map and folded it to our current area our purchase soon became known to the others. I noticed that another traveller was tracing our route on his map. I am not alone then.

Martina Franca.

Our next stop was in the ancient village of Martina Franca. It was not far from Ostuni. The sun was now higher in the sky but it was still only mid-morning.

Renzo dropped us off where he could in the centre of town before parking up a short way off. Serena shepherded us together and took us up the tree-shaded boulevard to the centre of town in front of the [another] cathedral while she explained its history. Naturally, Allen drank all this in while I as usual let my thoughts wander as I looked around—usually to find a seat in the shade.

Having some free time now to wander before our pick-up time, we strolled back towards the tree-covered square. I passed a well-dressed man in a white suit.

'Is he at a wedding?' I wondered to myself.

Then I saw a huge collection of white balloons outside a church, just the other side of the shady square. Yes, there was a wedding and the crowds appeared to be waiting for the bride and groom to emerge from the church. As the bride and groom stood on the steps laughing and smiling, all at once, there were loud noises as a type of firework was set off. In fact, they explode to send a shower of festive shapes and confetti-like stuff into the air. The balloons were released into the air while the bride gave her groom a big smacker of a kiss. All the guests cheered and clapped. Of course, I caught some of this on film. What a wonderful flavour of a typical wedding.

Alberobello.

Arriving back in Alberobello, Renzo had to park on the outskirts of the town in the quite large car/bus park. The walk to the town centre was uphill so we elected to go up in the mini bus, which Serena had thoughtfully arranged. Renzo came with us and pointed out a suitable trattoria/ristorante where we could eat lunch. This was another experience.

It was a typical Italian trattoria/ristorante with a wide and varied menu. As is usual, they serve bread, as this is part of the cover charge. Now in some establishments, the charge is per person and others, per table. It is a cover charge. The waiter asked if we wanted brushetta. Eager to try new things and savour our Italian experience I acquiesced and enjoyed. Service was a bit slow but they were busy and I think they forgot about us. A group from our coach came in and ordered. Some of them also thought they had been forgotten. Eventually we ate and the time to pay the bill arrived.

'How much?' many commented incredulously. There were many arguments at the till as most thought they had been charged for something they hadn't had—mainly from the cover charge. However, in the end you just pay up don't you, as they couldn't understand us? Serena, however, could translate for us but they insisted. Another couple had not heeded directions into this particular trattoria/ristorante but had gone across the road and found something much cheaper. There must be a moral to this story somewhere. Don't be frightened to explore must be one surely.

We met our guide just up the road in a small garden at the entrance to the UNESCO World Heritage Site of trulli houses. In the shade of the garden area, she told us the history of the trulli houses [singular is trullo.]. These houses are traditional Apulian, round, dry stone, conical shaped dwellings made of limestone. Painted white with grey stone roofs they are truly unique. Our guide explained how the area used to be a forest in years gone by. The peasants came and wanted to build a house.

However, there was a tax on houses, so when the local count or ruler came to collect his money they simply pulled out some stones whereupon the whole lot fell down. No house. No tax. Simple.

Eventually, the rulers realised that there was a settlement, and allowed the peasants to stay.

Wending our way into the hot sunshine of the village itself, we came upon street after street of trulli houses, all slumbering in the hot midday sun. One was open to allow visitors to peek inside and see how they lived. Moreover, they are still lived in today. Finding limited shade against a wall, Allen and I waited and sweltered.

(http://www.trullitour.com/english/trulli.htm)

A trullo house. Alberobello.

Following our guide, we came back into the more modern part of town. From a vantage point, we could see a huddle of conical rooftops across the town. This was another excellent reason to take photos before coming down into the centre where our guide pointed out other areas of interest. Truth to tell, by now we were all melting and drooping—young and old alike—and wishing for a rest. Eventually the tour was over and, stopping in the welcome shade of umbrellas under the trees, we thirstily drank our fill of a cold drink at the pavement cafés. This also was a chance to get to know more of our fellow travellers. We found a couple who had lived near to where our daughter used to live. It is a small world.

Having elected to go back to the coach in the mini-bus, we duly made our way back to the ristorante where we had eaten earlier while others strolled in the heat back down to the coach park. Serena came to wait with us; she began to be concerned that the bus was late and another guest had not arrived. As it was, it was fortunate that it was late as two ladies strolled up thinking they were early! After a few phone calls, all was well; our mini-bus turned up. We were soon safely back at the hotel where we were able to relax with a cool drink. It is important in these hot countries to avoid dehydration.

Dinner that night was a lively affair as we discussed our day. Our table [people] had gelled together and all were happy to share experiences and general chat.

Behind the scenes in Alberobello.

On the following day, Friday, there was an optional trip to Bari and Polignano a Mare. This is quite a big city on the Adriatic coast; it is also where the airport is situated but we declined to go on this trip; the hotel and the area were so beautiful we had decided that we would take the opportunity to explore more on our own. Therefore, courtesy shuttle bus it was as we, along with a few others, packed ourselves in, and rocked and rolled into town.

What a surprise we had. The driver took us along previously untravelled streets to come into Alberobello the 'back' way that gave us a glimpse of the town in general. Dropping us in the centre, we arranged a pick-up time before setting off to explore. We were able to get our bearings from the guided tour the day before where we had stopped outside the Police Station for a last chat, before dispersing at the end of the trip.

Using our street map—thoughtfully provided for us in the hotel—we meandered up the street towards the cathedral to be greeted by an unexpected change of scene! Everywhere on this main street, they were putting up street decorations. Workmen were erecting huge frameworks containing lights of various patterns. They were quite simple really, comprising of two poles with an in-fill of lights. These were erected and tied to the building at the side—a balcony, a railing, whatever. One on the other side of the road matched this. They were held together across the centre span in the middle of the road by another arched framework. It didn't take long as there was not a lot of actual construction work. It was amazing and it all looked so festive. The sun shone down from a bright blue sky, casting its warmth into our stiff joints and enclosing our backs in a comforting glow. (One of the perils of ageing.)

Making our way up to the cathedral, we entered the cool and quiet interior. The notice board gave us the answer to our queries. It transpired that the festival was to celebrate the patron saints of the cathedral and was quite a big occasion.

Coming down the steps into the bright sunshine once again, Allen just had to take photos of the outside. This imposing edifice with its numerous steps leading up to its great doors was topped by twin bell towers. These were unusual in that although they both had a clock face; one had a sundial while the other had a normal clock. Those bells must be quite a sound when they all ring out together.

Turning off the main street into a narrow meandering one, found us in the everyday part of town. Here there were boutiques, hair salons, car showrooms, garages etc, and the Fish Market. Consulting the map, we were easily able to find our bearings. To the right were the newer trulli houses, not the ones in the UNESCO Heritage Site, but in another part of town where they were newer. These were lived in. It was like another world. Stopping on the main street for a leisurely cold drink, we could see, around the corner, a lady doing 'knotting work' as she made strands of cotton into fabric.

A couple of our new friends joined us for a pleasant chat while they enjoyed ice creams. It was all very relaxed and pleasant. What was the rush anyway?

Deciding it would be a shame not to explore more in spite of the heat, we wandered up the side street into the trulli village. Long narrow streets greeted us. It was all so still, quiet, and unchanged. Many of the trulli were now devoted to crafts. Some had the strange symbols on the roofs, which our guide of yesterday had explained to us. At the far end, we came to some that were derelict. A lady asked us to take a photo of her outside a trullo (the word for one house). She reciprocated with a photo of us. It is a nice souvenir of our excursion into the far depths of Italy, where the family pressures of home started to recede into the distance.

We were going to eat in town but in the end, decided to go back to the hotel and have a toasted sandwich from the bar. While we waited for the bus, we noticed that school was out as children staggered past, shoulders bent under the weight of their backpacks.

'You would think they would have some books on electronic readers wouldn't you?' I observed as Allen commented that they would have bad shoulders when they were older.

It certainly is a reason for moving on with the times and storing textbooks electronically as I have read that one school has done.

We laughed at the antics of the lads who zoomed past on a pushbike. Only one bike you understand. Two boys, one bike.

The other balanced on the back and they had great fun as they swooped their wobbly way down the hill. Luckily, for them the police officers in the Police Station were not around. Where they having a siesta?

Back at the hotel La Chiusa di Chietri, we had a quiet lunch before Allen went to lie down. I took the opportunity to change into bathing things, grab a bottle of cold water, towel, and notepad to spend a few hours by the pool writing up our experiences so far. Finding a shady spot under the palm trees, I settled down. It was bliss. The pool looked inviting and, after sussing out the depth at various points around the pool, I ventured in. I am not a confident swimmer at all being more of a dog-paddler type of swimmer and like to be able to put my feet on the bottom. The water, although cold, was inviting and a welcome respite from the heat. A wonderful day doing just what we wanted to.

Trani.

Saturday dawned with another bright sunny day on the horizon. We were up early for breakfast as today we were off to the seaside, to Trani. Trani lies further north of the back of the heel of Italy, on the Adriatic coast. On the way back we were to have the opportunity to visit a Norman castle.

I mentioned earlier that our group had our own private buffet area for breakfast and dinnertime coffee. Well, there was a notice on the table to that effect but some of the guests from other tour groups who were seated near to us, decided that they would help themselves. Allen said that he just held up the notice and indicated that they should go away! I think they went.

The journey through the olive groves was again wonderful. Reaching the coast road, we drove along with the sea to our right. Serena explained some of the features of the area as we drove along.

Travelling along the coast road, I could follow on the map where we were. Polignano a Mare, Mola di Bari, past the great city of Bari with its industry and port, Molfetta, Bisceglie (here the road hugged the railway line whereas before it had crossed over and back along this most scenic route), before eventually reaching Trani.

Renzo had the route all planned out. Of course, they had reckoned without the sudden changes in the town, which could not have been expected and there were diversions! Our intrepid driver followed the diversion signs before reaching a very narrow street with cars parked on both sides. Here he demonstrated his extensive driving skills as, not content with parking where they shouldn't; some drivers had made it impossible to turn out onto the main road. Somehow, we came out of this entire shambles unscathed. All we could do was wait, laugh, and thank our luck that we had an unflappable chap up front.

Parking up in Trani, Serena explained the arrangements for the morning. Serena had maps ready for us and pointed out where we were to park up and meet later. She did not want us to get lost and was happy for us to wander off as long as we were back on time at the pick-up point. Following her explanations we could point out on the map where we were starting from, where we were making for and where the pick-up point was down a shady side street.

Trani is full of churches. It is built around a curve with the more modern part of town on one side and the old part at the far end.

Renzo, our intrepid coach driver whom we became convinced knew everyone in the area of Puglia, Calabria, and Sicily, pointed out a good restaurant for lunch. Renzo did not actually join us in the walk around the harbour from the bus park to the cathedral. No, no. He passed us on the pushbike which he must have had stashed away in the coach somewhere.

Quite sensible really as, after so much sitting and concentration, it was a chance for him to have some exercise.

The guidebooks describe Trani as being a port. In our earlier years of travelling by plane, we used the Michelin Green Books extensively, tending to rely on the descriptions in there as a pointer of where to plan trips. It describes Trani briefly, focussing on the historical aspect and importance in earlier years. Other places we visited on this trip did not appear in the guidebooks we had on the shelf at home and so would not have dreamt of visiting with only a small dot on the map to guide us. (I am talking pre-Internet days here.) At the time of planning and researching out this trip, we did not usually refer to our guidebooks for information, relying instead on the excellent notes provided by the tour company that were very user-friendly. We were more concerned with the location and terrain. The Internet was invaluable in sussing out these practicalities.

In reality, nothing could have prepared us for the sheer delightful, unspoiled charm of the town. A port—yes, but not a big port with big ships; it was more of a small town with a harbour/marina. Reaching the bustling harbour we were greeted by a cornucopia of boats tied up, boats on the harbour side with fishing nets spread out in the sunshine, lots of voluble chatter as Trani went about its workday life, and the usual noise of revved engines as cars and scooters zipped and zoomed past.

Making our way around the harbour, trying to keep to a crocodile formation as schoolchildren do, stepping over ropes, around parked cars etc. we came to the cathedral fronting a huge piazza overlooking the sea. It was enchanting and so unexpected! Not large, the building was more like a huge church but then, it is not size that depicts a church as a cathedral. At the side of this building of golden stone, rose the tall, square bell tower. No doubt, the bells were heard many miles away as they mingled with the bells of other churches in the town.

The front of the cathedral was approached by twin flights of steps; one side was decorated with candles and bowls of flowers tied with white ribbon on the steps. A wedding was imminent. It became a case of spot the wedding; we began to count them. Being careful not to disturb the arrangements, we used the steps on the other side to make our way to the great doorway. The cool interior was enhanced with magnificent arrangements of white flowers. The altar had been decked with acres of a sheer white gauze material, swathed around the top with a lime green fabric that ended in a huge bow. Two seats in front, for the bridal couple, were similarly decorated. No guests had arrived yet; all was quiet and still as it waited for the bride and the ceremony to begin.

As Allen went down into the crypt to explore further, I made my way down to the outside, strolling to the harbour wall. A thin, sinewy, man, his top half weathered nut-brown by the sun, wearing ancient, minimalistic bathing trunks, which didn't leave much to the imagination, and wellingtons (don't laugh, but it *was* a sight even if a sensible outfit for the job) was searching for crabs or other signs of sea life among the pebbles and rocks.

On the other hand, perhaps something for his dinner? He had rested a green container on the rocks into which he popped his finds as he scraped things off the rocks in the water. It was a timeless scene, far removed from the hustle and bustle of our daily grind back home.

By now, wedding guests were arriving, and what we would call an usher greeted them in the square by It could have been the groom. Another coach party arrived and well, what do you know? They, without a thought, went up the flight of steps that had been prepared for the wedding party, stepping among the bowls of flowers and candles. The candles I may add were lit.

'I wouldn't be happy if that was my son or daughter's wedding,' I commented to others who were sitting on the wall of the harbour. I was amazed at the thoughtlessness of it.

Our guide, seeming to know the general direction in which she needed to go, led us through the back streets of the town. We were happy to follow. Well, those of us who hadn't wandered off to our own devices.

We were in the old part of town where buildings were mellow in the sunshine; some had greenery sprouting out of cracks and crevices. Turning a corner, we came to an old synagogue. The door was open and ever nosy I wanted to peep inside. The building was very old, the stone a mellow gold. Inside was a wide covered courtyard. Here and there were potted plants in huge urns. Up above, plants and greenery tumbled down from the roof. Allen indulged me and did not complain as I peeped in apart from exhorting me to 'keep up with the rest'.

Eventually, we came out onto the harbour front, near to the ristorante, which Renzo had suggested. Was this another extended family member? He was a mine of information. Some tables were in deep shade under the arched and colonnaded entrance to the ristorante general. We were happy to sit in the sun as long as we could have a little bit of shade. The waiters were quick to serve cool drinks and take our order from the extensive menu. Settling for a pizza we sat back to enjoy the view and the life of Trani.

Lunch, as is normal in this part of the world, is unhurried. This means that service although good was not speedy although considering the numbers that had descended on them, we could not complain. It was the start of siesta time so restaurants became busy. Young couples on scooters zipped along and moved among the traffic as they paraded back and to along the front of the harbour. They were just showing off really. With lots of slaps on backs, old friends met and went inside. Our meal when it came was delicious. The bill included the usual cover charge but was not extortionate. We were in La Bella Italia. We followed their customs.

The harbour front had a wall with lots of covered arches, shielding open spaces underneath. Strolling slowly back along the harbour front I whipped out my camcorder.

'Look,' I called out, 'there is the bride. They are taking photographs.'

A little girl, wearing a lovely cream dress, sat quietly on a bench to one side, playing with her bouquet of red flowers.

Sure enough, there was the bride under the arches, posing for her wedding photographs. All brides are beautiful but this one was especially so. Looking back on my film, reminds me that she was tall, wearing a creamy, full-skirted dress. The strapless bodice appeared to be of fine lace, embellished with crystals, which set off the plain satin skirt. This in turn set off her deep golden complexion. Her jet-black hair, scooped back loosely before cascading into ringlets down her back, was held in place with her off-the face veil, which flowed over her hair following the line of the dress.

As photographers do, this one checked positions etc. On a signal, the bride ran across to change places with her bridegroom, who had been waiting on the other side, before meeting up with him for a smacking big kiss in her happiness. Some things don't change then. A wedding is a wedding and a lasting memento is the same the world over.

We continued to stroll back to the coach pick-up point and, as usual, someone was missing and Renzo only had so long to stop in that street before moving on. There is always one isn't there as you will see later.

Castel del Monte.

The next stop was Castel del Monte in the hills not far away. The heat of the day was becoming oppressive; we were thankful for the air-conditioning in the coach. As the coach travelled through the rich, green countryside Serena gave us more of the history of this castle. She also explained that we would park up in the coach/car park and a shuttle bus would take us up to the castle.

I elected to rest in the shade by the mobile shop in the car park, as I wasn't fussed about going up to the castle. Allen went but if he had known what was in store he probably wouldn't have as, once the shuttle bus stopped, he found that they weren't at the door but had a steep walk to the entrance.

Naturally, he soon found a seat to recover, as did quite a few others. He told me that the views from the top, were stupendous, providing an uninterrupted view across the hills. He was full of the history of the castle. I must say that I was surprised to hear that the Norman's had been active in this area. I thought they had only come to Britain.

Allen explained that the castle was in good repair and the photographs confirmed this. There was a huge imposing double door at the entrance. Inside the walls rose high into the sky around the courtyard. The inside of the castle was a surprise as, where you would think that there are two floors, one floor rose the height of two.

He explained to me later that the castle was hexagonal or octagonal and that the courtyard matched this design. Inside, there was no furniture but some good building features—not ornate but functional. He thought that it looked to be a transit stop for the Crusaders. If you check the Internet you will find pictures showing it to be octagonal and each corner has a round tower.

Norman castle. Castel del Monte.

Back in the car park I waited patiently and savoured some quiet time while I consumed a welcome bottle of cold water. The clouds descended and it started to rain.

This was most welcome it was as it washed away some of the heat and cooled the air.

The journey back to the hotel was uneventful as most of us went to sleep.

A quiet and lazy Sunday in Alberobello.

As weekend arrived, we were nearly the end of our time in Puglia. There was an optional trip to Lecce today. Lecce is reputed to be the Florence of the south. Being situated right under the heel of Italy, I was very tempted to go but we decided that a quiet day was in order. We do like our Sunday's to be like a Sunday if possible.

Booking the shuttle bus, we were able to pop again into Alberobello for Mass. As there were only two couples [from our group] wanting to go into town we found ourselves in the relative comfort of a car. I must also point out that the shuttle bus was complimentary for Saga guests; not having to pay made up for being a little way out of town so, no one could complain really. I doubt if such a hotel could be built in such an old town.

At the hotel, while we waited for the car to arrive, we had explained to the other couple the layout of Alberobello and where the other trulli houses lay, in relation to the UNESCO World Heritage Site that we had visited with the guide.

Arriving in Alberobello we arranged with our driver, using sign language and much watch pointing, a pick-up time before we parted company with our fellow guests. It was quite a pantomime to explain what time we wanted to be picked up. We wanted half past one but the driver seemed to want earlier. In the end, I pulled out my notebook and wrote it down.

After Mass, we decided that we would eat after all at the ristorante on the corner of the square near the Police Station. We knew it wasn't cheap but thought we would treat ourselves. Firstly, though we needed a cool drink, so settling ourselves down we enjoyed a spot of people watching as locals and visitors strolled about or found shade at the tables nearby. It was fascinating to watch as a young couple met someone and proceeded to do some business or other.

Chatting quietly we eventually ordered lunch, with the inevitable cover charge, before making our way across the square to sit on the benches under the welcome shade of the trees, to wait for our driver. He must have wanted his Sunday dinner as he was early but we didn't mind.

On arriving back at La Chiusa di Chietri, we elected to find somewhere cool in the gardens. These are extensive with quiet corners in which to relax and rest. Getting cool drinks from the bar, we meandered around to the back of the hotel. Allen had not ventured out here so was not quite sure where I was leading him.

'Follow me.'

I led the way to a delightful spot where we settled down for a quiet read. In truth, I fell asleep. The cushions were locked away after the wedding party of the night before so the seat was a little hard. It must be lovely to plan an outdoor reception and know that the weather will hold. It is a whole new ball game isn't it?

Eventually, we thought that we would go to the settees in the seating area near the entrance. We did try but it was too hot even though the sun had moved round. The only cool place was in the lounge area of the bar/reception. We more or less had it to ourselves until a coach party arrived to check in. All in all, it was a wonderfully relaxing day and we were so glad that we had taken the time to chill out and meander around a bit. It was our last day but there was enough time to pack in the morning.

Basilicata and Matera.

It was now Monday; a transfer to Altomonte in Calabria was on the menu. On the way, we were to experience Matera and the *sassi* houses in Basilicata.

http://www.sassidimatera.it/english/visitarematera.htm

http://en.wikipedia.org/wiki/Sassi_di_Matera

The sun shone as we gathered outside La Chiusa di Chietri to savour our last few minutes in this delightful part of southern Italy. As it was early in the morning the sun was not yet high in the sky. We had taken a last walk around the hotel grounds to drink in the peace and tranquillity. I had managed to capture quite a lot on film, without encroaching on the privacy of the diners who were seated around the various table settings under the umbrellas. The doors from the dining room leading to the outside area were wide open; it was all so relaxed and unhurried. The group of trulli houses that had been turned into guest accommodation entranced me. I must not forget to tell you that in the grounds is a massive, very old, olive tree, wide of girth and having a gnarled trunk that supported the mass of leaf-covered branches above. I wonder what tales it could tell.

Renzo brought the coach to the door and, while the porter marshalled the cases, Serena checked them off on her list ready for loading into the cavernous luggage space of the coach. We had been amused to see earlier, that there was a small private compartment in the side of the coach for sole use of the driver. We never saw Renzo's luggage but he was always smartly dressed; he had also stashed his bicycle somewhere; it made sense.

I was a little concerned that the luggage of the tour party who were leaving shortly afterwards would be mixed up with ours. But, no! The organisation and method applied was to be admired. Serena and Renzo had it all in hand.

Following the agreed rotation-seating arrangement, we settled ourselves on the left-hand side of the coach by a large window, which did not have the window frame to obstruct our view.

Bottle of water? Check! Camera? Check! Comfortable? Check! Everyone here? Check! With doors closing and into gear we slowly moved off.

'Buongiorno Renzo!' we chorused in what had now become a chant like small children in a classroom calling, 'Good Morning Miss'.

It became the high spot of the morning and always prompted a laugh. It certainly broke the ice.

With one last look at the wonderful hotel where we had spent our first few days in southern Italy, the coach turned out of the gates, onto the deserted road and soon hit the main highway to head south west, via Noci and Gióia del Colle into the region of Basilicata to Matera. There were olive trees everywhere. I commented that it was very pretty. I noticed one small farmhouse encircled by cypress trees and bounded by a stone wall.

As we left Puglia, Serena explained that the land here is not fertile with few animals to be seen. The fields are bordered with limestone walls. In Abruzzi, which faces the Adriatic Sea, the sheep go into the hills for summer. I noted that all around us was verdant green, rolling countryside where many groves of trees grew in abundance.

The Apennines are the backbone of Italy, stretching the full length of the leg; we were to travel to Calabria over the Apennines. This area is a watershed with the east of Italy being dry compared to the west; bad weather comes in from the Tyrrhenian Sea. Passing Gióia del Colle—a market town—we heard that it was a NATO Base. There was a castle built by Frederick II who had an illegitimate son with Bianca. He evidently locked her in a tower so that no one could see her. Perhaps he wanted to keep her to himself.

Most of the fields here were lying fallow, as they had been ploughed ready for planting. Heading west to Santéramo in Colle, we were near on the edge of the National Park of Murgia. This part of the region is more fertile with trees of fir and pine in abundance. We were entranced to see rows of vines forming a carpet above the ground as they stretched out to meet each other. Serena pointed out the prickly pears growing in the fields by the roadside. They are an orange/yellow fruit dotted with prickles or thorns—hence prickly pear. There were few cattle here.

In leaving Santéramo in Colle, we were leaving Puglia and entering the Basilicata region and the province of Matera. I noted that the road was the SP236. Serena pointed out the bottles in the limestone walls and explained that they do this when they build them so that they can be taken out when they want to put a pole in.

'A readymade hole, 'she explained.

As the morning progressed, the clouds rolled over; it became overcast. Renzo, who came from this area—we never did find out exactly which area, as he seemed to know everyone—said he was going to give us a treat. He had a surprise in store for us later.

Heading southwest to Matera in the foot of Italy, we passed huge factories with the name Natuzzi emblazoned across them. Natuzzi is the name of a Matera family, who are famous for making sofas. These factories lie between Santéramo and Matera.

Entering Basilicata, once known as Luponi, we heard that this region was one of the poorest until petrol was discovered. They do have water though. It comes down from the hills to Puglia and is more fertile now. There is also the Giuseppe Colombo Space Geodesy Centre due to an agreement between the Italian Space Agency and the region of Basilicata. Actually, it had never occurred to me that Italy had a space agency.

Matera.

In Basilicata, overlooking a ravine is the town of Matera. On the map of the foot of Italy, you will see Matera positioned where the inside of the heel rises up towards the arch of the foot before it sweeps down to the toe. As we approached Matera, the sky became overcast. The history of Matera is embedded in pre-historic times. We heard that it is a troglodyte [cave-dweller] settlement. Latterly, there have been many rulers and changes. The town is noted for its cave-dwellings or *sassi* houses. Driving along we were eventually confronted by a wall of rock with lots of what seemed like holes cut into it. These were actually the caves where peopled lived.

Before we reached the town, Renzo kept his earlier promise to give us a treat and swung his coach off the road to climb up and up through the mountains until we could see, far below, the whole panorama of Matera. The landscape around us was deserted and desolate. We would never have found it on our own, nor would we have known it existed.

'Did they used to live in those?' Pointing, I queried in amazement.'

'Yes,' a most definite reply came from beside me as cameras clicked all around.

'It is incredible,' commented Serena as she told us more about these cave-dwellings and the history of the area. With many gear changes, Renzo took us higher and higher to a spot where we could get some good shots of the modern town and Romanesque style cathedral with its beautiful high campanile above the *sassi* houses in the rocks below.

We all tumbled out to stand by the wall from where we looked down on the gorge and across to the town. The view we had was of a wall of rock with tiers of cave-like houses built into the rock in a formation of what seemed one on top of the other. They cascaded from the top of the gorge down as far as it was safe and feasible to be. The cave houses or *sassi* were not confined to one area; they were all around. Most were abandoned.

However, this area is now a UNESCO World Heritage site with the modern town and cathedral with its high tower, being on the plateau above. In recent years, many of these once-abandoned dwellings have been renovated and people now live in them. This area is now a tourist attraction.

The wind howled around us; cameras clicked furiously, and camcorders whirred as they zoomed in and out from our vantage point. Making our way back to the coach, we reflected on the incredibly, astounding scenes around us.

Arriving in the town, Renzo dropped us off by a café where a warm welcome awaited us. Another family member perhaps? By now, the rain had started to fall quite heavily.

A guided tour of the *sassi* houses.

After a welcome drink and comfort stop, we made our way to the centre of the new town—on the plateau—to meet our guide who would take us through the old *sassi* village. She pointed out important points of interest. Again, we could see that dominating the town is the old cathedral, high above the gorge with the caves below in the rock on which it is built. It was hard to imagine or work out not only where the caves where, but to appreciate that people actually lived in them.

The rain came down in earnest, forcing some of us to shelter in the doorways of old buildings nearby. Our guide suggested that, as the pathway was rough and downhill, some of us might like to forego the tour and wait in the nearby-disused church to admire the paintings.

As I am not noted for being nimble on my feet and not a lover of endurance tests, I elected to stay behind; but not before I had captured the scenes of the caves in the sheer wall of rock before us, on film. Allen, of course, was busy with his still camera as were many others.

A little exploration of the town.

While the main party had their archaeological and culture 'fix', I sheltered in a disused church with a few others. The rain slackened off and, one by one, we ventured out. In front of us was a long, wide, tree-lined street where one or two tourists had settled down at pavement cafés. Wandering off, I made my way past the many churches to the top of the street. Here it became very narrow as it rounded a corner. Not wishing to venture too far, I retraced my steps, peeking into one or two churches on the way back. It was a little oasis of 'me time', a personal adventure into this sparsely inhabited part of Italy.

There was no sign of the main party anywhere around. They had gone down some rough steps and disappeared into the past. Deciding that the sensible thing would be to retrace my steps to the cafe not far away where we were to meet up *(or at least I thought we had arranged to meet up there. I found later that Serena had expected us all to be waiting where she had left us)* I passed a few shops and found what I was looking for. It was now getting lunchtime and I knew that my other half would appreciate it if his lunch were ready. I ordered a drink, discussed what was on the menu, ordered and paid for hot sandwiches and snacks and found a place at a table. This is queue jumping down to a fine art! Well, it saved time later.

Arriving back at the starting point, Serena was devastated to find that the rest of the party had dispersed. There was no one around.

'They have gone!' White-faced, she turned with relief as one of our party came up the street.

'On, they are all in the restaurant,' he reassured. Her restraint was admirable.

The main group of the party soon joined us at the café glad of the wide range of instant food on offer. They really do have everything well sorted here. It was a simple job to pour wine into a carafe from a big bottle. It was good, cheap and just a lovely way to have lunch.

Over lunch, Allen was full of all that he had seen. He agreed that it was best that I hadn't attempted the walk down to the *sassi* as the steps and path were rough cobbles and slippy in the rain. Not feeling the need to watch out for me, he had been able to concentrate and enjoy the experience to the full.

What the guide explained as related to me.
Later, I had a full explanation from Allen of the houses as they are today.

'The guide explained that the houses were primitive but much advanced on how they would have been. One old cave has been re-furnished to show what a real peasant dwelling was like before the *sassi* were abandoned.

The animals lived in with the people in the cave. There was one room only and that was partitioned off for the animals.

They lived in the back. The people lived at the front. Cooking facilities were set out in a nook in a corner. Cooking pots hung high on the wall,' Allen went on. 'A double bed with striped cover, left enough space for a bucket with a lid to be placed at the side of the bed.'

Allen took photos to show how the living arrangements in the renovated cave-dwellings are today. All very compact and, to us, a bit primitive but a contrast to the furnished old cave which shows what a real peasant dwelling was like before the *"sassi"* were abandoned.

To Altomonte—a jewel of Calabria.

What a gem we found in the midst of the mountains.

Making our way back to where Renzo had parked the coach, we eagerly settled down for the long drive south through the mountains to Calabria and Altomonte. If you can picture a map of the foot of Italy, we were heading for the top of the foot above the arch, somewhere between the Ionian Sea and the Tyrrhenian Sea. This is a very fertile area with many mountains and plains. The roads tend to run from west to east across the foot and down the topside and underside of the foot.

Eventually, we reached the road running along the coast on the arch of the foot before turning inland at Marina di Sibari across the Piana di Sibari to the mountain town of Altomonte. It was very cloudy with rain now setting in so visibility obscured the wonderful views to a certain extent. We were however, able to see the rows and rows of peach trees and olive trees, which are abundant in this area. I was surprised to find that the dominant fruit was the peach tree as I had expected orange groves.

Following a tortuous route, we climbed higher and ever higher around the twists and turns of the narrow mountain roads into deserted countryside. We passed through olive groves, vineyards, fruit groves, and fertile fields growing an abundance of crops until, at last, criss-crossing the motorway to take us to the southern end of the town we eventually had our first sight of Altomonte in the distance as it perilously perched on the mountainside.

High, and proud, it stood on the hilltop, surveying all around. Built in a horseshoe shape around the mountains behind, it protected the plains below, that swept out to the Ionian Sea. Closer and closer we drove until, arriving on the edge of the town, we could see the old part where the church was perched on a sheer wall of rock. It was thought provoking to realise that this town had stood for centuries and remained intact. We were just a speck in the long line of its history and culture, which encompassed many turbulent times. Our guide eventually pointed out the Hotel Barbieri in the distance clinging to the rock face on the other side of the horseshoe.

'What views there must be from there,' I commented in wonder to my husband.

It was a scene out of a film and indeed, films have been made here.

Our driver, approaching the town from the south, needed all his driving skills and patience to take the coach along the narrow streets and the seemingly impossible corners of Altomonte as cars backed up and tucked themselves into the walls to accommodate him. It took all his skill to negotiate the seemingly impossible road up to the hotel. (I realised later when I looked at the map, that to arrive from the north would be impossible with such a long coach. The main road was twisty enough but the minor road to the town and hotel was even worse.)

The streets were narrow and, in the gaps in the mellow stone buildings were tantalising glimpses of the countryside down below. The views were out of this world. We all held our breath as we made our stately progress down one very narrow street, avoiding the overhanging roofs and balconies, parked cars— yes—parking restrictions appeared to be non-existent—people chatting etc., etc. Just where we thought we couldn't turn, we did; we turned left down the side of an ancient palazzo to find another building blocking our escape. All we could see was a huge, stone, wall rearing up in front of us to one side, and a sheer drop down to the plains below on the other.

The front of the coach overhung this drop as it perched perilously over the edge of the road. To cap it all, a car was coming in the other direction from around the corner. Oh! The driver must have been frightened to see this huge green monster of a coach bearing down. We needed to make a sharp right turn around the building in front which was bad enough and as we all held our breath wondering what was to befall us, our coach driver inched his way slowly around the corner onto the road up to the hotel.

With claps and cheers, we let out our breath as, with growing excitement and anticipation we found ourselves passing rows of flagpoles, which heralded the hotel entrance.

Making our way down the coach steps, we found that there was a smiling young lady waiting to greet us at the door. This was a good start to our stay in this family run hotel. Serena led us down a beautiful corridor lined with glass-fronted showcases, to a large function room at the end. This looked out over the plains, which today, were covered in mist. Our usual Saga welcome drink was waiting, as was Signore Barbieri.

What a larger than life persona! He is tall with a craggy but warm face. Dressed casually in raspberry coloured jeans and white shirt he offered us sparkling wine and red chilli crisps. I will call them chilli crisps, as I don't know the correct word. However, they were delicious and not at all hot. Signore Barbieri explained that they were cooked in olive oil, and when they were allowed to go cold, made a kind of crisp.

Alfredo, the Maitre D' bustled about with fresh supplies. He was a warm cuddly sort of person with a big smile, dark crinkly hair and a huge black apron with the logo BG embroidered on one side. His huge smile and desire to please became a hallmark of our stay.

With evident pride, Signore Barbieri proceeded to tell us about the hotel.

'From the hotel to the front, you can see the Ionian Sea and from the back the Tyrrhenian Sea.' (Altomonte lies in the middle of where the top of the arch of the foot meets the top of the foot; almost on a straight line from Sibari.)

His father had started the hotel, he explained and La Cantina Ristorante, where we were to eat on the last night, was part of his group. He was to take us on a tour of the town on our last day which would be quite special but more of that later.

At this point, Renzo, our driver, came to join us, letting out a smiling sigh of relief, wiping his brow and shaking his head in wonderment. The drive to the hotel was an unimagined feat with the sharp narrow bends taking us up to the entrance. (We think that he must have backed down again to park up below.)

Signore Barbieri took us on a small tour of the hotel. In the dining room to the left of the function room, he explained that,

'This is where you will have your meals.' He gave us the times of all the meals.

'Follow me,' he continued as he took us down the corridor to a small room. Hanging from the ceiling were rows and rows of red chilli peppers.

'They are hung up here when they are green and after about one month, they turn red.' *This was a revelation as most of us thought that the red and green ones were different peppers.*

'I will show you how to make the crisps you have just eaten. There will be a demonstration tomorrow night.'

Full of this knowledge we trooped out to check-in at the Reception desk and unpack.

First impressions count and WOW! What a first impression. At reception, we found that our own needs had been met with the requested easy access room and fortunately, there was a lift—but we had identified this during our web search as we planned the feasibility of the tour for us.

The reception area was to one side of the entrance hall /lounge. It was furnished warmly and traditionally. To one side there was a long corridor, which led to rooms at the far end of the hotel and the 'tower'. There must be fantastic views from there. The middle of the room has seats built around showcases. This separated the entrance from the lounge/bar area to the right with its cosy tables, chairs, and bookshelves.

We unpacked swiftly. As usual, I flung open the windows to take in the view. Our room was to the side of the hotel above the sloping red-tiled roof, which sheltered a covered area of the terrace. If I stretched out far enough I could just get a glimpse of the sea. Only just mind, it took a stretch of the imagination. The hotel staff had thoughtfully left a small, slim, bottle of sweet wine and some 'dunking' hard biscuits; something to try later.

We set off to explore the grounds and stretch our legs. The grounds were breathtaking in their abundance of everything and so unexpected, especially as we didn't know just what to expect right here deep in the countryside.

Leaving our room, we passed the lift and explored what was at the end of the passage. A door was open and to our surprise, we were looking out at a small terrace with many tables and chairs. They were all bedraggled after the storm but, what a charming area in which to relax.

Fronting the entrance, railings protect you from the sheer drop to the twisting road below and the Plains of Sibari that sweep down to the sea. With trailing plants everywhere, which dripped with raindrops after the earlier shower, flags of many nations moving wetly in the cool air, it was a most enchanting scene. To the right was a little secluded grotto with a water fountain and a plaque commemorating Signore Barbieri's parents. That was so private; it was a precious moment to be able to share in the history of the family. A gentleman visitor came out and told us that if we went through the gates at the side, we could pick fruit but only today. The gates, the gentleman informed us, would be closed in the morning. This was the private family residence but we didn't take up his offer; the drive that led to the gardens and peach groves was very steep.

Leaving the stupendous views behind, we rounded the corner of the hotel to be confronted by a huge terrace. They say that the Italians live outside and this was testimony to that. Why stay indoors when you can drink in the warm air and peaceful views. There must have been a heavy storm—in fact, the rain was heavy during our drive down to here—as the terrace was littered with branches and pinecones that had been knocked off the trees. I picked one up as a souvenir.

'That will do me,' I informed my husband. 'I am not worried about buying big souvenirs. We just need something to remind us of the place.'

At the end of the terrace, steps led down to the pool with more seating around. To one side of the terrace were more seating areas on different levels and a covered eating area. Everything was so fresh after the storm. The views were tremendous and one of our group pointed out the Ionian Sea in the distance. How good is that for contrast?

Clouds rolled in from the west; the sun pierced through, casting fingers of light across the mountains and valley below. It was almost as if the hand of God was shedding light to reveal the beauty of the land. I was actually waiting for a voice calling as it did in the bible. I was transfixed.

'You must take a photo of that,' I exclaimed.

Allen duly did his best. In fact, the photo has turned out quite well. In truth you could stand all day and be presented with a different, scene throughout it all. To the west, the verdant green mountains rolled down into the valley. Clouds gathered above; after pausing to survey the valley below, they blew, and fluttered on their journey to the Ionian Sea. A few of us took a seat and let the sun warm our faces.

From our vantage point in the hotel it appeared that the town circled the valley. Churches abounded, with bells ringing out at intervals. Most of the buildings were ancient with forbidding walls protecting their inhabitants from the elements.

That night, a thunderstorm again rent the air as lightning flashed and tress bent, groaning against the wind. After the drought of the last four months, the rain was welcome; it was much needed to save the olive crop.

The calm after the storm.

In the morning, Tuesday, the view from our window straight across to the town was changing by the minute. Wispy clouds, speeding over the mountains on their way to the sea, obscured the town. But, wait! All is clear again; the sky is blue with the promise of a fine day.

I was busy recording the scene and remarked,

'We are off to a liquorice factory near Sibari today before returning for a buffet lunch. This evening Signore Barbieri is going to teach us how to cook.'

The planned trip had been to visit Maratea on the Gulf of Policastro on the Tyrrhenian Sea. However, as this would have been a long, torturous, drive over the mountains with the subsequent long drive back, after discussion with the driver and her group, Serena changed it to a more leisurely drive to see how liquorice is made. We all, or at least most of us, remembered the liquorice sticks of our childhood and thought that this would be interesting.

'Buongiorno Renzo.' we greeted our driver.

Once again we negotiated (actually our driver did) the narrow winding roads. The journey through the mountains today was in bright sunshine. It was such a contrast from our arrival the day before. Along the way, we saw melons growing in the fields and pomegranates on trees. These we had never seen growing before. The land was so lush and rich; it was easy to imagine how the Greeks and Romans, dressed in their short tunics and sandals in the sunshine, would have tilled the earth to bring forth bumper crops of all things healthy. There were few sheep; this is not sheep country. Reaching Sibari, we turned onto the coast.

The Liquorice Factory and Museum.

The liquorice factory, situated by the Ionian Sea at Rossano, is small. Owned by the Amarelli family since the late fifteenth century—the original Amarelli was a Crusader and Knights Templar—the impressive family villa that sits on one side of the road now houses the company offices, museum, and a shop. Following directions to a tunnel that goes under the road, you quickly come out on the other side into a large car park and the factory. Behind iron gates in the factory yard, we saw huge mounds of straggly roots. The pervading smell was overpowering to say the least.

Our dedicated Amarelli guide gathered us around her with an introductory explanation of how they make liquorice.

'Follow me,' she instructed firmly. 'No cameras inside the factory, 'she warned.

Carefully entering the factory—it was a simple affair—our guide took us inside to the start of the tour, admonishing us to stay by the yellow lines on the floor. Explaining how the roots are transformed into a paste, she pointed out the store where the roots are received into the factory for the first process ready to transform them as a paste is extracted from them. Before us, we could see huge steel vats. The first one was half-full of a black tar-like substance that was being stirred around by massive paddles.

Peering over the side, we saw how the paddles in these huge vats turned this black paste, before it came out through other processes, into lumps of liquorice. Making our way down the factory as we followed our guide, naturally we were all inquisitive with many overstepping the marked areas of safety.

Walking further on, we entered another part of the factory. The liquorice paste was now been transformed into small lumps; the men were filling a kind of griddle with these small lumps. These were dull and indistinct. The two men obligingly demonstrated how the liquorice became shiny by passing the trays through steam. Of course, on this short tour of the factory, our guide did not demonstrate or take us around all the various processes and stages of production. This was simply a brief overview.

Later, having gone through the tunnel again to reach the other side of the road, we entered the museum where our guide continued with her dialogue and demonstrations to explain more of the history of the Amarelli liquorice organisation. On view, they had laid out ancient implements: horse saddles, cowbells, intricate gowns dripping with lace, worn by the ladies etc. All manner of things were on display, even down to leaflets advertising the product and of course the postage stamp.

'A postage stamp?' you are wondering. Our guide explained that in 2004, the authorities had dedicated a normal postage stamp to the Amarelli family. They are extremely proud of this honour; it is an indication of the importance and the contribution they have made as a whole to the economy and area.

Our last stop was the shop. Of course. You have to visit the shop at the end of the tour for a souvenir! This one was amazing and crammed full with all manner of unusual liquorice products: slabs of chocolate, tubes of toothpaste, bags of pasta, packets of almond cakes to name a few. The list was endless.

Making our way back under the road to where the coach was parked, I managed to snatch some photos of the vintage transport carts ranged around the yard along with a variety of old manufacturing vessels.

Later, with the clouds clearing as we left the liquorice factory, we stopped for a welcome comfort break at a huge retail outlet on the way back to Sibari. As to be expected, many of our group could not resist the opportunity to have some retail therapy. The selection of shops and café's was amazing and the supermarket was massive. Eventually, all the stragglers gradually appeared and we were on our way again.

Museum di Sibari.

On the way back to Altomonte, another 'must see' was the Museum of Sibari. The Greek city of Sibari is a very ancient place near the sea. It must have been idyllic for the Greeks and Romans to live here with the fertile earth producing crops and vines in abundance as they ripened in the hot Italian sunshine.

On display in the very modern museum, in vast glass cabinets were artefacts dating from around three thousand, seven hundred years ago. That is something like nearly four thousand years ago. It is hard to comprehend that such skill and artistry existed then when we tend to assume that we are the only ones today with the skills. In truth, many have been lost. My husband was in his element; I, on the other hand, was happy to rest on a seat in the corner. Museums are not really my thing. After a quick tour, I made my way back outside and sat on a wall in the midday sunshine, to reflect on this wonderful country and most beautiful, peaceful, unspoilt part of Southern Italy.

We arrived back at the Hotel Barbieri to be greeted by an excellent buffet selection for lunch. Served in the dining room overlooking the Plains of Sibari to one side and the town to the other, we settled ourselves at huge round tables. In this hotel we had a different mix of dining companions. Changing at each hotel was a good way of getting to know our fellow adventurers.

Alfredo brought out huge carafes of red wine. Most of us on our table plumped for white, which our waiter Alfonso readily brought. Some didn't mind either way but we found the red a bit sweet. On a side table was a selection of cold meats, cheeses, and a choice of soup from the tureens. This was starters. Then we had a choice of all manner of goodies and typical Italian food. Under a pristine white cloth at the side was a huge selection of fruits. Although a simple meal, it was more than adequate.

Replete after convivial conversation and good food, we had the afternoon free to wander as we pleased or rest. Before we drifted off Serena had a few words to say to her charges.

'Be down here well before dinner as you have a cookery lesson. Signore Barbieri is to show you how to cook the chilli crisps and then Signora Barbieri will demonstrate how to make gnocchi.'

An Italian cookery lesson.
When writing this I looked up the spelling of gnocchi on the Internet and found that there were many variations of these small dumplings. The ones we saw Signora Barbieri making that evening were very simple and it appeared that she used only flour. A temporary kitchen had been brought into the function room where we all gathered round for our Master Class of Italian cooking. Yes, even great pans of hot oil for the chilli crisps were on the table. The crisps were delicious and not at all hot.

Dinner again was excellent. As in the previous hotel in Puglia, we had to choose our menu in advance. This actually makes sense in a hotel of this size and keeps costs and waste down. You may say that there is no surprise and it is like being in hospital where you choose your following day's breakfast, lunch, and tea the day before. That is a point, especially when you have been used to resort hotels that have large kitchens. Mind you, if, like us, you forget what you have ordered, then the element of surprise is retained. Isn't it?

We rounded off dinner with a quiet drink in the bar before turning in. Tomorrow was destined to be an interesting day with a planned guided walking tour of the town. During the night, there was a huge storm. The wind howled as the rain lashed across the valley. The debris on the terrace in the morning was testimony to the fierceness of the storm.

Flavours of Altomonte with Signor Barbieri.

Altomonte is a medieval town built high above the Sibari Plain on the edge of the mountains of the Pollino National Park. Later, as I looked out of our bedroom window across to the old village of Altomonte where it clings to the precipitous mountainside, I reflected on our adventures of yesterday—the day after the storm.

Wednesday dawned in cloud with a threat of rain. A walking tour of the village was on our itinerary. (Sometimes the village was referred to as a town and the two descriptions became mixed up.) This was not your usual walking tour with the usual guide. This was a personal guided tour, through the history and traditions of the town. None other than Signore Barbieri himself, who obviously had authentic local knowledge, guided us

Most of the group walked down into town with him but a few elected to go by car, driven by a family member. Passing the walkers it swept out of the car park down a steep winding road from the back of the main entrance and up into the town square. The skill of drivers here has to be seen to be believed. They negotiate impossible junctions, switchback bends, and narrow streets where cars are parked at will.

I think I mentioned earlier that Signore Barbieri's father started the hotel and that there was a monument to both his parents in the hotel gardens. Well, the street leading down from the hotel was named Via Italo Barbieri after his father. What an honour!

I waited with a few others in the main square—Piazza Tommaso Campanella—in the newer part of the town, albeit still very old. Leaning over the railings I could see onto the road below and across to the panoramic views across the plain which swept down to the Ionian Sea. At this relatively early hour, the mist and low cloud after the storm of the night before still shrouded and obscured much of the view.

The town is dominated on one side by a castle and the old church —the Chiese di S. Francesco di Paola—which is now a museum. On the other side, in the Piazza where I am standing now, is the Chiesa di S.Maria della Consolazione, which is now the parish church and the centre of the community. As Signore Barbieri led the rest of the group to join us, he explained about the church, which used to be run by monks. He took us inside. It is simple yet at the same time ornate. We were privileged, on this personal tour, to be allowed into the area behind the high altar. This is an honour not bestowed to many.

Pulling back a curtain we filed through it to come upon a row of stalls which is where the monks sat. Of course, we all had to try them out. This was a perfect opportunity for a photo call. Behind this area, we found a room containing important objects. A glass case carefully protects the original statue of Saint Francis. Silently and in awe, we carefully made our way back into the church and outside, marvelling as we did on the utter simplicity of this ancient building.

Another treat was in store for us, one that was only possible due to the influence and position, which Signore Barbieri holds in the area.

Leaving the church, we entered another door into the cloisters of a building at the side of the church. This was the Chiotro Domenicani E Museo Civico. This building would originally have housed the monks i.e. it was a monastery. It now is the civic administrative centre of the town and a museum.

Cloisters always strike me as being so peaceful.

I remarked to Allen that 'they remind me of the cloisters in the church across from the Hotel Tramantano in the centre of Sorrento. Do you remember?'

The arches and columns of the passageway that ran around each side framed the cool foliage of the inner courtyard. Upstairs, we found that the rooms are now used for offices and the official business of Altomonte.

In effect, this is not only situated in the centre of the town; it *is* the centre, the hub which keeps the wheels turning. Our host very proudly explained the functions of the different rooms, greeting staff and other visitors alike as he led us on our tour. He took us into the (what we call in the UK) Council Chamber where all the important decisions to do with Altomonte are made. We found that apart from providing employment through his Barbieri Group of hotels and restaurants, he was also the Minister for Tourism. His passion for the town was apparent and shone through as he presented to us, various aspects of life in Altomonte. If you want more detail, you will have to pay a visit and get it all first hand. It is well worth the journey, I assure you.

As we came to a standstill outside the Mayor's Office, two well-dressed men approached quietly. Signore Barbieri introduced them as the current mayor and the future mayor before he allowed a peek into the inner sanctum of the Mayor's Office. In here, on display, are various important cultural awards.There is also a photograph of Queen Paola of Belgium whose family, we were told with great pride, came from Calabria.

Going downstairs by way of beautiful wide corridors (the upper floors of the Cloisters), we stopped for a moment to look out of the windows into the cool greenery of the ferns and palm trees in the courtyard below.

Finding ourselves back in the town square, we eagerly awaited our next adventure. Yes, there was another treat in store for us. The café's surrounding the square were by now showing signs of life and a stop here would have been nice. Indeed, we thought that those who didn't wish to climb the one hundred steps up to the tower would be resting here. But no!

The tower is in the old part of the town along with another church, the Chiesa di S. Francesco di Paola and the old parish church. This was the church, built on the edge of the wall of rock that we had seen when we had our first glimpse of Altomonte.

We had a choice. We could climb the one hundred steps of the tower or wait in the café at the bottom if we didn't want to do that. We thought he meant the cafe's in the square where we were gathered. But, no! Following our 'Pied Piper' who led us past the open air circular theatre with its tiered rows flowing down to the stage area [an amphitheatre], we negotiated all the twists and turns to the more medieval part of the town. He didn't tell us how many steps there were to get to the base of the church and tower; if we had have known some of us would have stayed where we were down in the square below.

The climb was well worth it though as, concentrating on one step at a time along the narrow twisting streets and pausing to admire the ever-changing scenery across the plain, we came to a small square with a café. The one and only café as it turned out. There was also a souvenir shop and a marvellous lookout point over to the other side of the town to the hotel and across the plain to the sea.

Around the corner was La Cantina, our restaurant for that evening and of course, part of the Barbieri Group. Family is very important in this part of the world.

Enjoying a coffee or a cold drink, we all sat in the cool air to absorb what we had seen that morning. We also had the chance to get to know other members of our party. It was all so unexpected and charming. It was as if we had taken a step-back-in-time and an experience we would never in a million years have dreamt we would be experiencing. Some of us elected to rest and relax some more while the energetic members of our group went into the church to explore.

We thought that the bell tower was the tower with one hundred steps. We found out later that it wasn't. It was another one.

The Amphitheatre. Altomonte.

The tiny souvenir shop was packed to overflowing with all manner of treasures but sadly, there were no up-to-date postcards of the area at that time. No doubt, this will be rectified eventually as tourism increases. The café service was quick and efficient with no pressure on us to hurry.

Signore Barbieri offered transport back for those who 'had had enough' so to speak and quickly rounded up transport from among his family members while others were exploring.

Eventually, a car hurtled into the square from the depths of a street so narrow you would not have thought a car could navigate it. (We were to find out at first hand that evening how possible this was.)

The journey down into the town and across to the Hotel Barbieri was an adventure in itself as Stefeno took the twists and turns of the narrow streets with practised ease. There was no room for cars to pass, you understand. Just a narrow steeply sloping street with cobbles in-between the path laid for carts—in days gone by—to run smoothly.

'It is a bit like driving through Cefn Mawr [North Wales] when you spend time backing up when a bus comes and pulling to one side when it is too narrow for two vehicles to pass.' I drily commented, remembering my very first bus ride through that village many years ago.

With a laugh, Allen agreed and concentrated on not being ill as we hurtled around corners.

As ever, as we turned towards the hotel, I wondered how on earth our coach driver Renzo, managed to nurse his coach around the 'dog's hind legs' of junctions without a scratch.

The hotel's terraces lend themselves to a quiet relax and chat with newly formed friends. We however, after another excellent lunch, elected to have a siesta in our very pleasant bedroom that looked out to the panoramic view of the village.

La Cantina Ristorante. Altomonte.

We prepared leisurely for our evening at La Cantina. Thankfully, transport was provided.

The charming La Cantina Ristorante is tucked away in the old village, around the corner from the café where we had relaxed that morning; it is formed from old cellars. It is an exhilarating journey where cars come from all directions as we turned to climb the steep narrow streets—surely that one is a dead end?—to the square. The old wine cellars have been turned into a delightful oasis of peace, charm, tranquillity, and ambience, where all manner of treats and delights can be savoured and enjoyed.

Alfredo, our cheerful smiling waiter from the hotel, was waiting to greet us. He is a mature man with a shock of greying hair, a beaming smile, and expansive welcome. There he was, dressed in his usual uniform of long black apron with the BG logo, over a white shirt and black trousers.

Great carafes of red wine sat on the tables waiting for thirsty diners to devour them. As many of us had found this a little sweet for our taste, opting instead at mealtimes for il vino bianco (white wine), I now asked for this.

The cellars were, as you would expect, small. They consisted of a series of rooms, one leading to another through an arched doorway; whitewashed walls were decorated with all things local and bottles of wine. Were some empty? We took over two rooms and as we waited for the other party to arrive, I chatted to Serena.

I told her what a wonderful job she was doing and commented that it must be hard keeping us all in order and where we should be.this was a new tour for her; it was a learning curve and of course, the original hotel had been changed to this one so Altomonte itself was an unchartered experience.

Neither she, Renzo, nor the hotel staff had let us down. It was all perfect and an excellent choice on behalf of Saga.

Soon, as the second party arrived, the rooms filled with the laughter and the chatter of many voices. With welcome speeches over, we heard the sound of music coming nearer, and nearer. Two locals (Albanian) serenaded us with traditional music—one with an accordion and one with a tambourine. This was to be the pattern of this wonderful night where a serenade of music preceded every course.

At one point, they came in with bagpipes. The bag was white and may have been a from a sheep's bladder. Well, so someone told me but it was a big one if it was. The bladder not the sheep. Well, come to think of it, the sheep must have been quite large as well!

After a selection of traditional meats followed by soup, a main course and dessert all washed down with copious amounts of vino, several of the party joined Serena and Alfredo for an energetic dance. The waiters came in with a very large square cake, iced and decorated with the words 'SAGA' especially for us. After it was cut, shared out, and we had devoured it, with hugs, kisses, and thank you to the waiters, singers, and especially Alfredo, we piled back into cars and wended our way back to the hotel and bed.

This was another wonderful experience in this mountain hideaway—it is an absolute jewel of southern Italy and Calabria.

Journey to the Very Tip of the Toe of Italy.

The following morning, Thursday, we were up early for breakfast and last minute packing. Leaving our cases outside our room as instructed ready for collection, Allen and I took a last stroll around the wonderful gardens. The palms and plants were dripping after the storm of the night, but today, the sun shone and the air was fresh. Settling our bill as we checked out at Reception and never one to miss a marketing opportunity, I left some information about our books with the receptionist, explaining what it was all about and how I was to include our wonderful stay in Altomonte in our next travel book. (It has just taken longer than anticipated.)

As the porter brought down the luggage, Serena checked it off ready for Renzo to load it carefully into the bowels of the coach.

Our journey today would take us right through Calabria through the Aspromonte, which is an area in the toe of Italy between two seas, right to the tip of the toe of Italy. Here we were to catch the ferry across to Sicily. As I mentioned earlier, Altomonte sits proudly between the top of the foot and the arch of the foot. We were now to travel down the front of the foot and along the toe. A long journey and one that needed careful co-ordination to make sure that we didn't miss the ferry.

We had visited Italy before, staying in Giardini Naxos on the coast. This tour itinerary had originally been planned to end at a hotel somewhere part way up Mt. Etna above Taormina, but the day before we left the UK, Saga had telephoned us of yet another change to our schedule. There was a problem with accommodation at the hotel so the hotel management had transferred us to a sister hotel on the beach near Taormina itself and was an upgrade.

What a gift this proved to be and set the seal on our holiday.

Meanwhile, we had a long journey ahead, so fasten your seat belts, and join us.

Once we were all boarded and settled, Serena counted her chicks and settled down. We all chanted our by now familiar,'Buongiorno Renzo!', as we set off with waves and smiles to the hotel staff lining the entrance.

Serena gleefully announced, 'Today we were off to Sicily.'

'Hooray,' we all cheered like children out on a day trip.

'I hope he gets this coach down safely,' I am heard to comment on film as Renzo inched his way down the drive of the hotel and along the narrow road leading into the town.

Serena explained that the plan was to travel down the west coast with the Tyrrhenian Sea on our right, until we reached Villa di San Giovanni. From there we would take the ferry to Messina in Sicily, a crossing that would only take half an hour. She asked us all to eat our lunch whilst on the ferry as eating on the coach is not allowed. On reaching Sicily, we would take the road to Taormina. We eagerly awaited this part of the tour as we had visited Taormina on our previous first visit under the care of Saga, when we had based ourselves in Giardini Naxos.

Leaving Altomonte in brilliant sunshine, I started to chat.

'This is where the fun starts.'

Renzo carefully and patiently eased and coaxed the coach down the narrow streets missing chatting villagers, around impossible junctions, past parked cars (just missing overhanging roofs and balconies) as we caught our last glimpse of this wonderful amazing place. With horn tooting, we wondered why we had stopped.

'Is there a car door open or something,' queried Allen.

'I don't know. It looks as if we are trapped in.'

I was amazed as a car carefully inched round the front of the coach and parked cars.

'They don't wait do they?'

I commented drily and, catching a glimpse of the countryside dropping into the plains below, exclaimed,

'It is a gorgeous view isn't it?'

We had a few moments to savour this due to the traffic situation. Moving on, we inched down the street.

'Look! There is the fruit and vegetable shop with rows of red chillies hanging outside.'

'Peaches, bananas, garlic,' I went on enthusiastically.

'There is the impossible uphill left turn we took last night up to the old town.' I chattered on as the coach slowly wended its way through Altomonte.

'There's the hotel,' I commented as, with gear changes on the steeply winding road, the wide windows of the coach gave us a glimpse of the Hotel Barbieri standing proudly on the edge of the mountain facing the Ionian Sea far below.

The beauty was timeless as the town slumbered quietly in the rising sun. The blue sky peeped through the tall trees that cast a welcome shade over the village. I wish we could have put this amazing scene of the village perched on the side of a mountain, into a bottle for keeps. I had to be content with capturing it on film. Eventually, craning our necks at our last view of the old town surveying the plains below, we left Altomonte behind. By now, it was but a distant view perched on the rock.

Facing forward now, I stopped bouncing around as we eagerly awaited our next experience on this wonderful Southern Italian and Sicilian adventure.

Leaving the treacherous mountain roads behind, Renzo soon joined the motorway. Geographically, we were heading down the very top of the foot of Italy down to the toe. At Cosenza, we passed through many tunnels cut into the rock.

These gave us glimpses of the green, lush, mainly pine, covered Sila Mountains which were on my left as we travelled south; lying on the bottom of the foot 'between Rossano to the north and Catanzaro to the south'.

The beauty, the sheer lushness of the land, and the fertility of the area that is now a National Park awed us. Opposite us on the coach was the stairwell for the back exit. This gave us a clear view through the wide window on the other side of the coach. I was therefore able to catch some of the wonderful views on both sides. To the right, we were now starting to hug the coastal motorway with clear views of the Tyrrhenian Sea as we headed towards the Straits of Messina.

Passing through many tunnels in the motorway cut into the side of the Aspromonte Mountains, we could clearly see the town far below. Soon it was time for a comfort stop. Serena had advised us to take advantage of this, as the facilities on the boat were not what we would expect. It was good to stretch our legs and relax in the shade of this glorious sunny day. It was hard to realise exactly where we were. After all a Shell Petrol Station is more or less the same the world over! However, here we were, at the toe of Italy where, as the old childhood rhyme says 'long legged Italy, kicking little Sicily right into the middle of the Mediterranean Sea'. Is it this simple childhood rhyme— designed to place the different countries—that fired my imagination all those years ago?

Surprisingly, this very tip of the toe of Italy appeared to be more populated and industrialised than we had found previously in Calabria. Our destination—the ferry port at Villa di San Giovanni—was a little further north than the larger Reggio di Calabria that lies on a wider part of the Straits of Messina and boasts an airport. Our ferry port, being directly opposite Messina in Sicily, would only take about thirty to thirty-five minutes with the boats plying back and forwards continuously.

Travelling on, from our height above coast, we could clearly see the port and across the water, yes, there is Sicily! Memories came flooding back of our first visit in 2005 and we got quite excited. The area became more and more built up, as you would expect from a ferry port. Far below, boats and ships of all sizes, ploughed their way through the waves towards the port of Villa di San Giovanni. Sicily lay in wait for the next boat to disgorge it load of cars, lorries, coaches and passengers. High above the coast, we travelled on towards the port and our passage to Sicily. The rock formations were fantastic. It was another timeless scene on this our adventure through history down the long leg of Italy.

Soon we ran alongside the railway where long trains, snaking along the many tracks, connected people to and from the mainland and the rest of Sicily at the Port of Messina. We had strict instructions to make sure that when on the ferry, we saw Sicily looming nearer, we were to head back to the coach immediately as once Renzo had the sign to move off, he couldn't wait. Of course there is always one isn't there.

Our packed lunch was excellent with a good variety of goodies. The Hotel Barbieri had done us proud. Seeing that Sicily was looming, we quickly put our lunch wrappers into the re-cycling bins and like good children, we all—or at least almost all—headed back down the stairs to the coach.

Into Sicily

Squeezing between the coach and wall of the stairwell in the gloom, we found Renzo waiting with the doors of the coach open. Serena, mindful of the timescales and disembarking arrangements, anxiously counted heads and, well would you know it; there was one missing.

Renzo kept his eye on the vehicles in front, as the great front of the boat slowly lowered down to form a ramp. Where was the missing passenger? Serena was in a quandary. She couldn't get off to look for him and she couldn't leave without him. Someone got off to look for the laggard. Then all at once, by the skin of his teeth, the missing passenger hurried up the steps onto the coach. He had been filming in another part of the boat!

Renzo moved off and down the ramp. I eagerly scanned the side of the quayside wondering if we would see what had truly amazed us in 2005.

'Oh, look! That is where that man was sitting on the ground, feet over the side, with his fishing rods trying to catch fish.'

A laugh from my husband was the answer.

It was clear that we were now in the rush hour as we ploughed our way through the centre of the city to reach the motorway above to take us to Taormina. There were so many memories now of when we had made the journey by train to Messina from Giardini Naxos to see how the land lay in the ferry port if we were able to come on the Gold Wing trike. There had been a student demonstration then and, as we waited to cross the road, a passer-by had admonished me to 'put that away', as she pointed to the camcorder slung around my neck.

Now, eagerly looking forward to our stay near Taormina we reflected:

'I wonder what our hotel will be like.'

As we ended our journey through to the very tip of the long leg of Italy, we were not to know what a gift awaited us on our latest island interlude.

The End

~~~~~~~~~~~~~~~~~~

References

References

Michelin Green Tourist Guide. Italy (1983)
http://www.aviewoncities.com/rome.htm
http://en.wikipedia.org/wiki/Swiss_Guard
http://www.vaticanstate.va/content/vaticanstate/en/monume
nti/giardini-vaticani.html
http://www.quirinale.it
http://en.wikipedia.org/wiki/Piazza_San_Marco
http://structural-
communication.com/Cultural%20Space%20Theory/Venice-
CST.html
http://www.lineamazzuccato.it/default3.htm
http://en.wikipedia.org/wiki/Florence_Cathedral
http://www.fodors.com/world/europe/italy/venice/review-
484157.html
http://goitaly.about.com/od/vaticancity/a/saint-peters-
square.htm
http://en.wikipedia.org/wiki/Pompeii
http://wikitravel.org/en/Pompeii
http://www.isolasangiulio.it/
http://www.sacrimonti.net/User/index.php?PAGE=Sito_en/s
acro_monte_orta&argo_id=6
http://www.kuriositas.com/2011/11/isola-san-giulio-italys-
fairy-tale.html
http://en.wikipedia.org/wiki/Adige
http://www.italyheaven.co.uk/lombardy/lake-iseo.html
http://www.alledolomiti.com/Molveno-e-dintorni/Molveno-
d-estate
http://www.tr3ntino.it/en/nature-and-landscape/lakes/lake-
molveno.html

http://www.tr3ntino.it/en/nature-and-landscape/lakes/lake-toblino.html
http://www.sassidimatera.it/english/visitarematera.htm
http://en.wikipedia.org/wiki/Sassi_di_Matera
http://www.italyheaven.co.uk/basilicata/matera.html
http://www.umfulana.com/italy/country-people/regions/sila-mountains/800967

Further Reading

Just Us Two Series.

During their first Gold Wing motorbike experience, finding that the words flowed when recounting their profound emotional experiences, Rosalie Marsh realised that there was the beginnings of a story. Eventually, their adventures developed into a travel series of which *The Long Leg of Italy* is the latest adventure. *Island Interludes* will round off the series when *Just Us Two Escape to the Sun* from the hectic pace and demands of life.

All books are in paperback and eBook formats for most devices. The photo illustrations are in colour in the eBooks.

Just Us Two: Ned and Rosie's Gold Wing Discovery.
ISBN 978-1-908302-12-0
Winner 2010 International Book Awards. Finalist 2009 Best Book Awards (Travel: Recreational category).

Ned and Rosie found their lost youth when, in middle age Rosie discovered a Honda Gold Wing motorbike. They set off to realise Rosie's dreams of finding her roots in Ireland before exploring Europe.

Chasing Rainbows: with Just Us Two.
ISBN 978 1 908302-00-7

Chasing Rainbows is the real ending to Rosie's Gold Wing motorbiking story as they mentally say good-bye to their beloved Gold Wing motorbike but until after more adventures.

Island Interludes: Just Us Two Escape to the Sun.
ISBN 978-1-908302-43-4 Pub Date t.b.a.

As their travel horizons widened and they continued to push back their boundaries Rosie took every opportunity to 'do what they could while they could and then they would not be saying "if only"'.

Fiction

ORANGES: A Journey. ISBN 978-1-908302-31-1
Marsh's debut fiction is a contemporary fantasy built on a dream. Introducing Charlotte to the world, this mixture of fact and fiction takes the reader into Portugal and Spain. But are they dreams? Or reality?

Lifelong Learning: Personal Effectiveness Guides.

The series draws on Marsh's extensive skills & industrial experience in sales management and work-based learning in adult and further education. Initially, the series looks at the background to lifelong learning and some research into various viewpoints.

The series continues with four user-friendly 'workshops in a package'.

Whom are these books for?
- Aimed at the Home Learner and designed to read in bite-sized chunks.
- Someone who is unable to attend formal courses.
- To fill gaps in underpinning knowledge and skills needed to 'get on in life'.
- Designed as a user-friendly support material for learners of all ages with a wide range of abilities.
- All books are in paperback and eBook formats for most devices. The illustrations are in colour in the eBooks.

Lifelong Learning: A View from the Coal Face
ISBN 978-1-908302-04-5

The springboard for the series is based on a research paper that looks at learning, opportunity, access, professional and personal development and asks if the initiatives in this area worked. The research is brought up-to-date with some post-research reflections in the light of the *Wolf Report*.

Release Your Potential: Making Sense of Personal and Professional Development.
ISBN: 978-1-908302-08-3

After looking at the process of professional and personal development, Marsh follows with an introduction on how to structure and develop your continuing personal development records.

Skills for Employability Part One: Pre-Employment.
ISBN 978-1-908302-16-8

Marsh looks at those skills for the future, which include preparing for work, Job applications, and successful interview, working effectively in the workplace and basic ICT skills in the workplace, legislation, and progression.

Skills for Employability Part Two: Moving into Employment. ISBN 978-1-908302-20-5

Marsh looks at the standards of behaviour and requirements of employers. These include Employment Rights and responsibilities, the business environment, working relationships, customer service, managing your money and healthy living before looking at progression.

Talking the Talk: Getting the Message Across.
ISBN 978-1-908302-35-9

Are you frequently in a situation where you have to give a talk, presentation or staff briefing? This book will help you to prepare well, become confident and overcome nerves, and deliver an interesting presentation that will be remembered for the right reasons.

C

Christal Publishing

www.christalpublishing.com